M000188574

POLITICS AND PIETY

Monographs in Baptist History

VOLUME 2

SERIES EDITOR
Michael A. G. Haykin, The Southern Baptist Theological Seminary

EDITORIAL BOARD
Matthew Barrett, California Baptist University
Peter Beck, Charleston Southern University
Anthony L. Chute, California Baptist University
Jason G. Duesing, Southwestern Baptist Theological Seminary
Nathan A. Finn, Southeastern Baptist Theological Seminary
Crawford Gribben, Queen's University, Belfast
Gordon L. Heath, McMaster Divinity College
Barry Howson, Heritage Theological Seminary
Jason K. Lee, Southwestern Baptist Theological Seminary
Thomas J. Nettles, The Southern Baptist Theological Seminary
James A. Patterson, Union University
James M. Renihan, Institute of Reformed Baptist Studies
Jeffrey P. Straub, Central Baptist Theological Seminary
Brian R. Talbot, Broughty Ferry Baptist Church, Scotland
Malcolm B. Yarnell III, Southwestern Baptist Theological Seminary

Ours is a day in which not only the gaze of western culture but also increasingly that of Evangelicals is riveted to the present. The past seems to be nowhere in view and hence it is disparagingly dismissed as being of little value for our rapidly changing world. Such historical amnesia is fatal for any culture, but particularly so for Christian communities whose identity is profoundly bound up with their history. The goal of this new series of monographs, Studies in Baptist History, seeks to provide these Christian communities with reasons and resources for remembering the past. The editors are deeply convinced that Baptist history contains rich resources of theological reflection, praxis and spirituality that can help Baptists, as well as other Christians, live more Christianly in the present. The monographs in this series will therefore aim at illuminating various aspects of the Baptist tradition and in the process provide the confessing church with a usable past.

Politics and Piety

Baptist Social Reform in America, 1770–1860

Aaron Menikoff

☙PICKWICK *Publications* · Eugene, Oregon

POLITICS AND PIETY
Baptist Social Reform in America, 1770–1860

Monographs in Baptist History 2

Copyright © 2014 Aaron Menikoff. All rights reserved. Except for brief quotations in critical publications or reviews, no part of this book may be reproduced in any manner without prior written permission from the publisher. Write: Permissions, Wipf and Stock Publishers, 199 W. 8th Ave., Suite 3, Eugene, OR 97401.

Pickwick Publications
An Imprint of Wipf and Stock Publishers
199 W. 8th Ave., Suite 3
Eugene, OR 97401
www.wipfandstock.com

ISBN 13: 978-1-62564-189-2

Cataloging-in-Publication data:

Menikoff, Aaron

Politics and piety : Baptist social reform in America, 1770–1860 / Aaron Menikoff.

xiv + 230 p. ; 23 cm. —Includes bibliographc references and index(es).

Monographs in Baptist History 2

ISBN 13: 978-1-62564-189-2

1. Baptists—United States—History—18th century. 2. Baptists—United States—History—19th century. 3. Church and Social problems—Baptists. I. Title. II. Series.

HN U6 M41 2014

Manufactured in the U.S.A.

For Deana,
my best friend,
thou excellest them all

Table of Contents

Foreword

WHEN ONE THINKS OF social reform and societal change, one usually does not think of southern evangelicals, much less Baptists, leading the way. Little wonder. On a popular level it is easy to get caught up in negative regional stereotypes that do not reflect reality. Even among scholars, the names and issues most commonly associated with the "Social Gospel" have tended to emphasize Northerners and their efforts to relieve the dispossessed, thereby reinforcing non-Southern or anti-Southern biases.

Yet, it is a mistake to assume that Baptists did not engage in concerted efforts to change their world. Among regional historians the past generation of scholars has begun to revisit southern evangelicalism and social activism. Happily, there now exists a body of scholarship that identifies and traces a southern Social Gospel in a variety of forms. In *Politics and Piety: Baptist Social Reform in America, 1770–1860* Aaron Menikoff goes a step further by identifying Baptists in the North and South as legitimate reformers whose legacy is rooted deep in America's antebellum era.

Menikoff maintains that America's antebellum Baptists engaged in a two-prong approach to society's problems. They preached a gospel of reconciliation to God that, they hoped, would lead to consecrated, orderly lives. Even so, Menikoff argues that America's Baptists were not bashful when it came to lobbying for socially oriented legislation at the local, state, and the national levels. Thus, when it came to direct involvement in social issues, Baptists may be considered both active *and* passive reformers.

There is much more to say but I will leave that for Menikoff. It is a story he tells well. In *Politics and Piety: Baptist Social Reform in America, 1770–1860* is a significant contribution to the emerging narrative of the complex interplay between individual belief and public behavior during what may be considered as America's most formative period. By any measure, this is a welcome book.

Keith Harper
Southeastern Baptist Theological Seminary
Wake Forest, North Carolina

Preface

MY FIRST EXPOSURE TO social reform came in the Hart Senate Office Building in Washington, DC, where I served as an aide to Mark O. Hatfield, a Baptist. The senator's religious convictions were widely known, as was his unwillingness to toe the party line. More than once he said with a sheepish grin, "The Lord baptized me, not my voting record." Hatfield wanted the citizens, churches, and the nation as a whole to express a social conscience. In *Conflict and Conscience* (1971) he implored the church to mobilize its members to serve the needy. In *Between a Rock and a Hard Place* (1976) he asked churches to apportion a percentage of their budget to ameliorate global poverty. Hatfield believed we could learn a lesson from men like William Wilberforce and a movement like the Second Great Awakening. Both inspired political change.

When I left the Senate, I kept an interest in the relationship between politics and religion. The books I read on the topic of social action in the nineteenth century generally fell into two camps. The first painted a rosy picture of social action among Christians—especially in the North where churches fought for the abolition of slavery. Donald Dayton's *Discovering an Evangelical Heritage* (1976) is a great example. The second camp argued that the church in the nineteenth century was socially sluggish, especially where political action mattered most. Ernest Trice Thompson, who helped unite the Presbyterian Church (U.S.A.), insisted that nineteenth-century Presbyterians invented the doctrine of the spirituality of the church as a religious justification for slavery. According to this doctrine, the church must confine its interest to preaching, evangelism, and personal piety. This left no room for dismantling that Peculiar Institution known as slavery.

In my own research, I expected to find that Baptists in the nineteenth century were largely unconcerned with meaningful, social reform. While I suspected there were many who cared more about building hospitals for the poor than evangelizing the lost, certainly the majority of Baptists had a view of the spirituality of the church that paralleled what Thompson had chronicled. To my surprise, I discovered that nineteenth-century Baptists in the North and the South were social reformers. Yes, they believed in a spiritual church—Baptist ecclesiology demanded it. For Baptists, a spiritual church simply meant a church whose membership was restricted to those whose profession of faith was genuine (i.e., spiritual). Rank and file Baptists cared about more than personal faith, they longed to promote a virtuous nation.

Baptists, like other evangelicals of the nineteenth century and like other Americans, were too often blinded by the sins of their age. The issue of the day was slavery, and Baptists failed to speak out in force against this hideous practice, just as they failed to speak out in force against the racism that permeated the South for over a century, and still flavors parts of America today. To claim without reservation that Baptists were social reformers when the Southern Baptist Convention was formed in response to slavery seems to fly in the face of common sense.

But to hear the Baptists speak for themselves is to better understand them. Admittedly, Baptist social reform was not primarily the renovation of social structures. First and foremost, a spiritual church nurtured pious individuals and these individuals changed society like leaven working through a loaf of bread. Individual Christians sought to edify the moral and social conscience of the nation and, for many Baptists, this was social reform. But Baptists did more than labor for souls with hope those souls would change the world. Baptists often engaged in more direct avenues of social reform. This included the political lobbying of Congress, the establishment of welfare committees within the church, and letters to the editor for and against participation in the Mexican War. Such examples may not be widespread but they were prominent and, albeit to my surprise, proved to be an important part of this narrative.

Baptists rarely agreed on how to reform society, and these disagreements are another aspect of the story that follows. Some preached that personal piety was the only biblical route to social change. Others pressed more vigorously for political solutions. But all accepted that, one way or another, society had to change; the American experiment was too important for the nation to drown in a sea of vice and immorality. The gospel demanded more of the new world's city on a hill.

There is no such thing as an objective historian. Though I was raised in the secular Pacific Northwest, I have been educated by Southern

Baptists and now even pastor a Southern Baptist congregation. Yet I have labored for objectivity. Historians do not serve their readers well by glossing over the sins of their subjects nor by failing to recount their achievements. I have sought to let the Baptists of a bygone era tell their own story on an important subject, one that I believe has yet to fully recounted.

Politics and Piety is about nineteenth-century Baptist social reform in America, North and South. I considered it appropriate to broaden the geographical scope of this study because the Baptists did not split until 1845, when the Southern Baptist Convention was founded. For much of the nineteenth century they saw themselves as one denomination, and I have treated them as such. My source material includes Baptist association minutes from Massachusetts, Rhode Island, and New York as well as Virginia, Kentucky, Tennessee, North Carolina, and South Carolina. I cite Baptist periodicals including, but not limited to, Boston's *Christian Watchman*, Richmond's *Religious Herald*, Washington's *Columbian Star*, and Savannah's *Analytical Repository*. When quoting from original texts, I usually kept the original spelling, but removed italics and block capitalization.

A book is a cooperative venture, and I am very thankful for the many individuals who have made this final product possible and who encouraged me along the way. The staff of the James P. Boyce Centennial Library at the Southern Baptist Theological Seminary provided crucial assistance. Archivist Jason Fowler did more than facilitate access to material, his expertise facilitated my research. Bruce Keisling, the seminary librarian, provided important resources, encouragement, and friendship. I am indebted to Gregory Wills for his incisive criticism. Though the failings are all mine, I do not hesitate to assert that the merits of this book are due to his investment. In addition, I appreciate the time and insight given to me by professors Thomas J. Nettles, Russell D. Moore, and Michael A. G. Haykin. A few churches deserve special praise. The members of Capitol Hill Baptist Church in Washington, DC, supported me throughout my seminary days, Third Avenue Baptist Church in Louisville, KY, provided a spiritual home, and the members of Mount Vernon Baptist Church in Atlanta, GA, welcomed a northerner into their arms. Finally, my family deserves special thanks. I am reminded of the many sacrifices made by my parents, Richard and Michael Messick. My father, Barry Menikoff, a professor of literature, offered scholarly advice. My wife, Deana, and our children, Rachel, Jonah, and Natalie, encouraged me more than they will ever know.

Senator Hatfield died before he could read this book, but I trust that he would have been surprised and pleased to learn a little about the many Baptists before him who sought to make a difference.

Aaron Menikoff
Atlanta, Georgia
May, 2013

1

Introduction

BAPTISTS WERE SOCIAL REFORMERS. In 1845 John Broadus, a struggling young Virginia schoolmaster, wrote home to his father. Broadus professed a longing for respectable piety: "The reflection that I have now arrived at an age when it is necessary that I commence striving to be what I wish to be, a man possessed of those solid qualities which alone can gain the esteem of the intelligent and virtuous, has often troubled me."[1] His troubled conscience soon gave way to the conviction that he was called not only to be virtuous but spread virtue abroad. In the first public speech of his career, Broadus did not address the Sunday school, though he went on to found a seminary. Nor did he preach before a congregation, though he became a renowned pulpiteer. He penned his first speech for the Berryville Total Abstinence Society: "I love the cause of Temperance and to its support and defence I am resolved to contribute my mite, how diminutive soever that mite may be."[2] Like so many other nineteenth-century evangelicals, Broadus labored for both personal and public virtue. His religion required it. He applied himself zealously to achieve these ends: the pursuit of pious living and political reform.

Broadus wanted his listeners to understand that the welfare of the nation depended upon their willingness to sign the abstinence pledge. Every American must take up "the cause of morality and philanthropy." The young reformer presented Babylon, Assyria, and Rome as case studies

1. Archibald Thomas Robertson, *Life and Letters of John Albert Broadus* (Harrisonburg, VA: Gano, 1987) 45.

2. John A. Broadus, "Address to Berryville Total Abstinence Society," May, 1846. Broadus-Mitchell Family Papers, Archives and Special Collections, James P. Boyce Centennial Library, Southern Baptist Seminary, Louisville, Kentucky. Broadus did not deliver the address as planned because rain canceled the event.

in wickedness. "When they became slaves to intemperance and vice, their power passed away." America must do better. Patriotism demanded her people to "labor for the good" of their fellow citizens.

Some Christians feared that engaging in the battle against temperance would sully their spiritual focus. Joining with tax collectors and sinners to spread virtue seemed unwholesome. Broadus disagreed. The danger of liquor called every patriot to duty. He insisted that those who would not fight the evil, even with unbelievers, lacked compassion: "Should a poor neighbor be so unfortunate as to have his house burned down, would you refuse to aid him in rebuilding it merely because men of the world contribute to it also?" If intemperance was a dangerous evil, Broadus was sure he could convince Christians to help: "O Christian, is it not your duty, as a patriot and a philanthropist, as a lover of your country and a lover of human kind, to unite with your fellow-citizens in putting a stop to the ravages of this cruel foe, this fell destroyer of the peace and the happiness of mankind."[3] The cause of social reform gripped Broadus. Piety stirred him to action. He was not alone.

This is the story of how American Baptists during the Second Great Awakening sought to reform the nation. Religious revivals began in earnest in New England and throughout the upper South and West at the start of the nineteenth century. The spiritual fervor associated with the revivals produced social reform. Revivalism and reformation depended upon established local churches for their support.[4] Therefore this study departs from 1770, when churches in the Kehukee Baptist Association of North Carolina were already organized, defining and defending the social impact of Christianity.[5] The study concludes in 1860, after the last great revival of the nineteenth century, but before the nation turned its full attention to the Civil War.

Baptists, North and South, believed that personal piety could never be merely personal, the conversion of sinners and the spread of their religion transformed communities. Personal piety was political in nature.

---

3. Ibid.

4. John B. Boles, *The Great Revival: Beginnings of the Bible Belt* (Lexington: The University Press of Kentucky, 1972) 9; and Donald G. Mathews, "The Second Great Awakening as an Organizing Process, 1780–1830: An Hypothesis," *American Quarterly* 21 (Spring 1969) 23–43.

5. *Minutes*, Kehukee Baptist Association, August 1770, 12. At this meeting the association debated the merits of playing the lottery, eventually concluding it to be both "unlawful and worthy of suspicion."

Baptists did not draw a sharp distinction between moral and social causes. The question remained how to channel that piety for the good of the country. Baptists promoted temperance, poverty relief, and Sabbath observance, but disagreed regarding the best means of advancing these agendas. All accepted the significance of individual conversions to Christianity. Such conversions produced personal peace and, indirectly, social good. Without personal transformations, other means of social reform were unlikely to succeed. Therefore, they prioritized the evangelization of sinners. However, some reformers wanted to do more than advocate social reform through the indirect method of evangelism. They sought direct action as well. By petitioning legislatures or forming church welfare committees, these Baptists sought to have an immediate and organized effect. Thus, all Baptists shared faith in the power of personal piety to indirectly reform society but many also advocated direct social and political action. When they disagreed it was usually over the strategy—direct or indirect—not the propriety of reform itself.

Powerful effects followed the Second Great Awakening. It was truly a national revival. Conversions multiplied in New England under the leadership of Timothy Dwight and Lyman Beecher, in upstate New York under the fiery preaching of Charles G. Finney, and in Kentucky under the guidance of Barton Stone and James McGready, and in a thousand other locales. Evangelical leaders organized a "benevolent empire" that emerged in the wake of the revivals. Sunday schools, tract societies, missionary societies, colleges, and seminaries made up this empire. Its soldiers fought gambling, fornication, theatres, novel reading, drunkenness, and poverty in an attempt to create a virtuous nation. They petitioned legislatures over matters of religious liberty, the Sabbath, liquor production, dueling, and taxation. This benevolent empire expressed the moral conscience of the evangelical churches, Baptists included.

Why did these evangelicals vigorously attend to social and political reform when the bread and butter of their work was preaching and praying? Historians generally appeal to two impulses in order to explain the work of reformers like Broadus. Some contend that they acted as agents of social control. Religion and the virtue it produced was a means to suppress vices detrimental to society's well-being or the merchant's bottom line. Others argue that the reformers were caught up in the nineteenth-century perfectionist movement, a theological vision that assumed a holy nation must precede the anticipated, second coming of Jesus Christ.

Neither impulse adequately explains why Baptists devoted their rhetoric and resources to the cause of social reformation.

Impulses for Reform

The social control theory has long been a favored explanation for the explosion of benevolent efforts during the Second Great Awakening. Early proponents like John R. Bodo presented the nineteenth-century clergy as architects of an American theocracy with themselves at the head. The infant nation suffered through a vacuum of leadership and pastors, or "theocrats," as Bodo called them, saw their power waning and sought to exercise control over an increasingly unruly population.[6] Twenty years later another social-control theorist, Paul Johnson, analyzed the Rochester revivals of 1830–31. He concluded the church was more interested in furthering middle class values than promoting the Beatitudes: "The religion that it preached was order-inducing, repressive, and quintessentially bourgeois."[7] Rank-and-file workers, who had a hard time keeping up with the demands of a budding industrial world, needed to be shaken out of their lethargy and laziness. They had to be taught the importance and value of hard work. Cunning religious leaders wielded revivalism as a tool to civilize society. Community leaders who controlled Rochester's resources "believed in their hearts that in proletarianizing workmen they were rescuing them from barbarism and granting them the benefits of Christian discipline."[8] Johnson's social control thesis endured several years of critique and he admitted, twenty-five years after its first publication, that his limited sources kept him from seeing the "democratizing and de-centering thrust" of the Awakening. In other words, the ruled classes of nineteenth-century America played a larger role in shaping their own destiny than Johnson was at first willing to admit.[9] Nonetheless, Johnson

6. John R. Bodo, *The Protestant Clergy and Public Issues, 1812–1848* (Princeton, NJ: Princeton University Press, 1954) 259.

7. Paul Johnson, *The Shopkeeper's Millennium: Society and Revivals in Rochester, New York, 1815–1837* (New York: Hill & Wang, 1978) 138.

8. Ibid., 6.

9. See Nathan O. Hatch, *The Democratization of American Christianity* (New Haven, CT: Yale University Press, 1989); and Gregory A. Wills, *Democratic Religion: Freedom, Authority, and Church Discipline in the Baptist South, 1785–1900* (New York: Oxford University Press, 1997). Hatch argued that the Second Great Awakening tore down the traditional, ecclesiastical walls of liturgy, governance, theology, and instruction and

refused to downplay the power of such luminaries as that great evangelist, Charles Grandison Finney, whose religion, Johnson quipped, was not merely the "dominant religion" of the North, "it was the religion."[10]

The second, popular explanation for the social reform movement of early America is the perfectionist impulse. Its advocates also lean heavily upon the revivalism of Finney, though their interest is more theological. Perfectionists believed that faithful Christians can actually achieve complete holiness in this life. If sin can be rooted out of the human soul it can surely be expunged from society as a whole. This optimistic view of humanity's ability to achieve spiritual victory and usher in the second return of Christ fueled a generation of social reformers. Gilbert Hobbs Barnes was one of the first to write about this perfectionist impulse in *The Antislavery Impulse* (1933). He looked at Finney's "Great Revival" of 1830 and observed how Finney freed himself and his followers from the shackles of Calvinism, a theological system much less optimistic about the moral ability of human nature. Finney and his disciples were convinced that personal salvation was nothing more than a stepping stone to social transformation: "Calvinism had made salvation the end of all human desire and fear of hell the spur to belief; whereas Finney made salvation the beginning of religious experience instead of its end."[11] But it was Timothy L. Smith in *Revivalism and Social Reform* (1957) who immortalized the perfectionist impulse as an explanation for social reform. The benevolent empire of antebellum America had been built upon the principles of a "democratically Arminian" creed: "Enthusiasm for Christian perfection was evangelical Protestantism's answer to the moral strivings of the age."[12] Jacobus Arminius, a sixteenth-century Dutch Reformed theologian, had a high opinion of human ability to attain salvation and perfection. Smith saw in the Arminian creed the best explanation for the massive nineteenth-century efforts at social reform. Barnes and Smith thus framed the discussion for more than a generation of historians who came to view evangelical life through the incomparable work of Finney.

---

replaced them with walls of popular opinion. Wills posited that Baptist churches, with a strong tradition of congregational and thus democratic leadership, valued ecclesiastical authority. In other words, church piety and church authority went together.

10. Johnson, *Shopkeeper's Millennium*, xvii.

11. Gilbert Hobbes Barnes, *The Antislavery Impulse, 1830–1844* (New York: D. Appleton-Century, 1933) 11.

12. Timothy L. Smith, *Revivalism and Social Reform in Mid-Nineteenth-Century America* (New York: Abingdom, 1957) 94, 146.

They characterized the reformers as adherents of a perfectionist tradition more suited to social transformation.[13]

The roots of perfectionism run quite deep. As George Marsden has noted, Finney's use of perfectionism is nothing more than the New Divinity or New England Theology repackaged and popularized for a mass audience.[14] In the years following Jonathan Edwards's death, three theological parties arose: the Old Calvinists, moderates who cherished traditional doctrine and resented the excesses of revivalism, Arminians, produced chiefly at Harvard and represented by Charles Chauncy and Jonathan Mayhew, and the New Divinity adherents, who counted Edwards their hero, Yale their school, and revival their goal. The New Divinity men embraced Edwards's teaching on divine sovereignty but added their own unique emphasis that the sinner had both the responsibility and ability, unaided by the Spirit, to repent. Men like Joseph Bellamy and Samuel Hopkins attempted to justify God in an "enlightened" age. Bellamy emphasized God's role as the "Moral Governor." Hopkins focused on God's work in regeneration and human activity in conversion, articulating the balance in such a way as to protect both sovereignty and responsibility and, concurrently, promoting revivalism and social reform. By 1828 the most famous New Divinity adherent, Nathaniel William Taylor, was teaching at Yale where he delivered *Concio ad Clerum* in which he denied the imputation of Adam's sin. In other words, he rejected the notion that, as the New England Primer put it, "In Adam's fall we sinned all." His New Divinity teaching made the Christian faith more attainable by making human nature less corrupt and, therefore, more likely to do good.[15] It is

13. Barnes and Smith were just the beginning. See also John L. Hammond, "Revival Religion and Antislavery Politics," *American Sociological Review* 39 (1974) 175–86. Anne C. Loveland, "Evangelicalism and Immediate Emancipation," in *History of the American Abolitionist Movement: A Bibliography of Scholarly Articles*, edited by John R. McKivigan (New York: Garland, 1999) 177. James Moorhead, "Social Reform and the Divided Conscience of Antebellum Protestantism," *Church History* 48 (1979) 416–30. Richard J. Carwardine, *Evangelicals and Politics in Antebellum America* (New Haven, CT: Yale University Press, 1993) 134. Douglas M. Strong, *They Walked in Spirit: Personal Faith and Action in America* (Louisville, KY: Westminster John Knox, 1997). Norris Magnuson, *Salvation in the Slums: Evangelical Social Work, 1865–1920* (Metuchen, NJ: Scarecrow, 1977) 38–44.

14. George Marsden, "The Gospel of Wealth, the Social Gospel, and the Salvation of Souls in Nineteenth Century America," in *Protestantism and Social Christianity*, edited by Martin E. Marty (New York: K. G. Saur, 1992) 7.

15. Some of the best works related to the New England Theology include *The New England Theology: From Jonathan Edwards to Edwards Amasa Park*, ed. Douglas A.

no wonder, then, that Charles E. Hambrick-Stowe, in his biography of Finney, presented the evangelist and activist as a practitioner of Taylor New Divinity.[16] Likewise, E. Brooks Holifield reached the salient conclusion that "somewhere in the deep background of even the holiness movement stood the unlikely figure of Jonathan Edwards."[17]

Linking the social reform of the Second Great Awakening to the New Divinity perfectionism paints the face of Finney on the movement much the way Edwards and Whitefield are forever associated with the First Great Awakening. Finney looms large in nineteenth-century America.[18] Historians have however unduly emphasized Finney's perfectionism as the primary impulse for social reform.[19] Many reformers did not

Sweeney and Allen C. Guelzo (Grand Rapids: Baker Academic, 2006); Bruce Kuklick, *A History of Philosophy in America, 1720–2000* (Oxford: Oxford Universtiy Press, 2001) 38–57; E. Brooks Holifield, *Theology in America: Christian Thought from the Age of the Puritans to the Civil War* (New Haven, CT: Yale University Press, 2003) 127–57; Sweeney, "Edwards and His Mantle: The Historiography of the New England Theology" *New England Quarterly* 71 (1998) 97–110; David W. Kling, *Field of Wonders: The New Divinity and Village Revivals in Northwestern Connecticut, 1792–1822* (University Park: Pennsylvania University Press, 1993); Joseph Conforti, "Edwardsians, Unitarians and the Memory of the Great Awakening, 1800–1840," in *American Unitarianism: 1805–1865,* ed. Conrad Edick Wright (Boston: Northeastern University Press, 1989); Sydney E. Ahlstrom, *A Religious History of the American People* (New Haven, CT: Yale University Press, 1972) 415–22; and Richard D. Birdsall, "The Second Great Awakening and the New England Social Order," *Church History* 39 (September 1970) 345–64.

16. Charles E. Hambrick-Stowe, *Charles G. Finney and the Spirit of American Evangelicalism* (Grand Rapids: Eerdmans, 1996) 31–32.

17. Holifield, *Theology in America,* 369. See also Leo P. Hirrel, *Children of Wrath: New School Calvinism and Antebellum Reform* (Lexington: University Press of Kentucky, 1998); William R. Sutton, "The Influence of Nathaniel W. Taylor on Revivalism in the Second Great Awakening," *Religion and American Culture* (Winter 1992) 23–48; Allen Guelzo, "An Heir or a Rebel? Charles Grandison Finney and the New England Theology," *Journal of the Early Republic* (1997) 61–94; idem, "Oberlin Perfectionism and Its Edwarsian Origins, 1835–1870," in *Jonathan Edwards' Writings: Text, Context, Interpretation,* ed. Stephen J. Stein (Bloomington: Indiana University Press, 1996).

18. Barry Hankins described him as "the most important figure in the Second Great Awakening and one of the most influential individuals of the nineteenth century." Barry Hankins, *The Second Great Awakening and the Transcendentalists* (Westport, CT: Greenwood, 2004) 51.

19. James David Essig argued that historians of Finney like William G. McLouglin and Charles C. Cole have depreciated Finney's antislavery commitments. Finney, Essig contends, was firmly committed to abolition. See William G. McLouglin, *Modern Revivalism: Charles Grandison Finney to Billy Graham* (New York: Ronald, 1959) and Charles G. Cole, *The Social Ideas of Northern Evangelicals* (New York: Columbia University Press, 1964). James David Essig, "The Lord's Free Man: Charles G. Finney

share the perfectionist impulse of Finney and his followers. Rank-and-file Baptists as well as their leaders held to the older Calvinist tradition that rejected perfectionism.[20]

This brings us to a third impulse to consider, independent of social control or perfectionism; an evangelical impulse. It is akin to that suggested by Beth Barton Schweiger in her study of religious life in nineteenth-century Virginia. Schweiger quoted the Virginia Baptist, James Taylor, who noted that "the Gospel worked up."[21] It had a spiritual and a temporal effect. Baptist and Methodist preachers wanted to do more than use their congregations as weapons in the battle for social control of the masses. They wanted their churches to understand the "public responsibility" entailed by their private faith.[22] By taking the convictions of these pastors and churches seriously, Schweiger countered the thesis of John Lee Eighmy who questioned the motivation of southern Protestants in general and Southern Baptists in particular: "One does not have to strain hard to conclude," wrote Eighmy, "that ethical responses arise more from custom and actually seeing need and suffering than from believing that this is profoundly a part of their obligation to Almighty God."[23] Schweiger's project is fundamentally more positive and productive: "Too often inquiries into Southern religious life have been narrowed to a single question: why did the white Southern church fail? . . . This study begins not with the question about these churches' failure, but rather by asking simply how did they work?"[24] When Baptists in the South and the North spoke about reform they related it to their desire to serve God and to obey both the principles of the gospel and the precepts of scripture. At times, this made them agents of social control. Their convictions could

---

and His Abolitionism," in *Abolitionism and American Religion*, ed. John R. McKivigan (New York: Garland, 1999) 319–39.

20. Holifield, *Theology in America*, 274. Nettles argued that "Calvinism . . . prevailed in the most influential and enduring arenas of Baptist denominational life until the end of the second decade of the nineteenth century." Thomas J. Nettles, *By His Grace and For His Glory: A Historical, Theological, and Practical Study of the Doctrines of Grace in Baptist Life* (Grand Rapids: Baker, 1986) 13. See also J. D. Nourse, "Calvinism," *Religious Herald*, 13 December 1849, 197.

21. Beth Barton Schweiger, *The Gospel Working Up: Progress and Pulpit in Nineteenth-Century Virginia* (New York: Oxford University Press, 2000) 6.

22. Ibid., 110.

23. John Lee Eighmy, *Churches in Cultural Captivity: A History of Social Attitudes of Southern Baptists*, rev. ed. (Knoxville: University of Tennessee Press, 1987) xiv.

24. Schweiger, *The Gospel Working Up*, 5.

be misplaced. At bottom however they believed that a virtuous nation, centered on the gospel, would prosper. They were motivated by a genuinely evangelical impulse. It caused them to work assiduously to establish a virtuous nation and they desperately feared the consequences of failure.

A Search for Virtue

Nineteenth-century Baptists rejected the notion of a private faith. They saw too clearly the link between politics and piety. Many pastors and other Christians sought for the well-being of society because they believed such a battle to be consistent with their duties as believers and Americans.[25] Virtue was the essential link between piety, evangelism, and social reform. The gospel renovated communities by improving character.[26]

25. Lois W. Banner, "Religious Benevolence as Social Control: A Critique of an Interpretation," *The Journal of American History* 60 (1973) 37.

26. The importance of virtue to the well-being of society has undergone something of a renaissance. Contemporary discussions of morality began with Alisdair MacIntyre's *After Virtue* published in 1981. He revisited and reaffirmed his thesis in 2007, arguing that society lost its ability to reason in moral categories. As "Enlightenment philosophers rejected tradition and turned inward, they failed to find a new foundation for morality. The legacy that survived was emotivism, "the doctrine that all evaluative judgments and more specifically all moral judgments are *nothing but* expressions of preference, expressions of attitude or feeling, insofar as they are moral or evaluative in nature." Alisdair MacIntyre, *After Virtue: A Study in Moral Theory*, 3rd ed. (Notre Dame: University of Notre Dame Press, 2007) 11–12. Many cultural commentators found his assessment persuasive. As emotivism grew in popularity, morality became an increasingly private matter, inappropriate for discussion in the public square and impotent to influence society. Done E. Eberly, "Preface," in *The Content of America's Character: Recovering Civic Virtue*, ed. Eberly (Lanham, MD: Madison, 1995) xi. Proponents of the public value of personal morality began to make civic arguments. Michael Novak saw a connection between private and public life: "How can a people govern a whole society that cannot, each of them, govern themselves." Michael Novak, "The Cultural Roots of Virtue and Character," in *Content of America's Character*, 59. John K. Roth contended that, from the birth of America to the present day, virtue is essential to the state: "A republican way of life depends mightily on the *virtue* of the people." Roth, *Private Needs, Public Selves: Talk about Religion in Ameridca* (Urbana: University of Illinois Press, 19978) 3. Other scholars argue that it is not simply virtue, or even any religion that serves the republic but, specifically, Christianity. This is Hugh Helco's point in *Christianity and American Democracy*. The very nature of Christianity drives believers to engage the culture: "Following the model of God's incarnation, believers are taught that the world is to be penetrated, lighted, and salted by their Christian lives." Helco, *Christianity and American Democracy* (Cambridge: Harvard University Press, 2007) 21.

For Baptists of the Second Great Awakening, republicanism implied
the centrality of virtue to social reform. They did not, however, limit their
motivation to republicanism. The evangelical impulse undergirded their
virtue.[27] Whether they debated slavery, Sabbath legislation, poverty, temperance, or war, they believed the gospel demanded virtuous living and
that virtue secured the success of society. Reformers wanted to do more
than alleviate temporal needs, they sought to improve the moral fabric
of the nation through the careful application of the gospel. Baptist editor
Henry Keeling agreed with the *Christian Spectator*, a Congregationalist
periodical, in an article instructing Christians on the finer points of religion and politics: "The gospel mingled with the laws, has thus been born
across the waters, and become the basis of our own legislation."[28] Many
southern Democrats objected to a republican mixture of church and
state.[29] But for most Baptists the promotion of virtue transcended party
politics and, as the author sought to clarify, true religion was worthy of
every patriot's support: "The sentiments which we have endeavoured in
this article to support, have simply been an expansion of the thought,
that the interests of the republic can be secured only by infusing true
religion into all the veins and arteries of the state.—We do not mean as
a matter of state patronage—but let its spirit ascend all our mountains,
and go down into all our vallies, and reign in the bosoms of our senators,
and statesmen; in our colleges, and schools; in every association, and at
every fire side."[30] Social reform required virtue and this was fueled by
"true religion."

27. A point also made by Mark Noll with regard to the formation of the American
republic. See Noll, "From the Great Awakening to the War for Independence: Christian Values in the American Revolution," *Christian Scholar's Review* 12 (1983) 99–110.

28. Henry Keeling, "The Influence of Religion on the Laws of Nations," *Religious
Herald*, 15 August 1828, 132.

29. Joel H. Silbey, Allan G. Bogue, and William H. Flanigan, eds., *The History
of American Electoral Behavior* (Princeton, NJ: Princeton University Press, 1978);
Seymour Martin Lipset, "Religion and Politics in the American Past and Present," in
Religion and Social Conflict, ed. Robert Lee and Martin E. Marty (New York: Oxford
University Press, 1964) 69–126; Richard L. McCormick, *The Party Period and Public
Policy: American Politics from the Age of Jackson to the Progressive Era* (New York: Ox-
ford University Press, 1986); Robert P. Swierenga, "Ethnoreligious Political Behavior
in the Mid-Nineteenth Century: Voting, Values, Cultures," in *Religion and American
Politics: From the Colonial Period to the Present*, ed. Mark Noll, 2nd ed. (Oxford: Oxford University Press, 2007) 145–68.

30. Keeling, "Influence of Religion," 132.

Real Social Reform

Baptists did not always agree how to promote the nation's virtue. The story of politics and piety in Baptist approaches to social reform is therefore more complex. All agreed that true religion was necessary for the sake of society but not all agreed how piety should exert itself in public affairs. This book is sensitive to this tension over the strategy of social reform. Some Baptists objected to direct political engagement, preferring private prayer to public policy. Others lamented the divorce of philanthropy from evangelism. The moment they sensed that the benevolent movement was no longer centered on the Christian message, they objected. Political, temporal reform without piety was worthless. Some believed benevolent societies usurped the church's mission to seek, save, and reform the lost. Others criticized churches for becoming benevolent societies. Baptists who urged withdrawal amid the zeal of the benevolent empire did not comprise the majority, but they forced the majority to reflect on the motives and character of the movement. They reminded their brothers and sisters that Christians and the churches to which they belonged had a sacred calling.

The tension over the strategy of reform and, in particular, between the spiritual and political mission of the church increased after the Civil War. Proponents of early forms of the Social Gospel raised the question not simply of social reform but of the theological category of social regeneration. The Congregationalist Josiah Strong, who prepared the nation for Walter Rauschenbusch, advocated a progressive view of social Christianity in his writings.[31] He is best remembered for the nationalist zeal displayed in his 1885 work, *Our Country*.[32] Strong pioneered the

31. Wendy J. Deichmann Edwards, "Manifest Destiny, the Social Gospel and the Coming Kingdom: Josiah Strong's Program of Global Reform, 1885–1996," in *Perspectives on the Social Gospel*, ed. Christopher H. Evans (Lewiston, NY: Edwin Mellen, 1999); idem, *Forging and Ideology for American Missions: Josiah Strong and Manifest Destiny* (Cambridge: Currents in World Christianity Project, 1998); Edwin S. Gaustad, "Our Country: One Century Later," in *Liberal Protestantism: Realities and Possibilities*, ed. Robert S. Michaelsen and Wade Clark Roof (New York: Pilgrim, 1986) 85–101; Ralph E. Luker, "Social Gospel and the Failure of Racial Reform, 1877–1898," *Church History* 46 (March 1977) 80–99; Paul R. Meyer, "Fear of Cultural Decline: Josiah Strong's Thoughts about Reforms and Expansion," *Church History* 42 (1973) 396–405; and Dorothea R. Muller, "Josiah Strong and the Social Gospel: A Christian's Response to the Challenge of the City," *Journal of Presbyterian Historical Society* 39 (1961) 150–75.

32. Josiah Strong, *Our Country: Its Possible Future and its Present Crisis*, rev. ed.

Social Gospel, thus spearheading a turning point in American theology. By 1880 in America the seeds of modernism had begun to sprout. Planted in Unitarianism and watered by evolutionary theory and the higher-critical approaches to interpreting the Bible, modernism emphasized "God's presence in the world and in human culture" and distanced theology from creeds and Calvinism.[33] Strong articulated the immanence of God and emphasized the necessity of works in a nation fractured by urban growth and in need of a compassionate touch.

Strong argued that Christians had separated the spiritual from the secular in their support of the benevolent empire. To deny the church's singular role in meeting temporal needs made as much sense as caring for the crop but being indifferent to the soil in which it grows.[34] Strong contended that the church was the proper place for the work of societies like the Young Men's Christian Association and the Red Cross.[35]

Strong also advocated a gospel of social regeneration in which the good news of salvation is more than individual. Society needed to be redeemed as well. Strong spoke of salvation in ethical, social terms:

> I saw that in order to have an ideal world, society must be saved as well as the individual, and that the body must be perfected as well as the soul, and that environment must be changed as well as character. Indeed, I have learned that environment is commonly (not altogether) decisive in shaping character, that the body profoundly influences the soul and that the individual is in very large measure what society has made him. It is evident, therefore, that the Kingdom of God cannot fully come in the earth until society has been Christianized, unfavorable environments transformed, and our physical lives raised to a much higher plane.[36]

Strong did more than present a postmillennial theology whereby Christians are exhorted to do good works in order to hasten the Lord's

---

(New York: Baker & Taylor, 1891).

33. William R. Hutchinson, *The Modernist Impulse in American Protestantism* (Durham, NC: Duke University Press, 1992) 79.

34. Josiah Strong, *The New Era or the Coming Kingdom* (New York: Baker & Taylor, 1893) 229.

35. Ibid., 238.

36. Josiah Strong, *My Religion in Everyday Life* (New York: Baker & Taylor, 1910) 50.

return. He socialized the gospel. Social reform became more than an implication of the gospel, it became the gospel.

Edwin Charles Dargan, a Southern Baptist pastor and professor, took exception to Strong's view of the gospel and the church while sharing his heart for society. Without ever mentioning Strong by name, Dargan attacked his views directly. He rejected Strong's identification of a regenerated society with the kingdom of God: "There are many who speak of the kingdom of God as if it consisted in good houses for the poor, improved sanitation, good municipal government, better distribution of the means of subsistence . . . and old clothes for the poor."[37] The kingdom of God, however, is not to be associated with the physical improvement of humanity but with the reign of God which is simultaneously and mysteriously within the believer and yet to come.[38] Whereas Strong invited secular ministries into the church, Dargan held the distinction tightly: "When we abolish the distinction in our own minds . . . we teach the world to regard nothing as sacred rather than everything."[39]

Dargan's view of the kingdom of God and the church informed his strategy of social reform. The church must be concerned with human society, though as a congregation the mission of the church requires a primary focus on individual conversion.[40] He warned against the church becoming simply another agent in humanitarian reform. Churches should be involved in the social reform movement, but their involvement ought to be indirect. A church building is the proper place for a temperance society to meet, but the church, as the church, ought not be a temperance society. Pastors and members of churches should be "intimately associated and concerned with any proper reform" taking place, but their association should involve them as Christians and citizens fundamentally and not pastors and members primarily. The church ought to change the face of the community, but it does so at the risk of ceasing to be the church.[41]

Dargan's concern for the purity of the church did not keep him from moving the Southern Baptist Convention in the direction of increased

37. Edwin Charles Dargan, *Society, Kingdom and Church* (Philadelphia: American Baptists Publication Society, 1907) 55.

38. Ibid., 53, 56.

39. Ibid., 55–56.

40. Edwin Charles Dargan, *Ecclesiology: A Study of the Church*, 2nd ed. (Louisville, KY: Charles T. Dearing, 1905) 539.

41. Ibid., 612–14.

social service. Upon his election to the presidency of the convention in 1911 he gave social Christianity greater visibility among Baptists North and South. He had already written *Society, Kingdom and Church* (1907) and he now sat on the Committee on Social Work of the Baptist World Alliance with E. Y. Mullins and Walter Rauschenbusch. He also supported the creation of the Southern Baptist Committee on Social Service in 1913, the genesis of the Christian Life Commission.[42]

The Social Gospel contributed to the dissolution of the benevolent empire, a fortress which united orthodox faith and social engagement before the Civil War.[43] Modernists who advocated the Social Gospel depreciated individual conversion while evangelicals magnified it—often to the exclusion of a social and political activism. Historians such as Rufus B. Spain have argued that although Southern Baptists attended to personal piety and morality during the formative years of the Social Gospel, they cannot be considered social reformers because they displayed little concern for social problems.[44] Spain's assumption has been challenged on two fronts. First, many historians have come to accept a connection between the promotion of personal piety and social reform. Such scholars allow Baptists to speak for themselves and Baptists believed their spirituality benefited society. Even during the heyday of Social Gospel liberalism when evangelicals often saw social reform stripped of its gospel roots, they still believed their private virtue would have a public effect.[45] Second, Baptists did the work of social reform. They did

42. John Miller Finley, "Edwin Charles Dargan: Baptist Denominationalist in a Changing South" (PhD diss., The Southern Baptist Theological Seminary, 1984) 170–72. The Christian Life Commission has since been renamed the Ethics and Religious Liberty Commission.

43. For a brief summary of this move and an analysis of its contemporary effects, see Christian Smith, *American Evangelicalism: Embattled and Thriving* (Chicago: The University of Chicago Press, 1998). See also George M. Marsden, *Fundamentalism and American Culture: The Shaping of Twentieth-Century Evangelicalism, 1870–1925* (Oxford: Oxford University Press, 1980); Joel A. Carpenter, *Revive Us Again: The Reawakening of American Fundamentalism* (New York: Oxford University Press, 1997); and Keith Harper, *Quality of Mercy: Southern Baptists and Social Christianity, 1890–1920* (Tuscaloosa: University of Alabama Press, 1996).

44. Rufus B. Spain, *At Ease in Zion: A Social History of Southern Baptists, 1865–1900*, 2nd ed. (Tuscaloosa: University of Alabama Press, 2003) 211.

45. Betsy Flowers, "Southern Baptist Evangelicals or Social Gospel Liberals? The Woman's Missionary Union and Social Reform, 1888–1928," *American Baptist Quarterly* (June 2000) 111; Paul Harvey, *Redeeming the South: Religious Cultures and Racial Identities among Southern Baptists, 1865–1925* (Chapel Hill: The University of North

more than pray and promote prohibition; they cared for the poor, established orphanages, and founded schools.[46] Historians have broadened the definition of social reform to include personal piety and in so doing have questioned the extent of fundamentalist withdrawal. Real social reform included a commitment to personal piety and evangelism as well as an activism that produced immediate results. This may have been difficult to see in the era of the Social Gospel, but it is obvious during the Second Great Awakening.

Summary

Baptists from the birth of the nation to the Civil War were social reformers. They evidenced a concern for society both indirectly, through a commitment to personal piety and evangelism, as well as directly, through a willingness to engage in social and even political activism. They often disagreed on the strategy of reform, and this is part of the story's texture, but they maintained that the transformation of society was a vital goal, an essential implication of the gospel. At times they argued that this reform ought to come about through direct aid to the needy or the lobbying of the powerful. More often, they chose the indirect route, choosing to change the nation one soul at a time. They believed that not only was the spread of virtue necessary for the health of the nation, but that free, independent congregations were best suited to encourage the piety the country needed. To these early American Baptists, "social Christianity" would have been a redundancy. Christianity, by its very nature, was social—it must have a public effect to be genuine. By embracing the historic tenets of the faith, they found a way to promote social Christianity.

This book examines the public thought and effect of Baptists through several key issues in American life. It begins with two chapters that speak less to what Baptists did and more to how Baptists understood their role in society. Chapter two examines the role of piety in Baptist life. It argues that far from forcing Baptists to withdraw from society and culture, their view of personal piety drove them into society. Chapter three considers the impetus for direct political engagement discussed by Baptists.

Carolina Press, 1997) 198.

46. Wayne J. Flynt, *Alabama Baptists: Southern Baptists in the Heart of Dixie* (Tuscaloosa: University of Alabama Press, 1998) 92–99, 266–98.

Chapter four explores the most controversial topic, slavery. By weighing in on the colonization scheme, religious instruction, and abolition, Baptists proved themselves to be both agents of social control and vital players in an effort to reform and remove the Peculiar Institution. By twenty-first century standards, colonization and reform can hardly be considered examples of social reform. But many Baptists in the nineteenth-century saw both endeavors as a means of mollifying and perhaps even ending the tyranny of slavery. Chapter five examines one of the most significant but least known debates of the antebellum period: the effort to end the delivery of mail on the Sabbath. Here Baptists joined their evangelical friends in pressing for a legislative end to what they deemed to be a social problem. Not all Baptists shared the conviction that Congress should interfere. The subject of chapter six is the evangelical crusade to battle poverty. Baptists spiritualized the effort. Fighting poverty meant encouraging conversion and promoting virtue. The war against poverty was an evangelistic mission. Chapter seven presents the temperance crusade as a spiritual and political effort. Baptists committed themselves to moral and political solutions. Temperance tested Baptist convictions more than any other philanthropic movement. The holy tension between the sacred and the secular and over the role of the church came to the fore as Baptists disagreed over the role of temperance societies. Chapters four through seven are case studies. Each of them, in their own way, make the point that Baptists did more than react to the world they found, they attempted to inculcate their own virtues, derived from their own Christian principles, in society. They wanted the nation to reflect their values. These values alone would secure the nation's prosperity. Without them, the nation would suffer destruction.

Rejecting party politics, Baptists knew they had a responsibility to engage the public sphere. Pastors looked for "the medium path" that embraced every topic worthy of sermonizing without degrading their ministry. Finding a balance was never easy, but it remained the calling of those who counted the following as touchstone truths: "Christ's kingdom is not of this world" and "righteousness exalts a nation."

2

Piety and Social Reform

IN THE AMERICAN BAPTIST story, religious liberty was central to the promotion of virtue because true piety was encouraged only where citizens worshiped God according to the dictates of their conscience and, more importantly, according to the precepts of scripture. The Baptist struggle for an independent church sheds light on the connection between personal morals and social change.

In May of 1789 President George Washington delivered an address before the General Committee of the United Baptist Churches in Virginia. Baptist preachers seemed an unlikely group to attract the attention of the nation's first president. They were generally "without learning, without patronage, generally very poor, very plain in their dress, unrefined in their manners, and awkward in their address."[1] One historian described them as "so few in number and unimportant that they were practically unnoticed."[2] Washington however honored Baptists as celebrated supporters of the republic.

Baptists had gained respectability, in numbers at least. They benefited from revival that swept through Virginia in the mid 1700s. By 1790 their numbers had swelled to over 20,000.[3] Many Virginians viewed the Baptist sect as a threat not only to the established church but to society itself: "It was even felt that the Baptists were planning the destruction of

1. Robert Semple, *A History of the Rise and Progress of Baptists in Virginia* (Richmond, VA: Pitt & Dickinson, 1894) 43–44.

2. Wesley M. Gewehr, *The Great Awakening in Virginia, 1740–1790* (Durham, NC: Duke University Press, 1930) 106.

3. John Asplund, *The Annual Register of the Baptist Denomination* (Goodlettsville, TN: Church History and Research Archives, 1979; originally published in 1791) 32.

the state."[4] As a result, the authorities arrested and imprisoned them for disturbing the peace. Still they grew. "Great congregations of people attended the Baptist meetings, while very few went to the parish churches."[5]

With growth came better organization. In 1783 Separate Baptists in Virginia formed the General Committee, a streamlined association which met annually. The Separate Baptists grew out of the New England revivals of the Great Awakening and moved South in the 1750s with a revivalistic and baptistic theology. One of the marks distinguishing the Separate from the Regular Baptists was the former group's reluctance to adopt a statement of faith. When the Separate Baptists adopted the Philadelphia Confession of Faith as their doctrinal standard they laid the groundwork for union with the Regular Baptists.

The General Committee had no qualms about direct political activity. In 1785 its delegates objected to a bill in the Virginia General Assembly to legalize state funded support of religious instruction. They decried the proposal as "repugnant to the spirit of the Gospel."[6] The committee sent its clerk, Reuben Ford, to petition against the policy. Baptists and numerous other evangelicals lobbied the Virginia legislature for religious freedom: "Presbyterian, Lutheran, and Baptist congregations and associations called for liberty of conscience."[7] The assembly refused to legislate state supported religious instruction. Instead, they established religious freedom:

> To compel a man to furnish contributions of money for the propagation of opinions which he disbelieves and abhors, is sinful and tyrannical; that even forcing him to support this or that teacher of his own religious persuasion, is depriving him of the comfortable liberty of giving his contributions to the particular pastor whose morals he would make his pattern.[8]

4. Gewehr, *Great Awakening*, 130.

5. David Benedict, *An Abridgement of the General History of the Baptist Denomination* (Boston: Lincoln & Edwards, 1820) 339. Vedder wrote, referring to Virginia: "In no colony were Baptists more oppressed." Henry C. Vedder, *A Short History of the Baptists* (London: Baptist Tract and Book Society, 1897) 208.

6. Semple, *History of Virginia Baptists*, 96.

7. Frank Lambert, *The Founding Fathers and the Place of Religion in America* (Princeton, NJ: Princeton University Press, 2003) 227.

8. "Bills Reported by the Committee of Revisors Appointed by the General Assembly of Virginia in 1776, 18 June 1779," appendix 3 in Daniel L. Dreisbach, *Thomas Jefferson and the Wall of Separation between Church and State* (New York: New York University Press, 2002) 133.

Evangelical opinion became public opinion, at least in Virginia, and in May 1789 Washington's address to the General Committee proved that democratic leaders must be responsive to popular groups, even groups that had once been persecuted sects.

In 1787 the names Regular and Separate Baptist were "buried in oblivion" and they now formed the United Baptist Churches of Christ in Virginia, the body Washington visited.[9] For half of the eighteenth century the Regulars and the Separates had refused communion with each other. However, the fires of revival, the shared experience of persecution, and the success of religious liberty diminished distinctions and contributed to harmony. With greater size and unity came respectability. According to Semple, "they were joined by persons of much greater weight in civil society."[10] Buoyed by popular and influential support they helped secure liberty of conscience.

It is no wonder, then, that Washington addressed the General Committee on the topic of religious liberty: "I beg you will be persuaded, that no one would be more zealous than myself to establish effectual barriers against the horrors of spiritual tyranny, and every species of religious persecution."[11] He knew his audience. Baptists supported the Revolution and their continued defense of the American experiment was contingent upon the government's commitment to liberty of conscience. Washington assured them of his personal convictions: "I have often expressed my sentiments, that every man, conducting himself as a good citizen, and being accountable to God alone for his religious opinions, ought to be protected in worshipping the Deity according to the dictates of his own conscience."[12] Such assurances, Washington hoped, would be enough to guarantee the support of Virginian Baptists: "I cannot hesitate to believe, that they will be faithful supporters of a free, yet efficient general government."[13]

Washington aptly summarized what became the Baptist disposition toward government and society from the late-eighteenth through the mid-nineteenth century. Baptists in Virginia and throughout the United

9. Semple, *History of Virginia Baptists*, 101.

10. Ibid., 59.

11. George Washington, "To the General Committee, Representing the United Baptist Churches in Virginia. May, 1789," in *The Writings of George Washington*, ed. Jared Sparks (Boston: Little, Brown, 1855) 155.

12. Ibid.

13. Ibid.

States faithfully supported the nation through preaching, evangelizing, and generally encouraging religious values. When it came to the rhetoric which undergirded the republic these Baptists remained Washington's "faithful supporters." With an evangelistic zeal, Baptists in Virginia and throughout the republic maintained that America's success depended upon the virtue of her citizens. And the virtue of her citizens depended on the piety that only the gospel could bring.

From the Revolutionary War to the dawn of the Civil War, Baptists showed their commitment to reform society by saving sinners. Virtue, rooted in Christian piety, and watered by the rain of religious liberty, lay at the core of Baptist social reform. Their decision to begin with the individual had nothing to do with distancing themselves from society. Baptists simply insisted that the nation would be made stronger through the movement of a spiritual church that is in but not of the world. When describing this spiritual church they regularly evoked Jesus' words from John 18:36: "My kingdom is not of this world." American Baptists lived and preached with the conviction that a transformed human life is effective, like leaven working its way through a loaf a bread—indirect but potent. However, the transformation was ultimately God's work. Any merely human change was temporary and ineffectual. This principle guided Baptist social reform for generations.

Virtue and Nationalism

The role of virtue was part of a larger question regarding the liberal versus the classical, republican tradition that influenced America's founding. According to Lockean liberalism, people will do what they most desire to do. A successful government recognizes each person's inherent selfishness and maintains certain checks to ensure the protection of individual liberties.[14] Republicanism, on the other hand, is dismissive of individual rights and emphasizes the importance of a virtuous population and especially, virtuous leaders.[15]

---

14. "Seen from a political perspective, this is supposedly the great realism of Lockean liberalism, for grounding rights on this single selfish passion marries rights to self-interest and thereby increases the odds that a government devoted to this end will succeed." Jean M. Yarbrough, *American Virtues: Thomas Jefferson on the Character of a Free People* (Lawrence: University Press of Kansans, 1998) 2.

15. Ibid., xvi.

Thomas Jefferson, argued historian Jean M. Yarbrough, struck a middle ground. He epitomized "The Liberal Ideal" that depended upon an innate virtue:

> The moral sense affirms society's collective judgment about right and wrong; it actively seeks the approbation of the larger community, though it must be emphasized to those who fear the danger of majority tyranny that the majority does not create these principles. They are inscribed in human nature by a Benevolent Creator so that human beings everywhere can develop the moral and intellectual capacity for self-government.[16]

For Jefferson virtue remained a private matter. He did not reject outright the public discussion of private virtues. Nonetheless, his criticism of administrations in which he served, his support for the infidel French Revolution, and his deistic philosophical speculations led many Federalists and pietists to conclude Jefferson was an enemy of the faith.[17] Washington, on the other hand, promoted private and social virtue to a level of regular public concern. He exhorted the young nation to exercise morality. In 1789 he called on the members of the Dutch Reformed Church to be good citizens for the sake of the nation: "You Gentlemen, act the part of pious Christians and good citizens by your prayers and exertions to preserve that harmony and good will towards men, which must be the basis of every political establishment."[18] Likewise, as he left office, Washington offered these closing remarks where he reiterated the necessity of virtue for the country's well-being: "It is substantially true, that virtue or morality is a necessary spring of popular government. . . . Who, that is a sincere friend to it, can look with indifference upon attempts to shake the foundation of the fabric?"[19]

After Alexis de Tocqueville visited America in the 1830s, he insisted that the nation was still preoccupied with virtue: "I consider mores to be one of the great general causes to which the maintenance of a democratic republic in the United States can be attributed."[20] By "mores," Tocqueville

16. Ibid., 193.

17. Lambert, *The Founding Fathers*, 273.

18. George Washington, "To the Synod of the Reformed Dutch Church in North America, October, 1789," in *The Writings of George Washington*, 167.

19. Washington, "Farewell Address," in *The Writings of George Washington*, 227.

20. Alexis de Tocqueville, *Democracy in America*, trans. and ed. by Harvey C. Mansfield and Delba Winthrop (Chicago: University of Chicago Press, 2000) 274.

meant "the whole moral and intellectual state of a people."[21] America's well-being depended upon her morality, according to the visiting French leader. Tocqueville's observation about virtue and nationalism had been argued by Baptists for decades.

One of the earliest and most forceful proponents of this principle was Isaac Backus, the Massachusetts Baptist who began as a farmer but emerged as a leading theologian and advocate for religious liberty. It is in the debate over the role of an established religion that his views of virtue and nationalism become clear. Baptists agreed with many Americans that the nation needed a virtuous population to succeed in politics and business. Where Baptists differed was regarding how virtue was to be promoted. Backus argued that the nation would be best served by independent churches, congregations with the freedom to exercise their faith unencumbered by interference from the state. By so closely tying the piety and independence of the church to the welfare of the nation, Backus and other Baptists presented themselves as early social reformers.

Backus repeatedly wrote against Article III of the Massachusetts Constitution's Declaration of Rights. Ratified in 1780 Article III established a state religion. It did so while articulating the link between morality and the well-being of society: "The happiness of a people, and good order and preservation of civil government, essentially depend upon piety, religion, and morality."[22]

Under the influence of John Adams, Massachusetts took a different approach to religious liberty than did Virginia, guided by Thomas Jefferson. Both Adams and Jefferson believed that individual citizens should be free to worship as they saw fit, but Jefferson rejected the establishment of a state church while Adams believed it to be commensurate with the public welfare. John Witte Jr. summarized Adams's position:

> The notion that a state and society could remain neutral and purged of any religion was, for Adams, a philosophical fiction. Absent a commonly adopted set of values and beliefs, politicians would invariably hold out their private convictions as public ones. It was thus essential for each community to define the basics of its public religion. In Adams's view, the creed of this public religion was honesty, diligence, devotion, obedience, virtue, and love of God, neighbor, and self. Its icons were the Bible, the

21. Ibid., 275.

22. Massachusetts Constitutional Convention, *Constitution* (Boston: Benjamin Edes & Son, 1780) 7.

bells of liberty, the memorials of patriots, and the Constitution. Its clergy were public-spirited ministers and religiously devout politicians. Its liturgy was the public proclamation of oaths, prayers, songs, and election and Thanksgiving Day sermons. Its policy was state appointment of chaplains for the legislature, military, and prison; state sanctions against blasphemy, sacrilege, and iconoclasm; and state sponsorship of religious societies, schools and charities.[23]

Adams wanted a civil religion, a society infused with Christian principles, led by Christian politicians, and sanctified by Christian ministers. Article III became the mechanism to make this vision a reality. Not only did society depend upon virtue, society depended upon government to deliver piety through religious structures. It required the taxation of every citizen to support Protestant ministers and demanded attendance at public worship services. Article III codified the colonial system of tithing to which Massachusetts citizens had grown accustomed.[24] Proponents believed government-sponsored religion served society's interests: "Though we are not supporting the Kingdom of Christ, may we not be permitted to Assist civil society by an adoption, and by the teaching of the best act of Morals that were ever offered to the World?"[25]

Article III displeased Baptists. It found a vigorous opponent in Backus who regularly promoted what William G. McLoughlin referred to as an "evangelical theory of separation of church and state."[26] In 1773, writing as a representative for the Warren Baptist Association, Backus penned *An Appeal to the Public for Religious Liberty* in which he addressed two legitimate but distinct forms of government, civil and ecclesiastical. Repeatedly citing John 18:36, Backus argued that since Christ's kingdom is not of this world, both the state and the church must operate in separate spheres: "The church is armed with light and truth to pull down the strongholds of iniquity and to gain souls to Christ and into his Church to be governed by his rules therein, and again to exclude such from their communion, who will not be so governed, while the state is

23. John Witte Jr., "A Most Mild and Equitable Establishment of Religion': John Adams and the Massachusetts Experiment," in *Religion and the New Republic: Faith in the Founding of America* (Lanham, MD: Rowman & Littlefield, 2000) 3.

24. Ibid., 13.

25. Ibid., 25.

26. William G. McLouglin, "Introduction," in *Isaac Backus on Church, State, and Calvinism Pamphlets, 1754–1789* (Cambridge, MA: Belknap, 1968) 1.

armed with the sword to guard the peace and the civil rights of all persons and societies and to punish those who violate the same."[27] Thus armed, an established church is a contradiction in terms.

In 1777 Backus devoted a circular letter of the Warren Baptist Association to the theme of religious liberty, again citing John 18:36. He contended that establishing religion through a ministerial tax is more absurd than the British taxing colonists without representation in Parliament: "For a civil assembly to impose religious taxes, is more certainly out of their jurisdiction than it can be for Britain to tax America; because the latter is only an extending of the power of one civil legislature into the territories of another of the same kind, while the former is for earth to encroach upon the authority of Heaven."[28] Backus decried the physical state supporting a spiritual religion: "But as the kingdom of Christ is not of this world, but spiritual, and he a spiritual King; so much the government of this spiritual kingdom under this spiritual King needs be spiritual, and all the laws of it."[29] A spiritual kingdom, argued Backus, ought not to look toward the state for succor.

Backus wanted his readers to understand the negative, social implications of an established church. He believed it encouraged hypocrisy and would eventually corrupt the society everyone wanted to support. His argument for a disestablished church was an argument for social reform. He believed that Adams and the advocates of Article III misunderstood the salient problem of establishment: it encouraged duplicity and thus undermined the virtue of the citizenry. This was the great irony, contended Backus, of civil religion. Though it presented the trappings of religiosity it confused its practicioners into thinking that by participating in the state they could gain righteousness: "What a temptation then does it lay for men to contract such guilt when temporal advantages are annexed to one persuasion and disadvantages laid upon another? i.e. in plain terms, how does it tend to hypocrisy and lying? than which, what can be worse to human society!"[30] Backus assumed society needed virtuous people, but he rejected the conclusion that an established church would produce them. Civil religion produces spiritual hypocrites, Backus

---

27. Isaac Backus, *An Appeal to Public for Religious Liberty*, 315.

28. Isaac Backus, "Circular Letter to the Churches," *Minutes*, Warren Baptist Association, 1777, 5.

29. Ibid., 6.

30. Backus, *Appeal to Public*, 335.

argued, by forcing citizens to participate in religious activities they did not necessarily support.

Not only did Backus stress the duplicity inherent in civil religion, he also maintained its implausibility. The state can restrain sinners but encouraging morality is the purview of an independent church and, finally, the act of a sovereign God. In making this argument, he tied social reform to theology: "The reason why piety, religion, and morality, are essentially necessary for the good order of human society, is because they are as much above the commanding power of man, as the showers and shines of heaven are."[31] Here Backus did more than simply agree with the assumption made by various religious leaders and politicians, he offered a theological basis for why society depends upon piety. His answer evidenced Backus's faith in God. He viewed society as a living organism, much the same way he viewed a tree. Just as man cannot take credit for the water that sustains a tree, people could not take credit for the virtue that improved society. Both found their source in God: "All which proves that piety, religion, and morality, are as much above the commanding power of men, as the showers of heaven are, or the sun in the firmament."[32]

Backus's writings indicate that from the earliest days of the nation, Baptists, like other Americans, held to the belief that America's success depended upon its piety. As Witte noted in his study of the 1780 constitution controversy, the question of the relationship between virtue and society never caused serious rancor: "None of these provisions establishing a public religious morality triggered much debate during the constitutional convention, and none of these provisions was amended or emended thereafter."[33] However, unlike many other Americans, Backus showed that Baptists differed on how piety ought to be encouraged. It was not enough to do good; Backus cared about why Christians chose to do good. Churches alone, seeking to be faithful to the commandments of God, could successfully inculcate virtue in America's citizens and prosper the young nation.

Article III remained a source of animosity, lawsuits, and debate.[34] In 1820 the editor of Boston's *Christian Watchman & Baptist Register*

31. Isaac Backus, *The Kingdom of God, Described by His Word, with its Infinite Benefits to Human Society* (Boston: Samuel Hall, 1792) 15.

32. Ibid., 18.

33. Witte, "Establishment of Religion," 21.

34. Ibid., 29.

criticized a Massachusetts chief justice for defending Article III.[35] Like advocates of ministerial taxes forty years prior, Chief Justice Parker argued that the civil government depended upon "piety, religion, and morality."[36] This is reason enough, he insisted, for the state legislature to require towns to establish churches and hire pastors.

The editors, following Backus's lead, summarized their disagreement with the chief justice in six headings. First, they noted that Christ's kingdom is not of this world and therefore the church must not in any way be governed by civil magistrates. Second, since the Bible teaches that religion is supposed to be "the holy and conscientious service of God, from a love to him," the legislature, which is not a Christian institution, must not oversee the church. Third, though it is true that the civil government depends upon the piety of its citizens, this does not imply an established religion: "We dispute not the principle, that 'the happiness of a people, and the preservation of civil government, essentially depend upon piety.'"[37] They refused to draw the conclusion, however, that the government must spearhead such virtue. Fourth, if the government has the right to establish religion then there is nothing to keep any government from establishing any religion. Fifth, and along similar lines, the government must also have the right to choose what religion is appropriate and arbitrarily exclude some worthy citizens from participation. Sixth, true religion should stem from an appreciation of God's authority and not from respect or fear of the state.

Massachusetts Baptists were social reformers because they linked personal piety, a free church, and the welfare of the nation. In a state that believed an established church guarded morality, Baptists needed to prove that their brand of civic polity would not corrupt the social fabric. Thus, they emphasized that the freedom to worship produced pious citizens. To the editors of the *Watchman*, religious liberty and virtue went hand-in-hand. In 1823 they called for the spread of piety throughout the land: "May Heaven grant, that virtue and knowledge may be so thoroughly diffused in all our population, that the period shall never arrive, when they will have to unlearn this lesson."[38] That "lesson" being the conviction that religious liberty undergirded a state's prosperity. A year later,

35. There is confusion regarding whether the editor of the paper in 1820 was Equality Weston or James Loring. For further discussion, see Albaugh, *History*, 2:933.

36. "Religious Liberty," *Christian Watchman*, 14 October 1820, 3.

37. Ibid.

38. "Untitled," *Christian Watchman*, 6 December 1823, 207.

citing a sermon by Dr. Rice of the United Domestic Missionary Society, the same paper noted, "A republic cannot exist without virtue. The law loses its energy, when it is not enforced by the sanctions of religion."[39] The success of the republic was linked to a virtuous population. The same point was made in 1833 when the editor of the *Watchman* connected a drought of pastors to a lack of virtue: "It is easy to perceive that without a proportionate increase of the means of education and religion, we shall be more than commonly liable to degenerate from virtue to vice, and from piety to irreligion."[40]

Baptists in Boston who argued against an established religion had a pressing reason to defend the necessity of virtue. However, Baptists throughout the nation in the early nineteenth century also made the case for a tie between piety and prosperity. They regularly articulated the connection between a virtuous society and a saved soul. Evidence of the relationship between personal spirituality and social reform outside of Massachusetts illustrates the point that for Baptists, social reform was more than a political debate, it was a theological necessity.

Henry Holcombe, pastor of the First Baptist Church of Savannah, Georgia, published the *Analytical Repository* beginning in May 1802. Though its subscription list never exceeded five hundred copies, it bears the distinction of being the first religious periodical of the South.[41] In its third installment, Holcombe addressed a lengthy essay "to the friends of religion" on the relationship between Christians and civil government. The Christian's character undergirded society, "his divine ambition is, to possess all the virtues, and discharge all the duties, which dignify and embellish civil and religious life."[42]

Though Holcombe called upon Christians to exercise virtue, he recognized that piety did not solve all problems. Depravity, not piety, necessitated government. Holcombe recalled the recent history of Baptist persecution and argued for a robust government willing to execute justice and capable of restraining vice: "Had man continued, as he was created, in the image, and subject to the laws of God, there could have been no necessity for punitive justice; and were all men genuine, and consistent

39. "Prospects for Our Country," *Christian Watchman*, 7 August 1824, 138.

40. Eubulus, "A Word to Churches—No. 2" *Christian Watchman*, 22 March 1833, 45.

41. Albaugh, *History*, 1:448.

42. Henry Holcombe, "Address to the Friends of Religion," *Georgia Analytical Repository*, September–October, 1802, 97.

Christians, there would now be no use for coercive power."[43] However, men are not consistent and therefore a government, even "badly administered, is preferable to entire anarchy" so long as the populace vests it with the authority to punish.[44]

Vice may explain why government is necessary but virtue caused government's success: "I need not prove, for it is evident, that without Religion there can be no virtue; and it is equally incontestable, that without virtue, there can be no liberty."[45] Thus, Holcombe defended Christians as "the most valuable citizens and the best soldiers in the world."[46] Were any of his readers unconvinced, he appealed to a higher authority, the "Great Washington" who, if "permitted to speak, once more" would say, "the preservation of your constitution, laws, and liberties, depends, under God, on the speedy union, and well directed exertions of your moral, and religious citizens."[47]

Holcombe's essay and the entirety of his short-lived periodical testify to the belief that virtue preserved liberty and was the bedrock of society. He intended the *Repository* to be "a confluence of numerous rills of virtue, piety, and salutary knowledge."[48] He used the power of the pen to distance true Christians from those who bore the name of Christ but lived in sin and, thus, corrupted society: "Many among us, improperly, called Christians, interpretively plead for prompt assistance. Engaged in no honest pursuit, and regardless of every call to common industry, they have ignobly yielded to the disgraceful, and ruinous dominion of their brutal lusts."[49]

Holcombe shared Backus's disdain for hypocrisy. True virtue—necessary for a successful republic—demanded genuine, individual conversion. He founded the *Analytical Repository* just after the great revival spread through Georgia. Holcombe believed that America was in its last days, and this conviction led him to do more than encourage evangelism; it caused him to seek a virtuous citizenship.[50] Empowered by the

43. Ibid., 99.

44. Ibid.

45. Ibid., 230.

46. Ibid., 232.

47. Holcombe, "Address to the Friends of Religion," *Georgia Analytical Repository,* January–February, 1803, 233.

48. Holcombe, "Preface," *Georgia Analytical Repository,* 25 May 1802, 10.

49. Ibid., 3.

50. John B. Boles, *The Great Revival: Beginnings of the Bible Belt* (Lexington: The

Holy Spirit, anxious to heed God's commandments, free to hear the Bible preached, these Christians did not need the state to encourage their piety. True Christians served society by pursuing personal virtue. Social reform began with the individual.

Quoting Francis Wayland, the editor of Washington's *Columbian Star* impressed upon his readers the necessity of a moral majority: "So long, then, as our people remain virtuous and intelligent, our government will remain stable."[51] A few years later, the *Star's* editor, W. T. Brantly, asserted that the "subversion of our institutions" is usually connected to a "decline of intelligence and virtue in the mass of society."[52] In Richmond, Virginia, the editor of the *Religious Herald* rooted America's success to its citizens' piety: "If ever this magnificent republic totters and falls, her overthrow will originate in the deficiency of intelligence, and industry and virtue, into which her sons and daughters will sink."[53]

No paper made the argument more forcefully though than the *Watchman*. In 1833, after a half-century of what Baptists considered religious oppression, the citizens of Massachusetts finally amended their constitution to disestablish religion. The commonwealth did not deny that society needed morality to succeed, it simply rejected the requirement of an established church: "As the public worship of God and instructions in piety, religion and morality, promote the happiness and prosperity of a people and the security of a Republican Government;—Therefore the several religious societies of the Commonwealth, whether corporate or incorporate, at any meeting legally warned and holden for that purpose, shall ever have the right to elect their pastors or religious teachers."[54] The editors of the *Watchman* continued to argue for piety's influence on society: "That a constant and powerful influence is to perform an important part in the salvation of man, and the moral renovation of the world, is too plain a proposition to be disputed."[55] Human depravity is always fighting against the positive power of a Christian. Nonetheless, "a pious influence, constantly and vigorously put forth, by prayer, by admonition, by exem-

University Press of Kentucky, 1996) 105.

51. James D. Knowles, "From Mr. Wayland's Sermons," *Columbian Star*, 18 June 1825, 100.

52. W. T. Brantly, "The Nation," *Columbian Star*, 4 December 1830, 353.

53. H. Keeling, "Religious Herald," *Religious Herald*, 18 January 1828, 7.

54. Cited by Witte, "Establishment of Religion," 29.

55. William Crowell, "The Power of Christian Influence," *Christian Watchman*, 6 December 1839, 194.

plary self-denial, will have its effect. As truth is the natural aliment of the mind, so an elevating influence is its natural stimulant. Truth, logically proved, may silence objections, and even produce mental convictions, but an active influence is necessary to arouse to action. Both are needed, with the blessing of God, to reform and sanctify men."[56]

A decade after disestablishment in Massachusetts, Baptists North and South continued, with equal vigor, to articulate the importance of virtue to America. In Boston the American experiment rested, argued Baptists, not on politics but on piety: "Political equality will not secure good government, unless wise and virtuous men form the majority, or exert a controlling influence. The form of republicanism, or democracy, may be a blessing or a curse; according as the people are ignorant or enlightened, good or bad. . . . The hope of our country, therefore, is in the advancement of true piety."[57] Likewise, down South on the eve of the Civil War, Baptists remained convinced that America's success was rooted in her religious heritage: "We must dig a deeper foundation for a lasting celebrity. Virtue can only make us free, freedom can only make us great, religion can only make us virtuous."[58] Baptists hungered for a righteous nation and a free church. They remained convinced that the two went hand-in-hand. Their doctrine of a spiritual kingdom did not lead away from social reform; it led them into it.

Faith and Pietism

As the nineteenth century progressed and Baptists grew in both numbers and prominence, their commentaries on virtue and society changed. Many grew weary of broad-based efforts at social reform. The same principles that led them to censure the established church now led them to criticize social reform. The vast machinery of social reform tended to draw citizens away from trust in the spiritual power of true piety and led them to trust the temporal power of benevolent societies. Ironically the benevolent empire was becoming a civil religion similar to the established religion Baptists had fought against so vigorously. Americans

56. Ibid.

57. William Crowell, "The Hope of Our Country," *Christian Watchman*, 15 November 1844, 182.

58. William Sands, "Effect of the Scriptures on National Character," *Religious Herald*, 26 August 1847, 133.

participated in the philanthropic enterprises of the day and assumed that such participation signified Christian faithfulness. Baptists generally responded to this danger not by repudiating social reform the way they repudiated the established church but by pleading for true social reform, for benevolence marked by sincerity. The only way for this to happen was to ensure that the Christian gospel motivated reformers to act. The piety that led to social reform had to be more deeply and clearly rooted in faith.

Claude Welch defined pietism at the turn of the eighteenth century as "a system of feeling" or "a theological mood and stance."[59] Pietism is more about the "inner conviction and peace . . . the intensity of feeling" than intellect, rationality, and orthodoxy. Protestants of the period prized the internality of the faith, its experiential aspects: "It was the inner experience of grace, the sure confidence of forgiveness and reconciliation, the full reliance on the blood of Christ, that was to be sought."[60] But pietism emphasized also right behavior. Welch described pietism as the "moralizing of Christianity . . . an emphasis on the outward shape of the good life that had much in common with the Enlightenment's desire to identify religion with morality. Christianity was not doctrine but life."[61] Baptists shared pietism's intensity, interiorization, and moralizing. However, Baptist piety was also doctrinal, it encompassed both life and truth. Social reform unguided by a pious faith was moralistic, hypocritical, and unacceptable. Baptist reformers sought to bring Christian spirituality and sincerity into the benevolent enterprises of the day. They aimed to make the gospel the principle of change. They worked to make evangelical piety the engine of Baptist social reform.

Many saw the rising tide of social reform as inconsistent with true Christian benevolence. Christian social reform must take into account, first and foremost, the salvation of the person and not simply the temporal crisis. As the *Columbian Star* argued, "there is one feature in the benevolent plans and exertions of the present period, which distinguishes them from nearly all the charities which have preceded them. It is now a leading object to remove the sufferings of mankind, by saving them from their sins."[62] The author expressed great confidence that salvation is what led to moral reform and prevented "crime and misery, by guiding youth

---

59. Claude Welch, *Protestant Thought in the Nineteenth Century* (New Haven, CT: Yale University Press, 1972) 1:27.

60. Ibid.

61. Ibid., 29.

62. "Christian Beneficence," *Columbian Star*, 12 October 1822, 4.

in the way of holiness and peace, and removing them from temptation."[63] Social reform that did not address the heart was impious and of little use: "Almost in vain is the penitent soothed in sickness, if the disorder be not eradicated. In vain is relief given by amputation of a limb, if the gangrene be left, extending to the vitals."[64] Some Baptists doubted that the social reform movement, divorced from an emphasis on personal conversion, could live up to its promises:

> Not unfrequently we meet with some zealous reformer, who would have us believe that the final triumph of Christianity depended, almost entirely, upon the success of his favorite scheme; while that scheme proposed for its accomplishment nothing more, than to correct some abuses, in the merest externals of our social relations. The friend of temperance, the abolitionist, the advocate of peace, they come successively before the public, too often leave the impression that unless their favorite schemes are carried, all efforts for the spread of Christianity will be but in vain; whereas, the great objects had in view by these friends of their race, depend exclusively for their success upon the progress of a pure Christianity.[65]

The editor of the *Watchman* believed that humanity needed a transformation of the inner nature—something the "zealous reformer" could not provide: "We believe in the depravity of man's nature, that as a moral being, he is utterly broken down and fallen into ruins—sinful, weak and even helpless. In such a state, the gospel comes to him as a sovereign remedy, quickening into life the energies of the soul, renewing and sanctifying every faculty which goes to constitute one a moral being."[66] The gospel, then, served as the principle of reform, able to transform society: "And, it is to the gospel, in its influence directly and indirectly . . . that we are indebted for every thing desirous in our civil and social relations, and in our condition as moral beings."[67]

For years, similar arguments found their way into the press. P. C., writing to the *Watchman*, agreed that the gospel is the best means of social reform: "Should the representative of moral reform, or of the abolitionist, or of the temperance man, or of the political agitator, or of

63. Ibid.
64. Ibid.
65. "Moral Reform," *Christian Watchman*, 13 March 1835, 42.
66. Ibid.
67. Ibid.

any other class of reformer, succeed in obviating the specific evils which they assail, the common source of these evils would still remain to break forth in other and equally disastrous forms of mischief and ruin. Nothing can prevent this result, but this radical renewal of the heart through the power of the Holy Spirit, which is the sole aim of Christianity."[68] Meanwhile, a few years later, J. C. feared that humanitarian efforts harmed the gospel by conflating social reform and Christianity: "The ideas of God and accountability, of heaven and hell, of the atonement, of regeneration and sanctification, of faith and pardon, of prayer and holy living, are ridiculed as abstractions, and are struck out to foist in a system of temporal improvement under the name of gospel."[69] Christianity was of great benefit to society. This J. C. did not deny: "It is true that Christianity promotes the temporal elevation of mankind."[70] However, the primary goal of the faith was salvation, "its main design . . . is to save sinners from eternal wrath . . . [Christ] was a Reformer, but one who laid the axe at the root of the tree, at the human heart, and who aimed at the renovation by a spiritual and superhuman power."[71] J. C. recognized that some pastors frowned upon the benevolent enterprises of the day. He did not. He simply identified a church devoted to the gospel as the ultimate source of relief and happiness: "The natural tendency of the gospel is to give increased breadth and tenderness to our social sentiments, and make us more completely human."[72]

New England pastor Lucien Hayden defended the pure church as the engine of social reform. In the midst of the din of a benevolent empire, he declared that without the church there was no empire. Hayden, who wrote of the atonement of Christ as the church's "vital doctrine," described the pious church as reform's only hope. Hayden argued that piety promoted social reform. The church could not allow the latter to take the lead, "Let not the sincere friend of humanity, then, whose heart glows with benevolent affection for the ignorant, the despised and the oppressed, be insidiously enticed, in an evil hour, to join in the insane cry, 'Down with the Church!'"[73]

68. P. C., "Simplicity of the Gospel In Its Tactics of Reform," *Christian Watchman*, 22 October 1841, 170.

69. J. C., "Social Reform, Not Christianity," *Christian Watchman*, 25 July 1845, 118.

70. Ibid.

71. Ibid.

72. Ibid.

73. Lucien Hayden, "The Pure Church, Characterized by Spirituality," in *Baptist*

When benevolence did take the lead, the social reformation appeared more secular than spiritual, and Boston Baptists feared the results: "We need not speak of the disguises and the speciousness under which many of these influences are set in motion. That their result in certain directions, unless checked, must be to sap the hold of vital Christianity on the people, appears to us undeniable."[74] The Boston Baptist Association refused to retreat from the call to serve society, choosing instead to educate its delegates regarding the proper relationship between piety and reform: "As those who have light from heaven which we shrink not to follow, and the spirit of Jesus in our hearts,—as those who profess to cherish a profound sense of the worth of man and his need above all things of the religion of the Gospel, as also that this, or nothing can conserve society, we cannot, nay we must not, yield up the reins of reform to the unbelieving and irreligious."[75] Instead of sounding the retreat, they chose to reform social reform itself. They sought to invest the movement with sincerity nourished by Christian spirituality. They returned to the argument that reform required virtue which could only be found in the exercise of personal faith. They held fast to the link between social reform and the tested principles of Christianity: "Apart from the cross of Christ as an exponent at once of love and law, of mercy and of justice, we look in vain for an element that can preserve society, either as settled or as agitated."[76] Religion and reform "can never be dissociated. They never should be separated. So much as the thought of their divorce should not be suffered."[77]

Boston Baptists persevered as social reformers even as they criticized the social reform movement itself. They remained convinced that social reform, separated from the cross of Christ, would prove ineffectual because outsiders would become disillusioned by the inevitable impiety

---

Pamphlets, ed. George W. Anderson (Philadelphia: American Baptist Publication Society, 1854) 44.

74. "Circular," Minutes, Boston Baptist Association 1846, 11.

75. Ibid., 13–14.

76. Ibid., 14.

77. Ibid., 15. All the efforts associated with reform are useless, the Boston South Baptist Association argued, without vibrant, evangelical Christianity: "Suppose, for example, that intemperance were banished from the land, or even slavery, what would be gained in the sum total of moral good, if, supposing such a consummation possible, the Sabbath and the ordinances of religion were at the same time to pass away, disrobed of their sacredness, and becoming a dead letter, should be lost to the present and to future generations?"

of the reformers: "They may hear us pray for the poor and oppressed, but they will despise us if they see us lack that piety which will lay partisan interests, political preference, and pecuniary interests, on the altar of benevolence, and humanity."[78] Christians who proved unable to unite social reform and piety were reminded of their error. In 1851 William H. Shailer called Boston Baptist churches away from greater philanthropy if such service was divorced from true faith and devotion: "This is emphatically an age of action. Many things tend to excite a love for humanity that do not excite a love to God. And as a consequence, there is by far more philanthropy than piety among us . . . while Christians are active they should also be pious."[79]

This emphasis on faith and pietism as the necessary precondition for true social reform was nothing new. Backus had already asserted that the Christian church is the organization best situated to serve human society when he described the gospel as good for humanity:

> For the proclamation of the gospel, believed with the heart, and obeyed in the church, without injuring any man in the world, as each one can answer it to God in the last day, is a glorious kingdom which cannot be moved. And if the church of Christ was governed wholly by his laws; enforced in his name, she would be an infinite blessing to human society.[80]

Backus had great confidence in the evangelical religion to redeem man and to transform the culture. One of Backus's contemporaries in the Warren Baptist Association, writing in 1788, expressed a similar trust: "It is the believers work to renounce and oppose these vices, and to exercise the contrary tempers of humility, love to God and mankind: denying self, taking up your cross, doing good as far as we have opportunity, to all men, especially to the household of faith."[81]

Speaking before the political elite of his day, Boston pastor Thomas Baldwin argued that the welfare of the government and society did not finally rest in the hands of the well-to-do. Should the people lose their faith, all is lost: "When a people give up their religion, and renounce the

78. "Circular Letter," *Minutes*, Boston South Baptist Association, 1849, 15.

79. William H. Shailer, "Report on the State of Religion in Our Churches," *Minutes*, Boston South Baptist Association, 1851, 8.

80. Backus, *Kingdom of God*, 14.

81. Edward Clarke, "The Circular Letter," *Minutes*, Warren Baptist Association, 1788, 10–11.

authority of God, they will not hesitate to overleap all bounds of law and morality, and destroy one another."[82] He preached this election sermon before the Massachusetts governor, council, and legislature in 1802, reminding them that "the religion of the Bible, above all others, has a peculiar tendency to cement and strengthen the bands of society, and promote the happiness of mankind. It inculcates the purest precepts, and exemplifies the most amiable virtues. Every man, let his rank in society be what it may, will here find his duty plainly pointed out, and illustrated by example."[83] Baldwin claimed Christianity and its attendant piety as the foundation of every social good.

William Fristoe, moderator and historian of the Ketocton Baptist Association of Virginia, also emphasized the importance of the Christian faith for society's welfare. Individual Christians "enjoy divine blessings peculiar to the Christian character." They are, as a result, "better able to support truth, and detect error" within and without the church and "so promote the general good." [84]

Some Baptists argued that Calvinism was the form of Christianity most likely to encourage this "general good." In 1822 Boston's *Christian Watchman* printed an article maintaining America, as a whole, favored the doctrine of predestination and then asked, "What are we to think of the morality of Calvinistic nations, especially the most numerous classes of them, who seem, beyond all other men, to be most zealously attached to their religion, and most deeply penetrated with its spirit? The author concluded that where Calvinist communities predominated, such as in New England, virtue abounded.[85] Most defenses of morality, however, were not explicitly rooted in Calvinism. The editor of the *Columbian Star* called upon his readers to change the world through example: "The humblest Christian can thus, by the 'mute eloquence' of his example, confound the wisdom and infidelity of the world."[86] He required fidelity to the gospel: "We have seen, in our reflections, thus far, that the Christian may essentially aid in promoting piety and happiness around him,

82. Thomas Baldwin, *A Sermon Delivered Before His Excellency Caleb Strong, Governor* (Boston: Young & Minns, 1802) 21.

83. Ibid., 18–19.

84. William Fristoe, *A Concise History of the Ketocton Baptist Association* (Staunton, VA: William Gilman Lyford, 1808, Reprint, Stephens, VA: Commercial, 1978) 82.

85. James G. Bolles, "Moral Tendency of Calvinistic Principles," *Christian Watchman*, 2 March 1822, 46.

86. "Christian Efforts, Continued" *The Columbian Star*, 25 May 1822, 3.

without departing a step from the path of ordinary duty. He has only to exercise piety in his own bosom, and the effects, to which we have been directing our attention, will calmly diffuse their influence on all around him."[87]

Similar sentiments blossomed in Richmond, Virginia. The "prosperity of the commonwealth" depended upon the faith of its citizens:

> Let its spirit ascend all our mountains, and go down into all our vallies, and reign in the bosoms of our senators, and statesmen; in our colleges and schools; in every association, and at every fire side. In one word, Christians will, of all men, be most obedient to the laws. They will by industry and frugality, do most to advance the prosperity of the commonwealth. They will be most decidedly on the side of learning, and good morals, and the tender emotions that do most to adorn the community.—They will, in fine, be foremost at the posts of war to defend their wives, their children, and their common country.[88]

Christians served the community by first purifying themselves. True social reform began with the believer: "The best reform will be, when every one sets about, in earnest, to reform himself. When everyone sweeps before his own door, we shall soon have a clean street; and when every man is what he ought to be, we shall have a whole nation fearing God and working righteousness."[89]

Baptists hesitated to separate moral from social reform. They feared that without changed hearts and renovated lives reformers would make a mockery of Christianity and a wreck of civilization. William Crowell, writing for the *Christian Watchman*, maintained that to change society Baptists had to follow in the footsteps of Christ who also prioritized individual regeneration and moral transformation: "The Saviour, therefore, though the greatest of all philanthropists and reformers, said very little about the existing relations of men, and forms of society; fruitful in evil though they were. He did not attack institutions, nor laws, nor masses of men. He adopted a more excellent way. He laid the axe at the root of the tree. He reproved individual sins to individual faces."[90] As the benevo-

---

87. Ibid.

88. "The Influence of Religion on the Laws of Nations," *Religious Herald*, 22 August 1828, 132.

89. "Christian Patriotism," *Religious Herald*, 30 May 1834, 77.

90. William Crowell, "The Gospel as a Reformer," *Christian Watchman*, 22 January 1841, 14.

lent empire grew and social reform became a staple of the Second Great Awakening, Baptists did not call for an end to the reform though they saw the danger in what appeared to be the establishment of a civil religion. Instead, they advocated for genuine social reform that began with the heart, demanded piety, and only then would secure a social benefit.

The Baptist focus on individual spirituality was not a means of shirking public duty. Spirituality produced order. The gospel "is the seminal principle in reform. It changes the face of society, spans the foundation of unjust laws and institutions, brings down kings from their thrones, and exalts the meek to the high places of power."[91] The gospel could not be reduced simply to meeting human, temporal needs: "The very moment it leaves its appropriate work on the heart to regulate the outward conduct, it is robbed of its strength and glory." When rightly wielded, the gospel accomplished more than salvation of souls: "It is thus the gospel is so eminently fitted to become the pioneer of intellectual culture, industry, social order, and good government. . . . In our view, the faithful laborer in the cause of Christ is doing more for the temporal, as well as for the spiritual good of his race."[92] Baptists saw the gospel as the harbinger of hope: "If any thing like a true Christian heart prevails throughout Christendom, we should have very little to fear for the civilization of the nineteenth century, with all its wealth, science, art, and enterprise."[93]

On the eve of the Civil War, one Baptist, J. A. James, described society as being in the hands of the pastor: "One truly faithful and zealous preacher of God's Word, to whatever section of Christ's church he may belong, does more to check the progress of vice and crime, to promote obedience to law, to aid the advancement of individual virtues, and maintain social order, than a hundred political essays, or than the utterance of the strictest views of justice, or the severest inflictions of judgment."[94] He described the pulpit as "the strongest pillar of human society."[95] His confidence in the power of the Christian message to bring reform to the nation was typical, albeit idealistic.[96] Social reform unchecked by sincere gospel piety was a travesty.

91. William Crowell, "The Gospel as a Reformer," *Christian Watchman*, 19 February 1841, 30.

92. Ibid.

93. "Christianity and Social Progress," *Religious Herald*, 30 November 1848, 189.

94. J. A. James, "Social Value of Preaching," *Religious Herald*, 2 July 1857, 101.

95. Ibid.

96. Presbyterian pastor Ezra Eastman Adams: "The pulpit civilizes by the

Political leaders from Washington to Jefferson and Baptists from Backus to James agreed that the happiness of the nation depended upon the virtue of her people. Baptists believed however that the gospel alone produced true virtue. They argued that the virtue of America depended on the Christian piety of the populace. They insisted that the best reform came indirectly as Christians lived lives in accord with the tenets of the faith once for all delivered to the saints. Social reform apart from the gospel's spiritual power would be hypocritical and ultimately self-defeating. They sought social reform rooted in Christian principles set free from political influence. When they saw a commitment to philanthropy eclipsing personal piety, they typically called the church to greater faith and more pious social service. Baptists argued for social engagement on the basis of the power of the gospel in the Christian life.

Withdrawal and Engagement

Their rhetoric however was often complex. Baptists contended, sometimes forcefully, that the church must attend to spiritual matters. Their language, if not read carefully, may lead one to argue that Baptists had only a secondary concern with society. Though this language certainly bore the mark of caution when it came to engaging the culture, even when they articulated the church as being a spiritual body, they often clarified that as a spiritual body it had a secular interest. A church even with a restricted mission remained the best hope for reforming society.

Richard Furman, pastor of the First Baptist Church of Charleston, described the role of the church for the Charleston Baptist Association. He argued that the church is appointed for two purposes, the preservation of the saints and the conversion of sinners:

> First, the preserving of a holy union and fellowship among subjects of grace, and their preservation, comfort, improvement,

---

benevolence it enjoins. In that condition of society which approaches nearest perfection, love is the bond of union. The rights of each citizen are felt and granted. In all the interchanges of life, trade, politics, and religion, that hallowed sentiment presides." Ezra Eastman Adams, *The Pulpit as Civilizer* (n.p., c. 1860) 8, 13. Gregory Wills argued that Southern Baptists, in their efforts to evangelize America, conflated "evangelizing" and "civilizing." See Wills, "The First Hundred Years of Baptist Home Missions in America: Civilization, Denominationalism, and Americanization," in *Baptists and Mission: Papers from the Fourth International Conference on Baptist Studies*, ed. Ian M. Randall and Anthony Cross (Milton Keynes, UK: Paternoster, 2008) 130–48.

while they are continued in the state of trial and ripening for the blessedness of Heaven. Secondly, the conversion of those who are yet in a state of nature; and the assistance of such who become concerned about their eternal interests, and enquire what they shall do to be saved.[97]

A couple years later Backus described for the Warren Baptist Association the duties of pastors. "A minister is bound to attend wholly and only upon his Calling in the Ministry, and not to entangle himself in the Affairs of Life, that he may please him by who he is called to his spiritual Warfare; and nothing but real Necessity may dispense with the contrary."[98] Pastors, according to Backus, must attend to "Gospel-service" and not to the "Cares of worldly Business" which only served to distract them "from that Study of God's Word and, Care of Souls, which the Duty of his Station engageth him to."[99] Such rhetoric severely limited the field of operations open to the church and its pastor. Spiritual, gospel service was the pastor's essential activity. Congregations and ministers must attend to their divinely commissioned spiritual task. Yet the duty of the Christian church and the responsibility of the Christian pastor, clearly articulated, did not conflict with the good of society. Baptists believed personal virtue was primary but they also clarified that a spiritual life did not contradict public responsibility. Ideally, in evangelical spirituality, personal piety produced temporal good:

> It is expected, and the expectation is a reasonable one, that the disciple of Christ will possess an excellent character, that he will be a good citizen, a good neighbor, an amiable and agreeable companion, but Christianity does not seek any of these external accomplishments as its end. Its aim is higher. It seeks as its end to bring the soul under the dominion of the grace of God, and then looks for every thing lovely and of good report in human character, as the necessary fruit of such a gracious state.[100]

Baptists repeatedly united gospel spirituality with secular prosperity. In 1854 the circular letter of the Elkhorn Baptist Association was

97. Richard Furman, "The Circular Letter," *Minutes*, Charleston Baptist Association, 1792, 9.

98. Isaac Backus, "Manuscript on the Support of Ministers of the Gospel," *Minutes*, Warren Baptist Association, 1789, 6.

99. Ibid.

100. E. Thresher, "The Design of a Christian Church," *Christian Watchman*, 22 December 1837, 202.

devoted to the church and, specifically, its spirituality as the author unpacked the sentence, "My kingdom is not of this world." It is the presence of the Spirit that makes the kingdom, in this case, the local church, otherworldly. First, "its spirituality is the life of the church."[101] The church, along with the individual believer, was animated by the Holy Spirit, a Spirit that was deposited in the believer upon salvation and was the gift of faith. Second, "in the spirituality of the church consists its unity."[102] Specifically, the author referred to a doctrinal unity into which every true believer was led by the Spirit. Third, "the efficiency of the church, will be first in proportion to its spirituality."[103] The churches that were the most successful evangelistically were those congregations most committed to remaining spiritual, focused upon the joy of salvation, and engaged in gospel matters. Fourth, "spirituality, is the perpetuating principle of the church."[104] So long as a church remained spiritual, it would survive. It was imperative in Baptist congregations where each member had responsibility for leadership in the body that each member be spiritual, "it becomes each, personally, to cultivate holiness—to strive for greater degrees of spirituality."[105]

These Kentucky Baptists argued that in a republic, where the people are sovereign, and in a church, "where every member has a voice," the spirituality of each individual is especially important. The polity of the church depends upon the godliness of the member just as the polity of the state depends upon the spirituality of the citizen: "When a single church is revived, a whole community feels its moral power, is brought under its influence, and conversions continually occur, as long as the church continues in that spiritual frame."[106] A church exclusively devoted to Christ can not be fairly accused of withdrawing from the culture. Spirituality does not lead to disengagement, at least in principle.

Lucien Hayden also argued for the secular benefits of a spiritual church. He used 1 Peter 2:5 as his text, "Ye also, as lively stones, are built up a spiritual house, a holy priesthood, to offer up spiritual sacrifices,

---

101. "Circular Letter," *Minutes*, Elkhorn Baptist Association, 1854, 7.

102. Ibid., 8.

103. Ibid., 9.

104. Ibid.

105. Ibid., 10.

106. Ibid., 9.

acceptable to God by Jesus Christ."[107] According to Hayden, a pure church was spiritual in its membership, its doctrine, its worship, and in all things. A spiritual church consisted of redeemed people, born again by the Spirit of God. Hayden asserted that his view of a spiritual church was a particularly Baptist idea. The pure church was full of the "regenerate, holy, heavenly."[108] The problem with Presbyterianism, Hayden asserted, was its polity that promoted a carnal church, for it assumed a spirituality that could be passed down through the family line. Piety, Hayden argued, did not run through the blood: "Relationship in the household of Christ is not carnal, but spiritual."[109] Only an exclusive commitment to being a spiritual church would tend toward a positive effect in the community. When the church changed the individual, he asserted, it could change the land: "By renewing the heart, she renews the entire individual man. By renovating individual after individual, she renovates the race. 'Ye are the light of the world.' 'Ye are the salt of the earth.'"[110]

Even when Baptists most clearly articulated the church as being a spiritual body, they did not deny that the church had a public responsibility. They rejected the category of cultural withdrawal. Baptists did at times, as we shall see, use the spirituality doctrine to restrict their social impact, though the principle behind spirituality did not demand this. Admittedly, engagement had its limits—some denied the appropriateness of political activism. Most rejected party politics.

Spirituality and Party Politics

If the purpose of the church is exclusively the edification of the saints and the conversion of sinners then there is no room for an explicitly Christian politics. Thus in 1842 the *Religious Herald* seemed to endorse an article originally published by the *New York Observer* that argued politics and piety do not mix: "It has become almost a settled opinion, that religion

107. Lucien Hayden, "The Pure Church, Characterized by Spirituality," in *Baptist Pamphlets*, ed. George W. Anderson (Philadelphia: American Baptist Publication Society, 1854) 3.

108. Ibid., 10.

109. Ibid., 26. Francis Wayland made the same argument three years later in *Notes on the Principles and Practices of Baptist Churches* (New York: Sheldon, Blakeman, 1857) 126. He argued that Baptists preserved the doctrine of the spirituality of the church by denying "hereditary membership."

110. Hayden, "The Pure Church," 43.

and politics are divorced; and the idea of re-uniting them, or suffering the former to influence the latter, has become obsolete."[111] Years of discussion about the role of pastors, Christians, and churches in politics culminated in this sweeping generalization.

"Timotheus," a pseudonymous reader of the *Christian Watchman* asked if ministers should take part in politics and answered strongly in the negative first, "because politics do not come within their province."[112] Pastors are called to preach the gospel, not to become administers in the civil government: "No where in the word of God do we find a warrant for ministers of the gospel to interfere in matters of civil legislation; but on the contrary, their duties are defined as relating immediately to the souls of men."[113] Second, pastors are not required to be involved in political affairs—others are more qualified: "They were educated for another purpose, and have been employed, or ought to have been employed, in subjects entirely foreign from those of a political nature."[114] Third, political involvement can harm a ministry: "How can he exhort those to place their affections on things above, while he himself intensely loves the world, and the things that are in the world."[115] Fourth and finally, the pastors with a political influence will lose influence in the church: "Many in our country, during the last war, by their injudicious zeal in political concerns, have fixed a stain upon their characters which time can never efface."[116] The pastor's domain was the church of God. That was his only vineyard:

> Let the minister of Christ then sacredly devote all his time, and all his labours to the interests of the church, and leave the concerns of the state to be managed by other men. Let him prove by his ardent and disinterested love for souls, and by his unwearied and laborious efforts in the cause of Christ, that he belongs to a kingdom not of this world; that instead of wishing to make the people patriots and statesmen, he above all things desires them to be saints of the Most High God.[117]

111. "Christians in Politics," *Religious Herald*, 22 September 1842, 149.

112. Timotheus [pseud.], "Ought Ministers of the Gospel to Take Any Part in Political Affairs?" *Christian Watchman*, 13 March 1824, 53.

113. Ibid.

114. Ibid.

115. Ibid.

116. Ibid.

117. Ibid.

Timotheus wanted pastors to make saints not partisans. God had assigned the church a spiritual task. Not all Baptists were as zealous as Timotheus to keep politics and piety separate. Nonetheless he represented many Baptists who believed a spiritual church excluded any political activism. As one Virginia Baptist put it, "The things of God are too holy and sacred with him, either to be mixed with, or truckled to the little low politics of men."[118]

Baptists repeated such sentiments frequently. The first issue of the *Columbian Star* announced to its readers that the editors would only engage religious affairs: "With politics we wish to have no concern. Willingly leaving to others the unprofitable conflict of partisan animosity, we shall keep entirely aloof from any alliances with political sects."[119] When discussing the presidential election, the *Star* warned its readers, "no Christian can, in our judgment, consistently participate in the eager excitements, and embittered animosities of political contests."[120]

Christian principles seemed to permit only the most limited engagement in the political realm: "We come, therefore, to the conclusion that Christians ought to be engaged in political concerns, no further than to exercise, conscientiously, their right to vote, determined as to their choice by the clearest light they can obtain."[121] Pastors were regularly exhorted not to persuade congregations in political affairs: "If there be a spectacle at which angels gaze with wonder and grief, it is that of an ambassador of Christ voluntarily descending from the dignity of his station and often prostituting the influence of his office, for the trifling object of aiding the election of a favorite candidate, or promoting the ascendancy of a political party!—How religion is scandalized! How professors are grieved! How churches are convulsed with factions!"[122] Baptists erected a barrier between the pew and partisan politics. In 1827 William Williams, a member of the Great Crossings Baptist Church in Kentucky, was so distraught for being "carried away by party feeling and shouting for his favorite candidate" at a political rally that he brought himself up on charges of church discipline. The church accepted his confession with satisfaction

118. "The Real Christian Loves His Country and is, Therefore, the Best of Patriots," *Religious Herald*, 29 February 1828, 29.

119. "To Our Patrons," *Columbian Star*, 2 February 1822, 3.

120. "Next President," *Columbian Star*, 7 September 1822, 3.

121. "Political Reflections," *Columbian Star*, 18 October 1823, 166.

122. Ibid.

and did not pursue any further action.[123] His troubled conscience testified that engaging in party politics was a sin to be avoided.

The *New York Baptist Repository* gave practical instructions for how to walk the tightrope between party politics and prudent citizenship, especially during an election season. First, vote. Second, vote for moral men. Third, avoid unfair politicking, "such as the use of ardent spirits, incendiary papers, and handbills."[124] Fourth, "adhere to principles rather than party." Fifth, keep church and state separate: "Guard against an amalgamation of religious and civil power."[125] The last admonition is telling. Baptists in the early and mid-nineteenth century had come to enjoy their religious liberty. They had united in opposition to an established church and they remembered the days when Baptist pastors faced jail time for preaching publicly. "Meddling with politics is no part of our business. Neither our inclination nor our duty lead in this direction."[126]

Baptists rarely identified themselves with a political party. Instead they professed their commitment to the constitutional ideals of republican democracy: "Is there a Baptist political position?" D. T. N. asked.[127] He reported hearing that if the Baptist churches are republican that Baptists, by political conviction must be republican: "Now I profess to be a republican, not in name only, but in principle and practice; and I wish all were such."[128] Nonetheless, he described Christians as being under no obligation to associate with any particular party and pastors were not to influence their flocks one way or the other: "It is not only inexpedient, but contrary to the spirit of our laws, and the precepts and practice of Jesus Christ and his apostles, for ministers and especially the pastors of churches, to use their influence directly or indirectly to bias the political opinions or votes of their people."[129]

Baptists prized the spirituality of the church. It focused their attention on missions and discipleship and it cautioned them against entangling the church in tense partisan politics. Spirituality also reminded them of the importance of personal piety, a piety best inculcated in communities

123. *Minutes 1813–1861*, Great Crossings Baptist Church, Kentucky, 18 August 1827, 157.

124. "Approaching Elections," *Christian Watchman*, 7 November 1834, 179.

125. Ibid.

126. Ibid.

127. D. T. N., "Mr. Editor," *Religious Herald*, 5 November 1840, 177.

128. Ibid.

129. Ibid.

that embraced religious liberty. Baptists knew, perhaps better than any other denomination, the dangers of social reform because the same insincerity Backus saw produced by the established church is the hypocrisy Baptists saw being encouraged by the new religious establishment, the benevolent empire. Nonetheless, instead of abdicating concern for social welfare, Baptists pressed ahead, committed to reform social reform itself. They charged the reformers to practice their philanthropy motivated by the historic Christian faith. They pleaded for sincerity. They encouraged social engagement, but on their own terms. They prioritized the conversion of the individual and the purity of the church without withdrawing from society.

The story, however, does not end here. Even as Baptists purposed to lay the axe to the root of the tree, they often took direct hold of the political levers to reform the nation directly. They turned their axes to branch and trunk.

3

Politics and Social Reform

PERSONAL PIETY WAS NOT the whole story. Baptists refused to restrict their influence to the pulpit, the prayer closet, and the mission field. They wanted more. The gospel working like leaven through society seemed too slow. They felt responsible for the welfare of the nation and employed the world's methods to advance it. They believed America was a Christian nation and sought to keep it that way.

Baptists viewed preaching and evangelism as their preeminent responsibilities, and contributed generously to missionary, Bible, and tract societies. But they saw the need for other more direct avenues of social engagement, including politics. Sometimes their commitment to social activism came in the most explicit terms, often in response to a political or social crisis like the 1854 Kansas-Nebraska Act, which allowed for settlers in a particular territory to determine through a popular vote whether to prohibit or allow slavery upon achieving statehood. That predicament elicited pleas for social activism:

> Many very worthy people reason that as the gospel is to renovate society, ministers must content themselves with preaching that, and thus 'leaven' the whole community. That is to say, they must aim exclusively at the conversion of men, in the confidence that, being made the subjects of regeneration, they will not fail of grace to do everything uprightly. Just as if the Bible were not full of instances in which good men committed grave errors! Nathan did not preach to David, generally, the duties of faith and piety, but charged his conscience with the sin that had awakened the divine displeasure. Now, the American people possess the attributes of sovereignty. As the prophet before the king, as the apostle before the procurator Felix, as the American minister

before the American people, should fearlessly rebuke the abuse
of their power.[1]

The author opposed the Kansas-Nebraska Act because it allowed
slavery into new territories, effectively repealing the Missouri Compromise. Though pastors in the North had divided opinions, they also largely
objected.[2] Long before the flare-up over the Kansas-Nebraska Act or
even the Fugitive Slave Law of 1850, Baptists in the North and the South
proved that though Christ's kingdom was not of this world, the Christian
was. Baptists believed that piety sometimes demanded political action,
proving politics and piety were not so far apart.

A Christian Nation

Benevolent reformers sought to do more than simply feed the hungry,
clothe the poor, and make the drunkard sober; they evangelized the lost.
They mixed spiritual and temporal needs. However, these reformers did
not see themselves as Christianizing America. They believed America
was already a Christian nation. Signs of God's providence abounded,
especially in the political liberties produced by the Revolutionary War.
Many Baptists understood that with American citizenship came political duties. In a Christian country, virtue was more than the fruit of the
gospel; it was a patriotic obligation.

Baptists engaged in political controversies because they believed
God ordained the American political system, and they had an obligation
to keep the nation mindful of its divine debt. In 1821, a few days after
celebrating Independence Day, the editor of the *Christian Watchman*
looked back to 1776 with more than admiration. He reflected on God's
hand in baptizing a country and freeing a continent: "On Wednesday
was celebrated the 45th anniversary of the establishment of the first
American Christian Nation, and the harbinger of the Independence of
the Western Hemisphere."[3] Just a few days later, the same paper argued
that the Fourth of July was a religious holiday and should be celebrated
as such: "We believe it would be far more becoming a *Christian* coun-

1. "What Have the Clergy to Do with Politics," *Christian Watchman and Reflector*,
March 1854, 30.

2. John R. McKivigan, *The War Against Proslavery Religion: Abolitionism and the
Northern Churches, 1830–1865* (Ithaca, NY: Cornell University Press, 1984) 154–56.

3. "American Independence," *Christian Watchman*, 7 July 1821, 119.

try, to spend this day in acts of solemn worship, thanksgiving and praise to Almighty God, for the blessings which He has conferred upon us."[4] Another Independence Day sermon, this one delivered by Baptist newspaper editor James D. Knowles in 1828, reached a similar conclusion: "If, then, we would preserve this anniversary from the fate which befalls human things, we must connect it with religion . . . by stamping on it the impress of a religious duty."[5] He considered America's independence to be evidence of divine favor: "His arm protected the little and adventurous bands, who, at different points along our coast, laid the foundations of this great republick."[6] To Knowles it did not bode well for the future of the country that many Americans no longer lived up to this religious identity: "Unless this country become a nation of Christians, not in name only, but in reality and power of pure and undefiled religion, it will not long retain its political liberty."[7]

Baptists in Boston had identified the people of God with the nation for decades. Preaching in 1795, the respected pastor of First Baptist Church, Samuel Stillman, saw a special providence in America's deliverance: "I bless God he ordered me into existence at a period, which gave me an opportunity of observing the origin, progress and glorious issue of my country's contest with her oppressors. She is free, happy and independent. Let the people praise thee, O Lord; let all the people praise thee!"[8] Stillman did not support a state church. There was no necessary tension between the religiosity of the nation and its religious liberty. In 1779, preaching before the Massachusetts House of Representatives, Stillman argued, with all good Baptists, "that the kingdom of Christ is not of this world. By his kingdom we mean his church, which is altogether spiritual."[9] Agreeing that religion is good for society, he suggested the magistrate should nonetheless encourage religion without establishing it. Stillman provided several examples. A magistrate should be personally

4. "Religious Celebration of the Fourth of July," *Christian Watchman*, 4 August 1821, 135.

5. James D. Knowles, *The Perils and Safeguards of American Liberty* (Boston: Lincoln & Edmonds, 1828) 6.

6. Ibid., 7–8.

7. Ibid., 22.

8. Samuel Stillman, *A Sermon Delivered the Day of Annual Thanksgiving* (Boston: Manning & Loring, 1795) 11.

9. Samuel Stillman, *A Sermon Preached Before the House of Representatives of Massachusetts-Bay* (Boston: T. & J. Fleet, 1779) 26.

interested in religion, concerned for the salvation of his own family, and exercise his authority to protect the religious rights of members of the state.[10] In all these ways, the magistrate could naturally encourage Christianity without favoring any one denomination.

The failure to encourage Christianity might lead America to lose favor in the eyes of God. In 1799 Stillman played the role of Israel's prophet. Only in this case, the "solemn assembly" of Joel 2:15–17 convened for a national fast by a recommendation of the President of the United States. Stillman argued that atheism was the great enemy of the nation and it had worked unspeakable woe:

> Never, till very lately, did we hear or read of the rulers of a whole nation espousing the cause of Atheism. This sentiment, as far as it is believed, destroys the foundation of moral obligation, and of all civilized life; and has already spread its horrid and destructive influence among thousands of unhappy people; and opened the way, in its progress, for those uncommon crimes which have marked the revolution of that nation.[11]

The sentiment of atheism had already produced God's wrath. Stillman cited a recent plague and asked, "Is there not a cause? Is there evil in the city, and the Lord hath not done it?"[12] Baptists stood in the tradition of the Puritans and could raise no objection to *God's Controversy with New England.*[13]

Thomas Baldwin, another prominent Boston pastor, promoted similar themes. In 1795 he preached from Psalm 33:12, "blessed is the nation whose God is the Lord." For a nation to have the Lord as God, it must acknowledge "the eternal God" as "Creator, Preserver, and Upholder of all things." That nation must agree that the "system of truth contained in the Bible" is true and that God "alone" is the object of religious worship and adoration." Furthermore, the nation must admit that his providence directs the affairs of all men.[14] A few years later, Baldwin

10. Ibid., 29.

11. Samuel Stillman, *A Sermon Preached for a National Fast* (Boston: Manning & Loring, 1799) 14.

12. Ibid., 15.

13. Michael Wigglesworth, "God's Controversy with New England," in *God's New Israel: Religious Interpretations of American Destiny*, ed. Conrad Cherry (Chapel Hill: University of North Carolina Press, 1998).

14. Thomas Baldwin, *A Sermon Delivered the Day of Public Thanksgiving* (Boston: Manning & Loring, 1795) 6–8.

delivered the annual Thanksgiving Day sermon before the Second Baptist Society in Boston taking as his text Psalm 144:15, "happy is that people whose God is the Lord." He preached that the nation as a whole must be marked by a devotion to God for its own good: "Governed by the sound morality of the gospel, and directed by its heavenly precepts, impartial justice will guide their intercourse with foreign nations; and a generous hospitality will alleviate the suffering fugitives who are cast upon their peaceful shores. Thus believing and thus acting, a people cannot fail of being happy at home, and respected abroad."[15]

Charleston's Richard Furman seemed to find something troubling about equating the nation to ancient Israel. He did it nonetheless: "Whatever specific difference may be noticed as existing, between the origin of the Jewish theocracy, and the rise, independence and establishment of these United States; yet it must be acknowledged there is a striking similarity: and if we have not received an express command to remember the day of our deliverance; yet, the analogy of holy writ unites with reason and gratitude to declare it a duty."[16] In the birth of America, Furman saw "the special agency of God."[17] He concluded this for several reasons. First, nothing takes place without God's permission. Second, Americans did not revolt until they were agreed the action was "justified in the sight of God."[18] Third, the unity experienced by the colonies was clearly a sign of "superintending Providence."[19] Fourth, the length of the war and the accomplishment of a federal constitution proved to be further evidence that God's hand was in it.[20]

Historians have long argued that religion played a prominent role in defining America in the nation's formative years.[21] These Baptists re-

---

15. Thomas Baldwin, *The Happiness of a People Illustrated and Explained* (Boston: Adam & Rhoades, 1805) 18.

16. Richard Furman, *America's Deliverance and Duty* (Charleston, SC: W. P. Young, 1802) 7.

17. Ibid.

18. Ibid., 10.

19. Ibid., 11.

20. Ibid., 13.

21. Some of the best examples include James H. Hutson, *Church and State in America: The First Two Centuries* (Cambridge: Cambridge University Press, 2008); *Religion and American Politics: From the Colonial Period to the Present*, ed. Mark A. Noll and Luke E. Harlow. 2nd ed. (New York: Oxford University Press, 2007); Matthew S. Holland, *Bonds of Affection: Civic Charity and the Making of America, Winthrop, Jefferson, and Lincoln* (Washington, DC: Georgetown University Press, 2007); Hugh

flected a larger trend attributing to God both the glory and judgment the nation deserved. For Baptists and most other evangelicals, God's interest in America required national interest in God, including gratitude and religious observance. Religion was the natural response to God's prior engagement with America. No wonder then, toward the end of his sermon, Furman assumed that every citizen should engage the political process, but without the partisan bickering that marked so many Americans.[22]

The Charleston Baptist Association took Furman's advice to heart. In 1804 it resolved to end dueling in South Carolina and petitioned the state legislature "for an act to abolish the bloody practice."[23] Over twenty years later, the zeal of the association on this matter had not subsided and it now found itself encouraging anti-dueling associations which, no doubt, promoted similar political measures.[24] A Christian nation, the association believed, depended upon politically active churches. However, finding the appropriate means never proved to be easy, and in 1844 the association sent out a letter to member churches that argued "a universal prevalence of political agitation" caused a "dearth of spiritual fruitfulness."[25] Even then, the association never went so far as to deny the importance of political activity.

Baptists knew they lived in a Christian nation and their identity as Christian citizens carried with it certain public responsibilities that went beyond preaching the gospel. They considered their political duties to be nearly as important as their private duties for they took to heart Proverbs 14:34, "Righteousness exalts a nation, but sin is a reproach to any people." Since Baptists remained eager to uphold and defend the spiritual nature

---

Helco, *Christianity and American Democracy* (Cambridge, MA: Harvard University Press, 2007); Mark Noll, *America's God: From Jonathan Edwards to Abraham Lincoln* (Oxford: Oxford University Press, 2002); Thomas J. Curry, *Farewell to Christendom: The Future of Church and State in America* (Oxford: Oxford University Press, 2001); James H. Hutson, ed., *Religion and the New Republic: Faith in the Founding of America* (Lanham, MD: Rowman & Littlefield, 2000); Conrad Cherry, ed., *God's New Israel: Religious Interpretations of American Destiny* (Chapel Hill: University of North Carolina Press, 1994); Mark Y. Hanley, *Beyond a Christian Commonwealth The Protestant Quarrel with the American Republic, 1830–1860* (Chapel Hill: University of North Carolina Press, 1994); Robert T. Handy, *A Christian America: Protestant Hopes and Historical Realities* (New York: Oxford University Press, 1971).

22. Furman, *America's Deliverance*, 20.

23. *Minutes*, Charleston Baptist Association, 1804, 2.

24. *Minutes*, Charleston Baptist Association, 1826, 4–5.

25. "Corresponding Letter," *Minutes*, Charleston Baptist Association, 1844, 5.

of their calling, their political identity, demanded by texts like this one, required careful thought and attention.

A Political Christian

When it came to their identity as political Christians, Baptists largely sought the middle ground. They engaged as political Christians, but they did so cautiously, always hesitant to avoid being labeled the promoter of a "soul-withering party spirit."[26] In 1796 Henry Holcombe addressed a circular letter to the Charleston Baptist Association on the topic of the civic and political interests of Christians. He introduced a theme that would come to typify Baptists for generations by portraying them as neither wedded to nor separated from the state. He described the Christian as the character who united "private and public, civil and religious life."[27] He painted the portrait of a political Christian.

Holcombe recognized that some Christians are overzealous and overcommitted to politics. However, he conceded that others have engaged in the opposite extreme and paid no attention "to their real and important duties as men and citizens."[28] Citizenship in a Christian nation demanded political action while membership in a spiritual church cautioned restraint. Holcombe envisioned a middle road, where the church engaged the political sphere and in so doing, followed in the footsteps of Jesus Christ who, after all, "contributed towards supporting the Roman government" and the apostle Paul who "frequently pled his privileges as a Roman citizen."[29] Far from being separate, Holcombe treated church and state more like two sides of the same coin. The state, he argued was necessary in a fallen world and it "is not capable of rectifying all the evils which exist."[30] However, religion was the only hope for morality, which the state was charged to uphold. As a citizen, every Christian had an obligation to support the state. And as a Christian, these citizens must provide this support in a manner faithful to their calling.

26. Ibid., 5.

27. Henry Holcombe, "Circular Letter," *Minutes*, Charleston Baptist Association, 1796, 4.

28. Ibid., 6.

29. Ibid.

30. Ibid., 9.

Holcombe's solution satisfied few Baptists. They continued to feel a strong ambivalence toward politics. First, they routinely discussed politics. Second, they routinely discouraged political debate. The Charleston Baptist Association commended the existence of "sober and healthy agitation" regarding politics in the churches. The nation's free institutions depended upon such "personal interest in the affairs of the country."[31] That same year "A Baptist" wrote Virginia's *Religious Herald* condemning his spiritual brothers for the amount of time they spent considering presidential politics: "If we may judge from the signs of the times, there are many in our churches who would be glad if all religious meetings could be suspended until after the November elections."[32]

This aversion to party politics had less to do with a hunger for "spiritual religion" and more to do with political climate of the day. In a speech from 1826, John Leland described the political setting of America after the Revolutionary War. There existed a general sense that Great Britain had done everything it could to sabotage America's international trade, making another war inevitable.[33] President Washington disagreed and he appointed Chief Justice John Jay to negotiate with America's former enemy. As Leland noted, the event stirred division from beginning to end: "Mr. Jay was confirmed by the Senate; but many questioned the constitutionality of appointing a Judicial officer to manage Executive business."[34] The final treaty "tested public opinion." The slaveholding states reacted vehemently against the treaty because it included no compensation for slaves the British took at the end of the Revolution. As Leland reported, "the value of 30,000 slaves was therefore lost in the treaty."[35] However, the pact secured payment of debts to British subjects which outraged Republicans who consequently lambasted the Federalist supporters of the treaty.[36] The debate spilled over into the church: "For twenty years the

31. "Corresponding Letter," *Minutes*, Charleston Baptist Association, 1844, 5.

32. A Baptist [pseud.], "Politics Against Godliness," *Religious Herald*, 26 September 1844, 153.

33. John Leland, *Part of a Speech Delivered on the First Jubilee* (Pittsfield: Phinehas Allen, 1826) 8.

34. Ibid.

35. Ibid., 9.

36. Estes confirms the significance of the Jay Treaty as an event that raised partisan politics to unprecedented levels of acrimony, moreover, it changed the political landscape of the nation: "The Jay Treaty debate, long recognized as a watershed in the growth of party warfare, did more than solidify partisan divisions and rivalries: it altered the entire political system within which the nascent parties operated." Todd

pulpits rang and the presses groaned with anathemas to each other."[37] Baptists, mindful of this era of animosity, warned pastors against entering similar, acrimonious debates. They were inspired to formulate and publish guidelines for appropriate civil engagement. The church realized that that politics could have a deleterious effect on piety.

One such treatment of the political duties of Christians came in a series of articles printed in Boston's *Christian Watchman* between November 1844 and March 1845. The author began by arguing that every Christian is a politician to the extent that civil society is ordained of God and the Christian is part of society. He should thus "be acquainted with the principles of governments, with the individual rights of community."[38] In so doing the Christian was following the example of Christ who "could not have been unmindful of political relations, because he was obedient in all instances to the civil requirements of the Jewish polity, as modified by the Roman."[39] The author of the essay, "M," refused to countenance partisan politics for the "partizan," as he called him, blindly adopted policies to secure the success of certain candidates. This was not the Christian way.

Next, a Christian ought to show an interest in politics. By not voting, the uninterested citizen allowed the state to be led by a tyrannical minority: "A danger always to be apprehended in our country, is, that the sovereignty will pass from the many to the few, from the million to the one. Let each citizen be well informed of his duties, and we may hope that this danger will be so well guarded against, that our present means of social and moral improvement, and our spheres of usefulness, will always be enjoyed."[40]

Estes, *The Jay Treaty Debate, Public Opinion, and the Evolution of Early American Political Culture* (Amherst: University of Massachusetts Press, 2006) 213. Estes described the democratization of popular politics.

37. Ibid.

38. M [pseud.], "Political Duties of Christians: The Christian's Relations to the Civil Government," *Christian Watchman*, 15 November 1844, 181.

39. Ibid.

40. M [pseud.], "Political Duties of Christians: No. 2: The Consequent Duty of the Christian to be Interested in Politics," *Christian Watchman*, 22 November 1844, 185. Similar sentiments were printed a few years later: "A great duty, which every Christian citizen owes to himself, to his children, and to his country, is to keep his mind well-informed respecting the constitutions of the Commonwealth, and of the nation; respecting public men and public measures." "The Christian Citizen's Duty," *Christian Watchman*, 22 June 1848, 98.

The third essay describes the political duty of obedience. "M" put it bluntly: "There is no lawful way of breaking a law, as there is no holy way of committing a sin."[41] Unless a religious belief was being denied, the magistrate was to be obeyed—and not because the civil law spoke to the matter, because the Bible did: "The Bible has spoken so definitely upon it; and must regard him as being either ignorant or irreverent, who can feel that no crime against heaven is committed, when his mind fondly devises plans to demolish the authority of laws, or rejoices in their inefficiency."[42] The author called for obedience of the hands and of the heart, a Christian citizen inclined not only to follow the dictates of his civil leaders but to declare, to the extent the laws don't violate the Christian's conscience, that they are good.

"M" turned next to the disposition of the Christian. The ultimate goal, he argued, was a state that preserved the rights of conscience. Each citizen must therefore "love and defend those laws by which [the rights of conscience] are embodied and protected. We thus own a positive good will to our State Constitution, and to the Constitution of the Federal Government."[43] The overall tone of the essay was altruistic: "If it were right and proper for any one to withdraw himself from all sympathy with official fidelity, the right and propriety would be due to the Christian last; for he is supposed to know better than others the demands of duty, and to be more ready than others to make sacrifices for the general good."[44] A Christian citizen has a responsibility to serve his Christian nation.

God's providential relationship to America shaped the Christian's relationship with the state. Since God dealt with the nation corporately, Christians bear a unique responsibility in averting national judgments: "Jehovah is a God of nations, as well as individuals, and chastises national, as well as individual sins."[45] Christians must urge the nation to repent when necessary and pray that such repentance would be sincere.

The last three essays explore the great problem facing the Christian citizen: civil disobedience. Christians live under the weight of Romans

41. M [pseud.], "Political Duties of Christians—No. 3: Obedience to Law," *Christian Watchman*, 27 November 1844, 189.

42. Ibid.

43. M [pseud.], "Political Duties of Christians—No. 4: Duty of Respect to Rulers," *Christian Watchman*, 6 December 1844, 193.

44. Ibid.

45. M [pseud.], "Political Duties of a Christian—No. 5: The Christian's Duty in Respect to National Sins," *Christian Watchman*, 13 December 1844, 197.

13, well aware that the civil government had been established for their own good. Baptists also knew that the civil government did not always serve the good of humanity in general or Baptists in particular: "How would it be if the laws and magistrates were so changed as to infringe upon the rights of conscience. Is a man bound to obey a law which compels him either to pray or blaspheme? Which fixes his faith to a particular creed, or which compels him to go through certain specified forms, or use a particularly obnoxious mode of speech?"[46] He did not equivocate. Though the general duty was to obey every law, matters of conscience proved to be an exception. Should the state bind one's conscience in matters pertaining to religion, the citizen was permitted to break the law so long as he is willing to "submit to its penalty, with petitions and protestations, and prayers against its injustice." He must "oppose the law in a lawful way."[47]

Pressing the question further, when was it allowable to resist the civil order? "Is it morally wrong to disobey any law besides one which encroaches upon conscience?"[48] Here the answer was still yes, though the reasoning sounded less Christian and more American: "It is morally right to resist (in some manner and under some circumstances,) any government which tramples upon constitutional prerogatives."[49] "Constitutional prerogatives" are those rules established to protect life, liberty, and the pursuit of happiness. Citizens have a "moral obligation to resist and oppose" that authority which "breaches upon immutable justice" by ignoring these standards of humanity.[50]

The manner by which America was founded implied an inherent right of revolution. Having laid out the duty to obey the civil magistrate so forcefully, the author ended his series by establishing three conditions that must be met before a revolution is morally acceptable. First, "the highest tribunals must have pronounced the enactments unconstitutional."[51] Second, every effort to change the law must have been attempted. Third,

46. M [pseud.], "Political Duties of Christians—No. 6: In What Circumstances May Law be Disobeyed," *Christian Watchman*, 7 March 1845, 37.

47. Ibid.

48. M [pseud.], "Political Duties of Christians—No. 7: What Constitutes Justifiable Cause of Resistance?" *Christian Watchman*, 14 March 1845, 43.

49. Ibid.

50. Ibid.

51. M [pseud.], "Political Duties of Christians—No. 8: The Right of Revolution" *Christian Watchman*, 28 March 1845, 49.

a constitutional majority, composing two-thirds of the revolting population, must be united. The American Revolution, "M" argued, met
each condition. Nineteenth century Baptists lived in the shadow of the
Revolution. They loved their country and knew its origin was rooted in
a violent act of civil disobedience. As Christians, this action could not be
swept under the historical rug. Moreover, it offered a blueprint for the
possibility of revolts in the future.

Pastors wondered if their own office allowed for greater involvement
in political affairs. Should local church shepherds become politicians?
Baptists knew that the Presbyterian clergy took a stand against such action. The *Christian Index* reported in 1833 that the Presbyterian synod
comprising ministers in Mississippi, South Alabama, and Louisiana had
resolved "that the Synod have hitherto deemed, and now deem it highly
inexpedient for ministers to seek or accept civil office."[52]

Just a few years earlier, Francis Wayland offered every indication
that he agreed. He believed that the political office was a worthy occupa-
tion for the Christian, at least in principle: "Now, whether a Christian
may or may not be a politician, I have no question whatever to raise. It
must be left to his own conscience and to the providence of God, and may
be innocent or praise-worthy, or wrong, according to the circumstances
of the particular case."[53] Wayland delivered his sermon at First Baptist
Meeting House in Boston on July 4. He argued, however, that the pastor
should not leave the pulpit for political office. Moreover, behind the pulpit, ministers should be careful to avoid damaging the reputation of the
pastorate by aligning it with a particular party. It is hard to imagine how a
pastor could avoid this if he ran for office himself. Wayland lamented the
Federalist/Republican party spirit that for so many years had infected the
churches. The moral compass of ministry, he argued, had been replaced
with a political compass: "You would hear a congregation of immortal
beings, nay, you would hear pious men, asking concerning a minister
of the gospel, not, Is he devout, but, What are his politics? The very
sine qua non of his acceptableness, as his supporting of their candidate,
and approving their measures; and it was not serious disqualification if
he were prepared, when the occasion presented, to anathematize their
opponents."[54] Wayland's opinion was consistent with the answer given

---

52. "Ministers of the Gospel and Civil Offices," *Christian Index*, 5 January 1833, 14.

53. Wayland, *The Death of Ex-Presidents*, 93.

54. Ibid., 88–89.

by Kentucky's Elkhorn Baptist Association to a question regarding the propriety of Christians entering the military or politics. The association responded positively but excluded ministers of the gospel.[55]

By the middle of the nineteenth century, enough Baptist ministers concluded they could best influence society through political office that the editor of the *Christian Watchman* felt compelled to write an editorial discouraging pastors from this practice: "Christianity only became corrupted when political influence began to work upon its professors. Its self-denying doctrines were gradually lost sight of in the scrambles of ambition, and Popery, with its unhallowed reachings, tore off the graces of simplicity and truth which the Apostles and disciples had worn, and put in their place the meretricious ornaments that now . . . sully the name of Christianity."[56] The editor did not intend to draw pastors away from a robust engagement with the public sphere. He viewed pastors as walking a tightrope, entering politics just long enough to become educated in the things of the world and, to a degree, shaping the world for the good of the church. All the while pastors had to refrain from becoming so enmeshed in the world that the mission of the church became subservient to merely human goals. Seeking the middle path did not excuse the pastor from using the pulpit to do more than calling sinners to repentance. The middle path meant preaching politics to the extent that preaching must touch "boldly and warmly on all moral questions, however intimately they may be mixed up with politics. . . . A preacher who does his duty fearlessly is no political clergyman, but a true disciple of his Divine Master."[57]

New York pastor William R. Williams also embraced this middle way. He would not sever entirely the relationship between church and state because he believed matters of state required the morality that fell under the purview of the church: "No State can, in the present age, live without morality. . . . And morality, to find living and permanent roots, must resort to Christianity, and in it recognize the ripest and truest morality of all the earth."[58] The church, argued Williams, was the "guardian of order, the witness of truth, the bringer of peace, and the pattern of benevolence."[59] Moreover, in times of crisis, the church must serve as the

55. *Minutes*, Elkhorn Baptist Association, 1785, 419.

56. "Political Clergyman," *Christian Watchman*, 29 November 1849, 90.

57. Ibid.

58. William R. Williams, "The Church in Its Relation to the State," in *Madison Avenue Lectures* (Philadelphia: American Baptist Publication Society, 1867) 441.

59. Ibid., 444.

nation's prophet, "as fearlessly as did Nathan, a prophet of the old dispensation." Those politicians who maintained the church has strayed from its appointed task were mistaken: "These critics forget that its very errand from Heaven is to preach repentance as the only escape from individual perdition—national repentance as God's appointed and only way for escaping national judgments and national overthrow."[60] Williams knew that Baptist history was replete with examples of the church speaking on issues of policy, sometimes to rebuke and sometimes to encourage the policies of the state. He urged Baptists to continue to do both. The line between preaching piety and politics was sometimes razor thin.

Many Baptists in the early to mid-nineteenth century wanted, a bold faith and a brave pulpit. They decried a "religious party in politics," that reeked of an established religion, but they quite happily embraced a Christian influence both in the church and at the voting booth. As one editor put it, "By no means would we urge the organization of a Christian party, but we would urge the Christianizing of an organized party."[61] Committed to influencing the culture through the leaven of the gospel, Baptists attempted more. They aimed to shape the country as Christian politicians, not through the party spirit they deplored but through measured political activity. Political Christians were the light of the world and the salt of the earth.

Politics and War

Some issues seemed suited to elicit a political response. The delivery of mail on Sundays and intemperance were two such issues. War was another. Each displayed the depravity of mankind. They caused irreparable harm and threatened the stability of the nation. They represented therefore the kind of civil crises that demanded action from the church. In the mind of some Baptists social reform must only be indirect. They trusted that personal piety would eventually have every desired public effect. Others however identified themselves as political Christians with the responsibility to lead their constituencies to act politically. The issue of war demanded a Christian response.

60. Ibid., 445.

61. William Crowell, "A Christian Politician," *Christian Watchman*, 14 August 1840, 130.

When it came to the War of 1812, Baptists did not remain neutral. The Revolutionary War had yet to fade from the collective consciousness of the young nation. In the mind of most Americans, Britain still symbolized political domination. The War of 1812 brought Federalists who opposed it and Republicans who supported the war into bitter conflict. Nonetheless, by the time the war ended and the Treaty of Ghent secured the state of affairs prior to the war, the partisan politics at least temporarily subsided and America entered the Era of Good Feelings.[62] Historian William Gribbin argued that religion was central to support for the war: "Most men of 1812, like those of the atomic age, could not make the total commitment that is war without the psychic support of a system of values and hopes, whether it be called religion or philosophy or ideology."[63] Living in a Christian nation and seeking to be faithful political Christians, supporters of the war largely depended upon the church's understanding: "There was probably no organization as representative of a community's stated values as the religious organization."[64]

The Elkhorn Baptist Association in Kentucky, which in its long history rarely addressed matters of politics, made an exception to express its support for the war: "War in any shape is a curse. . . . But to resist the lawless aggressions of our vindictive enemy, is certainly commendable. We are contending for rights ever dear to freemen."[65] Baptists in Concord, Tennessee, urged their churches to discipline any member "unfriendly" to the government. This apparently meant persons unsupportive of the war: "Resolved therefore, that this association do earnestly recommend to the churches they represent, to keep a watchful eye over their respective churches, and should they discover any of her members unfriendly to the great gift of heaven, our republic form of government, that they forthwith exclude such a person from fellowship as unworthy of the society."[66]

---

62. Leland noted the many deleterious effects of the Jay Treaty and the positive ramifications of the Jefferson administration that persisted well into 1826 in what he described, quoting from a Boston newspaper editorial, the "day of good feelings." John Leland, *Part of a Speech Delivered on the First Jubilee* (Pittsfield, PA: Phinehas Allen, 1826) 10.

63. William Gribbin, *The Churches Militant: The War of 1812 and American Religion* (New Haven, CT: Yale University Press, 1973) 7.

64. Ibid., 9.

65. "Circular Letter," *Minutes*, Elkhorn Baptist Association, 1814, 5.

66. *Minutes*, Concord Baptist Association, 1813.

Many New England Baptists, however, did not support the war. They spoke out in opposition to the government's actions, loudly enough to draw the criticism of John Leland. Looking back at the war in an Independence Day address in 1830, Leland recounted how both citizens and churches in Massachusetts, unwisely in his opinion, rejected the war. He rebuked them for their shortsightedness. Leland believed that in a fallen world war is often necessary, a point he made several years earlier in a separate address.[67] However in this sermon he marveled not only that the citizens did all they could "to paralyze the arm of Congress" against the war but that even the churches joined the fight for peace: "The pulpits were ringing, the presses groaning, and misrepresentation was the order of the day."[68] Indeed, for Leland, the role of the Christian, at least in this instance, meant defending not decrying the actions of the national government. He admitted that in a republic, when the interests of the state and federal governments clash, serving the constitution is difficult but must be attempted: "We all wish to be loyal subjects to the constitution and constitutional laws and measures of this Commonwealth; and likewise to the constitution and constitutional laws and measures of the United States, (which are supreme) but how all is to be done when the State and General Governments clash, is not easy to say."[69] Baptists took more than an interest in the war, they made their views known. They advocated from the papers and their pulpits. Political activism stood under the banner of social reform.

The nullification controversy, begun in 1828, also attracted the attention of Baptist churches. When the United States Congress passed what came to be known in the South as the "tariff of abominations," citizens and congregants rose up in dismay and alarm. The tariff rate had been a national concern for several years. High tariffs cut off British competition, a great benefit to the burgeoning manufacturing industry in the Northeast, but protectionist policies spoiled markets for agricultural regions in the South and no state felt the pain worse or struck back harder than South Carolina which sought to "nullify" the federal tariff. The state promised to secede if President Jackson attempted to collect the tax. The governor raised a volunteer army. Eventually, U. S. Senators John

---

67. John Leland, *Free Thoughts on War* (Pittsfield, PA: Phinehas Allen, 1816).

68. John Leland, *Short Sayings on Times, Men, Measures and Religion* (Pittsfield, PA: Phinehas Allen, 1830) 11.

69. Ibid., 13. For a thorough discussion of Baptist support for the War of 1812 see Gribbin, *The Churches Militant*, 78–89.

C. Calhoun of South Carolina and Henry Clay of Kentucky reached an agreement that postponed a national disaster.[70]

Baptists however did not wait for politicians to solve the problem. The political crisis demanded a response from the church. In 1830 the Saluda Baptist Association issued several resolutions regarding the Tariff and Internal Improvement Act passed a couple years earlier. The resolutions indicated a Baptist desire to walk the middle ground in defense of both the spiritual and political nature of the church. First, the association resolved that the entire unfortunate tariff situation "demands our serious and prayerful attention."[71] After disclaiming "all intermeddling in the political views, which are entertained by our statesmen and citizens at large," the association asserted that the present state of affairs resulted from America's "pride, our extravagance, and our abuse of [God's] rich favors both in our national and individual character."[72] Second, the association committed itself to fast and pray in order to secure God's pardon. Third, its members resolved to unite as believers throughout the state in their spiritual concerns. Fourth, they decided to send a copy of the resolutions to the current governor that he might know not only how these Baptists were praying, but how they interpreted God's providence in the current trial.

A few months later, the *Columbian Star* included a report repudiating the tariff law. Though the editor tried to maintain some semblance of neutrality—"on the question of the existing duties laid to protect American manufacturers, we pretend not to express an opinion"—he failed, for he kept publishing the antitariff argument.[73] The report's author maintained that the "the vigor of the laws is a moral force" and he urged his readers to take action: "As men and brethren we appeal to you then to unite your efforts with ours in the correction of this abuse. A system which is unequal in its operation, and therefore unjust; which is oppressive . . . such a system, if persevered in, must alienate our affections from each other . . . and lead inevitably . . . to the most awful of all calamites."[74] By publishing these views, the Baptist paper called Christians to action.

70. William W. Freehling, *Prelude to Civil War: The Nullification Controversy in South Carolina, 1816–1836* (New York: Harper & Row, 1966) 263, 275, 292–93.

71. "Miscellaneous Record," *The Columbian Star*, 4 September 1830, 146.

72. Ibid.

73. "The Late Anti-Tariff Convention," *The Columbian Star*, 15 October 1831, 250.

74. Ibid., 250, 251.

Northern manufacturing interests supported the tariffs and Baptists in the North did not share the animosity toward the legislation. Writing in 1833, the editor of Boston's *Christian Watchman* dismissed the secessionist threats made by South Carolina. He criticized the southerners' actions as "ill-advised" while displaying faith in the longevity of the Union: "We cannot but regret the ill-advised measures, which were contemplated and threatened in that one to which we allude; but if our country is wise, the evil may and will be overruled for good. Our Union, like the sturdy oak rocked by the furious storm and tempest, may now take deeper root, and spread abroad its branches with increasing greatness."[75] Baptists did not remain aloof during the nullification crisis. They did not see piety and politics as mutually exclusive. Baptists believed that the nation could benefit from their sage counsel.

The Dorr Rebellion of Rhode Island also led Baptists to speak out and exercise their political voice. Rhode Island's charter, issued in 1663, had yet to be modernized and the criticism most often leveled against it pertained to its requirements for suffrage. Only landed freemen and their eldest sons could vote in an election and by the 1830s only one half of Rhode Island's males met these qualifications.[76] In October 1841 a popular movement led by Thomas W. Dorr drafted and ratified an alternative constitution which granted suffrage for all white males. This movement wanted more than a new constitution. It sought a new government and proclaimed Dorr governor. He delivered his inaugural address on May 3, 1842. However a few days later, when Dorr led a group of supporters to take control of the state arsenal, he met resistance from the establishment. His leadership came to an end shortly thereafter, he fled from Rhode Island to avoid capture, and he soon surrendered.[77]

Baptists marveled at divine providence in Dorr's fate. Francis Wayland thanked God for the way Rhode Islanders rose up in defense of the state and in opposition to Dorr. Wayland did not hesitate to speak with absolute assurance that justice had been done in Dorr's defeat: "God has, in this transaction, revealed to us the firm and unalterable attachment of this people to the cause of constitutional law. We all believed that

75. "Our Country is Our Glory," *Christian Watchman*, 22 March 1833, 46.

76. Marvin E. Gettleman, *The Dorr Rebellion: A Study in American Radicalism: 1833–1849* (New York: Random House, 1973) 6–7. See also Peter J. Coleman, *The Transformation of Rhode Island, 1790–1860* (Providence, RI: Brown University Press, 1963) 274–94.

77. Ibid., 119–38.

this attachment existed, but never before has it been put to so stern and actual a trial."[78] Wayland used Dorr's rebellion to remind his listeners that the church must be bold, and that pastors must be willing to issue proclamations beyond the gospel for the good of society. It is, Wayland insisted, unbiblical to assert that religion has nothing to do with politics: "I grieve to say that the pulpit has failed to meet such sentiments at the very threshold, with its stern and uncompromising rebuke. From fear of the reproaches of men falsely professing godliness, it has been silent when it ought to have spoken out plainly."[79] The church did not explain the political duties of the Christian:

> It has failed to set before men their duties as the New Testament sets them forth. Hence in the midst of the Christian land, in the very home of the Puritans, we find men so ill-instructed in the obligations which they owe both to God and to each other, so utterly unaware of the duties which Christianity enjoins upon parents and children, upon husbands and wives, upon buyers and sellers, upon employers and employed, and upon magistrates and citizens. If this be so, I say the pulpit is grievously in fault, and until the fault be amended, the ministers of the gospel will not be held guiltless before God."[80]

Rhode Island's Warren Baptist Association also took the occasion of the Dorr Rebellion to commend the action taken by the First Baptist Church of Providence, a congregation which sided against Dorr. First, the congregation resolved that allegiance to the civil government is a Christian duty "enforced by many precepts and sanctioned by the whole spirit of the gospel." Second, it resolved that any members of the church who "aided or countenanced the late insurrectionary movements in this State, as having grievously erred; and as bound in duty to their brethren and to the cause of Christ, to repent, to confess, and to renounce their error."[81] Though the church spoke only to its members, an action consistent with its polity, its statements nonetheless indicated the church's refusal to take a neutral stand on a political issue. The local church maintained that "obligations to Christ" made insurrection the equivalent of disobedience

---

78. Francis Wayland, *A Discourse Delivered in the First Baptist Church on the Day of Public Thanksgiving* (Providence, RI: H. H. Brown, 1842) 3, 11.

79. Ibid., 22–23.

80. Ibid., 24.

81. "First Providence," *Minutes*, Warren Baptist Association, 1842, 13–14.

and demanded the action of the member. Dorr incited more than armed combat—he prompted political activism on the part of Christians.

The Mexican War brought similar controversy. Politically, it expanded the United States westward, challenged the power of a military thought incompetent during the War of 1812, and with the debate over the extension of slavery into Texas, laid the groundwork for the Civil War. Spiritually, the Mexican War tested the willingness of Christians to engage the public sphere. It did not have the support, within or without the church, which the War of 1812 received even though the outcome, in terms of territory gained, was an unqualified success.[82] When the House of Representatives declared war on Mexico in 1846, some Baptists protested.[83] Whether supporting or opposing, Baptists who spoke out regarding the Mexican War evidenced once again that their piety was not restricted to the prayer closet; it demanded national, political concern.

Boston Baptists argued that the war, in principle, contradicted the precepts of Christianity: "The law of Christ which requires all men to love their neighbors as themselves, is as applicable to the nations as to individuals, and this nation has acknowledged it to be so by sending two national ships with food to Ireland, but we strangely contradict ourselves by sending cannon, bomb shells, and licentiousness to Mexico."[84] This Boston Baptist critic saw in the Mexican War a Christian nation taking the military offensive, invading and subjugating another nation when, "if any nation can afford to be forbearing, to be magnanimous, and generous, it is ours."[85]

In North Carolina the editor of the *Biblical Recorder* also spoke against the war. Thomas Meredith described the violence as something to "be deeply regretted by all the friends of humanity and national prosperity."[86] Writing almost two months after a battle that took place at Rio Sacramento, when over 500 Mexican soldiers were killed, wounded, or captured, J. T. S. wrote to the *Christian Watchman* to express his outrage over the war and to censure those pastors choosing to be silent:

82. See David S. Heidler and Jeanne T. Heidler, *The Mexican War* (Westport, CT: Greenwood, 2006) 141–42.

83. McCafferey argued that the popular opposition to the Mexican War was limited by its short duration. McCafferey, *Army of Manifest Destiny: The American Soldier in the Mexican War, 1846–1848* (New York: New York University Press, 1992) 205–6.

84. "The War with Mexico," *Christian Watchman*, 15 October 1847, 166.

85. Ibid.

86. Thomas Meredith, "War with Mexico," *Biblical Recorder*, 23 May 1846, 2.

If I were to press these questions, I might be thought to be entering upon politics, which every body knows is forbidden ground to the religious press and the pulpit. But then I hope it is not political for me to say, here is murder being committed, and that some individuals are guilty of it; and that possibly, when the Most High makes inquisition for blood, it will be found that there are more murderers, both in high stations and in low, than many people who are afraid the pulpit and the religious press will transcend their proper limits, are willing to believe.[87]

Francis Wayland offered more than a veiled criticism of the war in 1847 when he, too, distinguished between conquest and defense. The magistrate, he argued, "is authorized to use national force, in order to defend us from external injury; but this confers upon him no authority to use that force for the purpose of conquest. The guilt of such an abuse of power is enormous, when war is provoked by the infliction of aggravated injury; but how greatly is this guilt increased when it is waged for insufficient cause, and yet more in the perpetration of atrocious wrong."[88] These Baptists joined many Americans who opposed the nation's policy: "There were Americans from all sections and from all political persuasions who simply as a matter of principle favored a more just and humane policy toward Mexico and who therefore viewed annexation with disfavor."[89]

Not all Baptists opposed the war. "A Lover of His Country" took umbrage against those who argued that the Mexican War was a symbol of American immorality.[90] If anything contributed to furthering violence, he suggested, it was those who chose to attack the government's military policies: "I have seen nothing so likely to produce much blood-shed as the opposition to the war and the spirit that is thereby infused into the Mexican ranks."[91] He sought to convince his readers that America had just cause to enter the war with Mexico: "Our national honor had been trampled upon, our innocent citizens abused, and finally, our

87. J. T. S., "National Sins," *Christian Watchman*, 23 April, 1847, 65.

88. Wayland, *Duty of Obedience*, 24.

89. Gene M. Brack, *Mexico Views Manifest Destiny, 1821–1846: An Essay on the Origins of the Mexican War* (Albuquerque: University of New Mexico Press, 1975) 124.

90. A Lover of His Country [pseud.], "A Reply to Mr. Watchman," *The Biblical Recorder*, 27 April 1847, 3.

91. A Lover of His Country [pseud.], "In Reply to Mr. Watchman's 2d & 3d Numbers," *The Biblical Recorder*, 10 July 1847, 2.

ambassadors insulted, and the United States, as a nation, only demanded satisfaction for this conduct."[92]

"A Lover of His Country" did not merely defend the war. He attacked the use of a religious periodical to critique it. He questioned a pastor's suitability to prosecute a political discussion, especially when clergymen claimed to know God's will in such a complicated matter like a national war: "I wonder if he or many other ministers are sufficiently well acquainted with the state of affairs between the two governments to have decided what was the will of God. I doubt his knowledge upon this subject. And if he is, is it consistent with ministerial duties, to engage in political matters?"[93] Previously, he had censured Meredith for allowing such a discussion in his *Biblical Recorder*: "To yourself, bro. Meredith, I would say, I fear you will suffer the cause of religion, the Baptist cause, and your own interest to be injured by admitting such communications in your column."[94] Meredith, having already established himself as being opposed to the war, replied directly. He saw no compromise to spiritual religion in printing correspondence related to the morality of war in general and the Mexican War in particular:

> We would ask him, whether, in his opinion, national wars—national sins, supposing them to exist—the moral and religious conduct of rulers, &c. &c., are not proper points of inquiry for religious readers, and of course proper subjects of discussion for the religious press? It is the duty of christians to pray for their rulers; may they not be permitted to inquire whether the conduct of such rulers is just or unjust—righteous or unrighteous? . . . Our principle is, to give ample scope to free inquiry, on all subject properly belonging to a religious paper.—and we are unwilling that any subject should be suppressed, or that any writer should be thrown overboard, merely from a selfish fear of losing a few subscribers.[95]

In a pattern that has become familiar, some Baptists supported the war, others opposed it, and still others remained neutral. Each national crisis tested their identity as citizens of a Christian nation and as members of a Baptist community. The Tennessee Baptists of 1813, for example, urged friendliness to the government as a condition of membership

92. Ibid.
93. Ibid.
94. A Lover of His Country [pseud.], "A Reply to Mr. Watchman," 3.
95. Thomas Meredith, untitled editorial, *The Biblical Recorder*, 27 April 1847, 3.

and the First Baptist Church of Providence, Rhode Island, rejected the political usurpation of Thomas Dorr. Civil crises compelled associations and churches to act. At times, they led Christians to be silent. Still, one cannot fairly argue that Baptists refused to engage the culture or that they betrayed a lack of interest in political matters. They embraced a political role. They saw themselves as political Christians living in a Christian nation. Their allegiance to a spiritual church cautioned them against party politics and encouraged them to embrace indirect routes to reform but did not finally chasten them against exercising a political voice. Baptists saw themselves as social reformers. They may not have always been convinced they would finally change the nation, but faithfulness demanded that they try.

After the Civil War, Southern Baptist John A. Broadus addressed the question of politics and preaching and asked the question: "How can the preacher do most to further patriotism and political purity?" He answered that pastors best served their churches when they preached on the "general principles of political duties in the light of Christian teaching." He emphasized that it is a subject worthy of the pulpit "for religion has relation to everything in the whole realm of life and thought. There is absolutely no subject in regard to which it may with propriety be said, that of this subject a religious instructor has no right to speak." Nonetheless, Broadus counseled wisdom on the part of the preacher, noting that Jesus and Paul restrained themselves from discussing political matters.[96] Broadus, like so many other Baptists of the nineteenth century, wanted to find that middle road where they engaged society directly but prudently and cautiously. Though they knew that "righteousness exalteth a nation," they sought to conform their actions to Christ's words "my kingdom is not of this world."

---

96. John A. Broadus, "On Sensation Preaching," Manuscript Notebook, The John A. Broadus Collection, The Southern Baptist Theological Seminary Archives, Louisville, Kentucky.

4

Slavery, Spirituality, and Social Reform

AT THE BOSTON PREACHERS' Meeting in 1858, Father Henson, a black minister, told a story about a day years ago when he was forced to pray. Henson was, at the time, a slave, and he was well aware that this public act of piety might make him more attractive to his potential buyers who wanted their slaves to fear God since that meant they were less likely to steal or worse, kill, their masters. The young Henson was taken by flat boat on the Mississippi River from Kentucky to New Orleans to be sold. He and his master stopped in Vicksburg, Mississippi, where his owner hoped to sell Henson there and avoid a lengthier journey south. At a landing place, the master commended the qualities of his slave. He was "honest as the Bible, and he could preach and 'pray like a steamboat.'" But the shoppers wanted evidence of this piety, so they cried out, "'Let us hear him pray!'" Henson heard their appeal, but he struggled with what to do. His Christian faith kept him from killing his master and running away. Now his prayer could earn him a place in the home of an even more unscrupulous owner:

> After having been strongly tempted to kill my young master at night when I had good opportunity to do so, but being held back by religious principle, [I was] now commanded before the profane rabble to pray, that two or three hundred dollars more might be bid on my head! Should I do it? Was there any God, and if so, would he allow me to be so tormented? I had not time to think—hesitation would only provoke violence, resistance would be death—I would not be martyred for not praying, and I therefore fell down on my knees before a log and poured out my soul in supplication.[1]

1. "One of the Slaveholder's 'Legal Rights,'" *Christian Watchman*, 7 October 1858,
1.

After the prayer, the "profane rabble" wanted nothing to do with the pious slave, and he walked his young master back to the flat raft. Though in this instance a slave could be too pious, slaveholders were typically convinced that those slaves who feared God the most worked the hardest. As Henson told his fellow pastors that night in Boston, a revival on a large plantation "must net the owner some thousands of dollars."[2]

A society that allowed slavery, and a religion that refused to fight for its end, desperately needed to be reformed. Most Baptists did nothing to bring down the Peculiar Institution. They accepted it as a necessary if not inevitable part of American life. And as Henson's own experience illustrates, many used religion as a weapon to keep slaves docile and safe. But not all Baptists resigned themselves to the existence of slavery. Some worked to return slaves to Africa. Others worked to educate slaves, not merely for the good of the owner, but for the good of the slaves themselves. Still others saw slavery as the scourge of eighteenth and nineteenth centuries, and fought to make it illegal.

When Baptists discussed slavery, three discrete topics emerged: colonization, religious instruction, and emancipation. Colonization was the attempt, officially beginning in 1816 but with antecedents in the eighteenth century, to relocate blacks to Africa. Efforts for the religious instruction of slaves elicited debates over the appropriateness of slave education. Some white southerners believed slaves to be incapable of a moral education. Others feared a religiously educated slave to be a threat to a peaceful society. Emancipation or abolition was unsurprisingly the issue over which Baptists disagreed most stridently. A tiny minority of southern Baptists, until about the 1830s, and numerous northern Baptists, carried the banner of abolition. Given the low percentage of Baptists who opposed slavery, it is too grandiose to claim that the "crusade against slavery is perhaps the most evident example of the denomination's struggle to achieve human rights."[3] However, as Baptists promoted colonization, religious instruction, and to a lesser degree abolition, some even exemplified a strong impulse for social reform. Each of these three issues uncovered a Baptist spirituality focused on personal piety and evangelism but cognizant of wider social concerns. In Baptist thought and life, slavery tested and, in the South especially, challenged the impulse toward social reform.

2. Ibid.

3. William H. Brackney, *Baptists in North America* (Malden, MA: Blackwell, 2006) 229.

Colonization and Reform

Baptists considered the colonization of Africa one avenue of social reform. The American Colonization Society (ACS) was established in 1816 to arrange the transportation of free blacks to Liberia and encourage the manumission of slaves. It was not uncommon for a slaveholder's will to grant slaves freedom on condition that they go to Africa.[4] However, interest in colonization predates the nineteenth century. Though the majority of free blacks of the revolutionary era wanted to integrate into the fledgling country, some petitioned to return to their homeland. White northerners like Noah Webster of Massachusetts joined other philanthropists in introducing one of the earliest plans to make colonization possible. In 1787 Thomas Jefferson, who saw dangers in immediate emancipation, suggested colonization as a safer alternative. After the War of 1812, colonization proponents avoided discussing emancipation and emphasized the expatriation of free blacks. In 1816 Virginia politician Charles Fenton Mercer and others formed the American Society for Colonizing the Free People of Color of the United States.[5] The leadership included some of Washington's most powerful men, including Secretary of the Treasury William Crawford and Speaker of the House Henry Clay.[6]

The society attracted little support initially and had meager success. It competed with the abolition cause. Between 1820 and 1830 only 154 free black northerners sailed to Liberia. Meanwhile, in the same decade, 720 free black southerners made the arduous journey. When Nat Turner's 1831 rebellion incited white backlash against blacks, interest in colonization exploded. According to an 1832 report of the ACS, the insurrection "gave a new impulse to the subject of colonization, and turned the popular feeling in its favor."[7] Thirteen hundred black southerners left for Liberia between 1831 and 1833. Its popularity was brief. Many abolitionists dismissed it as an instrument of racism and slavery, and many

4. In 1837, the *Biblical Recorder* printed an article listing several cases of deceased slave owners whose executors made application to the Colonization Society to take the former slaves. See "Emancipation," *Biblical Recorder*, 15 July 1835, 3. See also Eric Burin's discussion of "postmortem emancipations" in *Slavery and the Peculiar Institution: A History of the American Colonization Society* (Gainesville: University Press of Florida, 2005) 53–56.

5. Burin, *Slavery and the Peculiar Solution*, 6–19.

6. P. J. Staudenraus, *The African Colonization Movement, 1816–1865* (New York: Columbia University Press, 1961) 30.

7. "Colonization Society," *Religious Herald*, 6 July 1832, 102.

southern whites came to view it as a tool of abolitionism. Poor reports from Liberia, ties with family in America, and domestic economic opportunities compelled free and manumitted blacks to stay home.

Baptists provided leadership in the colonization movement from the beginning. Obadiah Buel Brown, pastor of First Baptist Church in Washington, DC from 1807 to 1852, served as one of the founding managers of the ACS. Both the ACS and Brown were strategically situated in the nation's capital.[8] William Staughton, the British born minister who became the first president of Columbian College, a Baptist school that Brown helped start in 1821, presided over a local auxiliary of the colonization society in 1823.[9] Further south, Virginians Robert Semple and Andrew Broaddus were vice-presidents of another auxiliary society. At a Fourth of July meeting in 1862 they both preached and enlisted sixty-two new members for the society.[10] Jeremiah Bell Jeter also promoted the cause in Virginia. In 1836 during a meeting of the Colonization Society of Virginia, he introduced a resolution commending the movement to "the pious and philanthropic."[11]

Colonization appealed broadly to Virginia's Baptists. One of the readers of Virginia's Baptist paper, the *Religious Herald*, complained in 1832 that the paper ignored the topic of colonization: "While I rejoice to see the columns of the Herald devoted to the cause of Missions, Temperance, and much that promises to benefit mankind—I deeply regret the little interest that is shewn on the subject of African colonization."[12] Many Baptist leaders responded by promoting the cause with zeal. When the Baptist Association of Fredericksburg gathered on June 2, 1853 to discuss colonization, William Broaddus proposed "the subject of African colonization is in our judgment a wise measure of state policy, and a worthy object of Christian sympathy and support." The delegates passed the resolution and went on to encourage their churches to take up an annual collection for the ACS of Virginia.[13] Northern Baptists similarly called on

8. "Colonization Society," *Columbian Star*, 6 December 1823, 195.

9. "Colonization Society," *Columbian Star*, 20 December 1823, 203.

10. "American Colonization Society," *Columbian Star*, 6 August 1825, 127.

11. "Colonization Society of Virginia," *Religious Herald*, 15 January 1836, 6.

12. C. T., "The African Colonization Society," *Religious Herald*, 2 November 1832, 169.

13. "African Colonization," *Religious Herald*, 21 July 1853, 114.

their readers to view colonization as a "subject of deep interest to every patriot and philanthropist."[14]

Compassion for blacks motivated many Baptists to support the colonization movement.[15] They believed colonization was necessary to keep blacks from occupying an "inferior position" in society. When H. B. B. wrote to Boston's *Christian Watchman*, he described the discrimination endured by blacks: "I would seriously ask, whether Christians have regarded the people of color in this city, as their neighbors? If so, how happens it that they are so much neglected, despised, ridiculed, and shunned?"[16] In Virginia the Baptist teacher and preacher, John Broadus, summarized but did not accept the popular opinion that blacks were too backward to be educated: "Some persons, indeed, are so much impressed with the difficulties attending the work, as to be almost ready to pronounce it impracticable. The colored people, they say, are often so stupid, so devoted to mere excitement, so easily deceived and so ready to become deceived and so ready to become deceivers, so hard to be bound by the straits of morality, that we can scarcely hope to do much in the way of making them genuine Christians."[17] Promoters of colonization took all these factors into account and concluded the social conditions of the United States limited the potential of blacks. Integration with whites set a plateau on how much blacks could achieve. "Here, the colored man must ever occupy an inferior position," argued representatives from the Colonization Society of Virginia. "In the land of his forefathers, he has free scope and every inducement to develop his faculties, and raise himself to the highest station."[18] Instead of blacks remaining inferior and underfoot, the Colonization Society of Virginia resolved to do all it could to send them to the "flourishing" colony at Liberia.[19] Many advocates of colonization believed their support to be an act of mercy toward the black who did not, and probably would not, receive just treatment in America.

14. "Colonization of Liberia," *Christian Watchman*, 9 December 1825, 2.

15. Mitchell Snay also noted that the reforms saw colonization as a form of "Christian benevolence toward blacks." See Mitchell Snay, *Gospel of Disunion: Religion and Separatism in the Antebellum South* (New York: Cambridge University Press, 1993) 23–24.

16. H. B. B., "Who is My Neighbor?" *Christian Watchman*, 9 January 1835, 7.

17. John A. Broadus, "Of the Committee on the Religious Instruction of the Coloured People," *Religious Herald*, 23 October 1856, 165.

18. "Colonization Society of Virginia," *Religious Herald*, 1 May 1851, 70.

19. Ibid.

The decision to support colonization in order to provide blacks a better life in Liberia is a perfect example of benevolence as a means of social control. White Baptists believed they knew the best place for blacks to prosper, and they supported this particular engine of reform to make the transfer possible. Colonization, they thought, promised to solve the problems involved in governing a black underclass. Jesse Mercer, president of the Georgia Baptist Convention, writing for Georgia's *Christian Index*, shared the opinion that colonization served free blacks and the social order: "Every man who looks at this subject rightly, knows and feels, that if the black man is free, he ought to be in his own country—in the land of his fathers! Amalgamation and promiscuous intercourse, are out of the question. . . . There the free Negro can go and act for himself, perfectly untrammeled by the superior advantages of his white neighbor."[20] White Baptists wrongly perpetuated the judgment that blacks were inferior, and expected their neighbors to treat them accordingly. In that sense, colonization was both social reform and a means of social control. Baptist advocates of colonization displayed a genuine if misguided evangelical compassion for the downtrodden blacks facing what many Americans considered to be the impossible task of social integration.

Baptists also supported colonization because it promised to become a great engine for the evangelization of Africa. Three years after the movement began, the *Watchman* published a Baltimore article that encouraged colonization for the sake of the gospel: "We plant the standard of our Redeemer on the shores of Africa; her sable sons were torn from thence, enveloped in all the darkness of ignorance; they are returned with minds radiant with the beams of intelligence."[21] Baptist editors in Boston, Washington, and Virginia solicited their readers to donate to the cause.[22] As one agent for the ACS so directly asked, "Is there a soul who loves the Lord Jesus Christ, who mourns over the multitudes now under the dominion of the evil one, that will not joyfully embrace this opportunity of dispelling the darkness which covers the vast continent of Africa?"[23] They

20. Jesse Mercer, "African Colonization," *The Christian Index*, 15 June 1837, 372.

21. "Colonization Society," *Christian Watchman and Baptist Register*, 25 December 1819, 3.

22. "Colonization," *Christian Watchman & Baptist Register*, 1 January 1820, 2; "American Colonization Society," *Christian Watchman & Baptist Register*, 12 August 1820, 2; "Colonization Society," *Columbian Star*, 8 May 1824, 73; "American Colonization Society," *Columbian Star*, 26 August 1826, 135; R. R. Gurley, "To the People of the United States," *Religious Herald*, 6 July 1832, 103.

23. "Colonization Society," *Columbian Star*, 14 August 1824, 129.

received news of ACS ships sailing for Liberia loaded with emigrants ready to start a new life, equipped "to spread the blessings of Christianity and civilization in an heretofore benighted and savage region."[24]

When Baptists received reports of the meeting of the New York Colonization Society in 1824, its members emphasized colonization's three goals: first, the suppression of the slave-trade, second, the civilization of a "barbarous portion of the world," and third, "the giving to her tribes that religion which a Saviour brought us from Heaven."[25] Baptists approved the first two, but the third stirred them to action. The editors of the *Religious Herald*, for example, accepted colonization as a "barrier to the slave trade" but urged its defense on evangelistic premises: "This colony is entitled to the support of every lover of his country and his species. But on the Christian it has a still higher claim; as the planting and increase of these colonial settlements must exert a salutary influence on the neighboring tribes, and materially aid in the introduction of the gospel into that region of more than midnight darkness and death."[26] Baptists saw in the birth of the American Colonization Society the hand of God stretching itself out into the recesses of Africa. They had reason to believe revivalism was a global, not simply a local, phenomenon. Baptists knew God had wonderful plans in store for Africa, but wondered what he had in store for the Africans who remained in chains in the United States. This question would test their view of social reform.

How reformers defended colonization had much to do with their geography. ACS agents were known to change their message to fit their audience. Northerners, sympathetic to abolition, would likely be told that it was a movement supportive of emancipation. Southerners would be told that even the slaveholder could support colonization because it was a movement concerned only with free blacks.[27] When the colonization society reported in Virginia it stated: "Let it be distinctly understood that the society aims at the removal of the free people of colour, and that in no instance, whatever, does it interfere with the rights of property, or exercise compulsory measures in removing those already free."[28] These southerners were told not to worry about colonization's impact on slavery.

24. "African Colony," *Columbian Star*, 14 January 1826, 6.

25. "New-York Colonization Society," *Columbian Star*, 5 June 1824, 89.

26. "American Colonization Society," *Religious Herald*, 16 June 1837, 95.

27. Ellen Eslinger, "The Brief Career of Rufus W. Bailey, American Colonization Society Agent in Virginia," *The Journal of Southern History* 1 (February 2005) 39–40.

28. Philanthropos [pseud.], "Colonization, No. 2," *Religious Herald*, 26 February

Southern whites remained unconvinced. They generally saw colonization as a first step towards emancipation and were often therefore hostile to colonization.[29] The editor of South Carolina's *Columbia Telescope* noted in 1827 that colonization implied the eradication of slavery: "To countenance the American Colonization Society will be to proceed upon the principle, that slavery is a rank weed in our land." The editor appreciated the fact that South Carolina laws forbade emancipation and believed that the ACS was fundamentally an association that moved in the direction of abolition.[30] In similar fashion, S. J. M'Morris, editor of South Carolina's *Southern Times and State Gazette*, lamented what he saw as the inevitable connection between colonization and freedom: "The object of the Colonization society, as avowed by its founders and supporters, is the 'gradual emancipation of Slavery.' . . . Are we willing to stand idle while this process is going on?"[31] M'Morris pinpointed the real cause for concern: the fear of emancipation won through revolt. Slaves who sensed the possibility of colonization would stop at nothing to gain it: "When . . . the blood of murdered innocence smokes to heaven from the ashes of our dwellings—it will be too late to execrate the fanaticism of the North."[32]

Many Baptist reformers similarly linked colonization and emancipation. For example, the editors of Washington's *Columbian Star* approved of an 1824 Rhode Island gradual emancipation law that utilized colonization: "It would work the redemption of many an oppressed African, and finally free our nation from the curse of slavery, than which deliverance nothing can be more desirable."[33] On November 18, 1835, in the course of canceling his subscription to Boston's *Christian Watchman*, one southern reader explained that he based his decision on what he considered to be the paper's radical support of abolition. Like many southerners, he believed slavery to be "a great evil," but viewed immediate abolitionism as the wrong remedy. He regarded "the American Colonization Society as the only means of eradicating the evil." He continued, "Let a colony be established firmly in Africa, and intercourse between Africa and this

---

1830, 29.

29. Burin, *Peculiar Solution*, 163.

30. *Columbia Telescope*, 22 November 1827, 224.

31. S. J. M'Morris, "Colonization Society," *Southern Times and State Gazette*, 7 October 1830, 2–3.

32. S. J. M'Morris, untitled article, *Southern Times and State Gazette*, 2 February 1831, 3.

33. "Emancipation," *Columbian Star*, 5 June 1824, 90.

continent become frequent, as it must necessarily become, and you will
see thousands flocking to Liberia." He believed that God had established
this colony for two purposes. First, "to undermine slavery in this country," and, second, "to evangelize Africa." The last thing this reader, who
favored gradual emancipation, wanted to see was his goal undermined by
radical abolitionists.[34] In 1847 the *Watchman* published an article from
the *New York Observer* that argued the emigration of blacks would soon
lead to the end of slavery: "Three millions of instruments placed in our
hands, to sharpen, polish, and prepare for the subjugation of a continent
for the prince of peace!" Only God knew the timetable. It was enough,
the author argued, for zealous reformers to know it was neither the work
of a day nor a year; they must not become impatient, "though His chariot
wheels may seem to move slow." The ultimate release of the slaves portended the salvation of a continent:

> Yes, they have here in the South the grand lever for raising Af-
> rica; let the foot of it be placed at Liberia; let Christians, and
> patriots, and philanthropists throw their weight upon this end
> of it, making the Bible the fulcrum, and ere long, Africa, with
> her sable millions, will be seen emerging from the long night of
> cruel tyranny and barbarism into the pure sunlight of Christian
> civilization; annexing herself by indissoluble bonds of grate-
> ful affection to this, her sister patron-republic; and with her
> churches and schools, her colleges and legislative halls, her ports
> and her orators, take a proud and enviable position among the
> enlightened and civilized nations of the earth. The Lord hasten
> it in his time, and to Him be the glory.[35]

Many saw colonization as a stepping stone to the end of slavery and the
Christianizing of a foreign nation.[36]

34. "Slavery," *Christian Watchman*, 27 November 1835, 190.

35. E. W. Sawtell, "Facts Concerning Slavery at the South," *Christian Watchman*,
17 September 1847, 149.

36. David T. Bailey argued that the relationship between colonization and emancipation among southwestern ministers was a complex one. They generally did not view
it as an engine for emancipation and yet abolitionists supported it. "The colonization
movement provided ministers with a safety valve, a means of draining off some of the
internal pressure brought on by doubts about the morality of the peculiar institution,
and it was valuable largely because advocates only rarely suggested that it would end
slavery. Indeed, ministers who opposed abolition gladly joined the cause." See David
T. Bailey, *Shadow on the Church: Southwestern Evangelical Religion and the Issue of
Slavery, 1783–1860* (Ithaca: Cornell University Press, 1985) 142–43.

Some Baptists objected to colonization for pragmatic reasons. "A Baptist" concluded that if 100,000 slaves could be extradited a year at a cost of sixty dollars each, starting with 2.5 million slaves in 1833 and factoring in a growth rate of 60,000 a year, it would take one hundred years and six hundred million dollars to transport them all to Africa, making colonization a politically unpromising solution.[37] He shared this view with other Baptists in Boston: colonization would never lead to the removal of millions of blacks.

Some slaveholders might have embraced colonization anyway, but they did not know how to orchestrate the details. One Virginia master had thirty slaves he hoped to free and send to a colony in Africa. However, they had intermarried with neighboring slaves and preferred slavery in America to freedom overseas. The owner wanted to do God's will, which he felt certain did not include immediate abolition, but in this case could not include colonization either.[38] J. B. Jeter expressed similar concerns: "The manumission of my slaves to remain in the State was not to be thought of. Should I send them to Liberia? Some of them were in a condition, but none of them desired, to go. If sent, they must be forced to leave wives and children, belonging to other masters, to dwell in a strange land." Colonization often foundered on these practical realities.[39]

In short, colonization proved to be a difficult issue with which Baptists had to contend. Some opposed colonization because they defended slavery while some, ironically, because they disdained slavery and supposed that populating Liberia with America's free blacks would only engender antipathy towards the remaining African-American population. Supportive Baptists expressed compassion for blacks even when their brothers and sisters in Christ accused them of fighting to bring down the Peculiar Institution.

All Americans found reasons to embrace and oppose colonization. But the possibility of evangelizing a continent proved an irresistible inducement for many Baptists. They jumped on the colonization bandwagon and linked their yearning for the spread of the good news with social program that some believed would precipitate emancipation itself.

---

37. A Baptist [pseud.], "View of Slavery," *Christian Watchman*, 6 December 1833, 193.

38. "Slavery-Colonization," *Christian Watchman and Reflector*, 5 February 1852, 22.

39. Jeremiah Bell Jeter, *The Recollections of a Long Life* (Richmond, VA: The Religious Herald, 1891) 68.

Those Baptists who supported colonization hoped that Liberia would be a new front for global missions. Africa, like America, could birth its own Christian nation if the Holy Spirit saw fit, and the colonization effort was just the type of social reform movement to make this dream of evangelistic conquest a reality. Not surprisingly, a heart for evangelism led Baptists to promote religious instruction.

Religious Instruction and Reform

The religious instruction of slaves was often rejected as a pathway to revolt or accepted as a means of social control. The popular sentiment existed that an educated slave would grow discontented with his shackles and seek an opportunity to rebel against his master. It became standard fare in the religious newspapers for northerners and southerners to trade barbs regarding the treatment of slaves, northerners emphasizing the cruelty of slavery and southerners defending the humanitarian character of the institution. Southern and northern Christians alike agreed that the slaves ought not to be treated harshly, and many accepted that slaves ought to be given a religious and moral education. Still, most masters saw educated slaves as threats to society, anxious to foment revolt. Others used religious education as a whip to keep their slaves docile. It is also true that many Baptists considered the religious education of slaves to be a moral imperative. In that sense, they saw it as way to bring some degree of reform to the blight of slavery.

After reading *The Religious Instruction of the Negroes* by the Presbyterian Charles Colcock Jones, James Petigru Boyce described it as "the best and oldest treatment of the subject and should be reprinted for its intense interest, data, and fairness."[40] Its publication in 1842 gave Jones nationwide notoriety as the "missionary to the slaves." Jones rejected an offer to teach sacred rhetoric and ecclesiastical history at Columbia Theological Seminary in Columbia, South Carolina, in order to devote himself full time to the gospel ministry among slaves in Liberty County, Georgia. In the estimation of northerners and southerners alike, he chose a noble

40. From an inscription in Boyce's copy of Charles Colcock Jones, *The Religious Instruction of the Negroes in the United States* (Savannah, GA: Thomas Purse, 1842) Archives and Special Collections, James P. Boyce Centennial Library, Southern Baptist Theological Seminary Archives, Louisville, Kentucky. On Jones, see Robert Manson Myers, ed., *The Children of Pride: Selected Letters of the Family of the Rev. Dr. Charles Colcock Jones* (New Haven, CT: Yale University Press, 1972).

life of self-denial and hardship to labor among the "degraded" blacks of his homeland.[41]

Jones called the Christian church to action in defense of the moral and religious development of nearly three million slaves. The Baptists, he lamented, had not one society or association committed exclusively to the conversion of blacks, although Baptist associations and conventions occasionally discussed the propriety of evangelism among slaves. Converted slaves became Baptists in large numbers. According to Jones, "there are more Negro communicants, and more churches regularly constituted, exclusively of Negroes, with their own regular houses of public worship, and with ordained Negro preachers, attached to this denomination than to any other denomination in the United States."[42]

Sadly, Jones's desire for the evangelism of the slaves cannot be separated from his promotion of racism. Despite their "own regular houses of public worship," the slaves, Jones insisted, had a desperate need for the white preachers to bring them the pure gospel. Blacks, he argued, had no control over their morality: "Whatever is idle, dissolute, criminal, and worthless, attaches to them."[43] He catalogued their various sins. They were "proverbially thieves. They steal from each other; from their masters from any body. Cows, sheep, hogs, poultry, clothing; yea, nothing goes amiss to which they take a fancy; while corn, rice, cotton, or the staple productions, whatever they may be, are standing temptations, provided a market be at hand, and they can sell or barter them with impunity."[44] Such characterizations affected the content of religious instruction the slaves received. Lucretia Alexander, a freed slave, gave a first-hand account of the moralistic sermons white evangelists preached: "The preacher came and . . . he'd just say, 'Serve your masters. Don't steal your master's turkey. Don't steal your master's chickens. Don't steal your master's hawgs. Don't steal your master's meat. Do whatsoever your master tells you to do.'"[45] Preachers addressed what they perceived to be the needs of the slaves, a personal morality that better served their masters. Such preaching helped also to quiet the anxieties of suspicious masters.

41. "Missionary to the Slaves," *Christian Watchman*, 3 February 1843, 17.

42. Jones, *Religious Instruction*, 94.

43. Ibid., 103.

44. Ibid., 135.

45. Quoted in Albert J. Raboteau, *Slave Religion: The "Invisible Institution" in the Antebellum South* (New York: Oxford University Press, 1978) 214.

Given this moralistic preaching, it is somewhat surprising that many southern slaveholders were nonetheless suspicious of evangelicals and their desire to encourage religious instruction to the slaves. Some simply questioned the possibility of the slaves' character ever improving. The morally bankrupt could not recover. Others suggested that the inherent inferiority of blacks implied laws, not education, must regulate their behavior. But it was pride that prohibited many southerners from allowing the religious instruction of their slaves.[46] For years northern reformers had insisted that a lack of religious instruction marked southerners as vicious to their servants. To change course would be to admit wrongdoing and prove the North correct.[47] As imposing as these obstacles may have been, they paled in comparison to the possibility, a probability in the minds of many white southerners, that religious instruction would promote slave rebellions.

To gain support among white slaveholders for preaching to slaves, Jones addressed the fear that religiously instructed slaves would fight for their freedom. He discounted the possibility by asserting the mission of the church is purely spiritual. Jones decried what he saw as the growing trend in which pastors dismissed their role as society's leaven and chose instead to play the role of the politician's prophet. He expressed the pervasive attitude southerners had toward the political thrust of many northern sermons:

> As ministers or missionaries to the Negroes, in the discharge of our official duty, and in our intercourse with the Negroes, we should have nothing to do with their civil condition. We are appointed of God to preach 'the unsearchable riches of Christ to our perishing fellow-men. We are to meditate upon the duties and responsibilities of our office; and to give ourselves 'wholly' to it. We shall, by so doing, in the most effectual manner subserve the interests of masters and servants, for time and eternity. It is too much the fashion of late years, for ministers (I speak not of all,) to consider themselves, *ex-officio*, the supervisors of human affairs, the conservators of the theological, the civil and the political interests of society, and of course, as possessing

46. Pike Powers, for example, argued pride was the primary reason white Americans failed to improve the moral condition of their slaves. They did not want to demean themselves by becoming slave teachers and they especially did not want to be cajoled into any action by their abolitionist critics. Pike Powers, "The Religious Instruction of Slaves," *Religious Herald*, 15 March 1839, 41.

47. Jones, *Religious Instruction*, 103–7.

the wisdom, experience, and observation sufficient 'to entitle them to be heard.' Any subject, any object of pursuit, however, remotely touching upon the religion or morals of the people, is considered as legitimate 'work' to which they may conscientiously devote all the powers which God has given them.[48]

This was southern evangelical philanthropy. For Jones, improving the spiritual status of slaves was a question of duty, not utility. Meddling with their civil status, however, was simply out of the question—a misappropriation of the pulpit. Slaveholders could rest assured, insisted Jones, that their morally instructed servants would be healthy, happy, and well-adjusted slaves, encouraged by the precepts of the gospel to support the domestic arrangement God saw fit to ordain.

Such thinking epitomized by Jones and commended by Boyce can hardly be categorized as "reform." Most southern Baptists did not challenge the social system that secured slavery. They did, however, seek to convert individuals, black and white, and in so doing, perhaps unwittingly, they laid the foundation for what Donald G. Mathews called a "biracial community."[49] Blacks and whites shared very little in the Old South, but with the advent of religious education they shared scriptural truth—the closest thing to equality proslavery advocates allowed.

Some slaves accepted the Christianity taught by their white evangelists even though they recognized that their earthly masters often promoted religious education for self-serving reasons. Albert J. Raboteau thus perceived two religions existing simultaneously in the southern slave society. The first religion was taught by the master. It was a pacifying faith, designed to suppress an inclination for freedom. But the slave experienced a different religion altogether. It was a personal faith, a religion of the heart that transcended the motives of their first teachers. "The religion of the slaves," in Raboteau's words, "was both institutional and noninstitutional, visible and invisible, formally organized and spontaneously adapted. . . . Preachers licensed by the church and hired by the master were supplemented by slave preachers licensed only by the spirit."[50]

The existence and tenor of religious instruction depended upon the slave owner. As a historian of North Carolina slavery argued in 1899, if

48. Ibid., 241–42.

49. Donald G. Mathews, "Charles Colcock Jones and the Southern Evangelical Crusade to Form a Biracial Community," *The Journal of Southern History* 3 (August 1975) 299–320.

50. Raboteau, *Slave Religion*, 212.

the master was "humane and intelligent [the slave] fared well. If he were otherwise the slave fared poorly."[51] Southern Baptists accepted the authority of the slaveholder but urged benevolence. In 1856 John Broadus chaired a committee for the Albermarle Baptist Association to investigate the religious instruction of slaves. He concluded that its necessity had become a foregone conclusion among Baptists. He disagreed with the common opinion that blacks were incapable of learning and thus the committee encouraged religious education: "The able reports of several years past have been sufficient to remove any remaining doubt or excuse.—Masters are bound by this duty, with reference to their servants, as a part of their families."[52] Broadus did not question the hierarchy of the slavery institution, but he argued the institution demanded responsibilities from owners as well. He called slaves "family servants," and expected owners to treat them as more than property. Masters had a "duty to give the colored people religious instruction" just as a father was obliged to teach his son or daughter.[53]

Similarly, others Baptists refused to let fear dissuade masters from religiously educating their slaves. Many slaveholders saw themselves as progressives, "active participants," as Eugene Genovese described them, "in the material and moral march of history." They believed the institution of slavery secured a "Christian social order."[54] Many slaveholders believed religious education planted insurrectionary thoughts in the minds of slaves and, therefore these masters denied their servants an education. They contended the Christian social order depended upon keeping the gospel from their slaves.

Some Baptists managed to see in religious education more than simply a means to keep slaves silent. Richard Furman argued it was a moral responsibility rooted in what blacks and whites both shared: the image of God. In 1822 Richard Furman asked the governor of South Carolina to appoint a day of public humiliation and fasting. The state had recently experienced two perils that called for, in the opinion of the South Carolina Baptist Convention, a public declaration of the fear of God. In Charleston earlier that year, Denmark Vesey, a free black and

51. John Spencer Bassett, *Slavery in the State of North Carolina* (Baltimore: Johns Hopkins University Press, 1899) 82.

52. John A. Broadus, "Of the Committee on the Religious Instruction of the Coloured People," *Religious Herald*, 23 October 1856, 165.

53. Ibid.

54. Genovese, *The Slaveholders' Dilemma*, 13, 38.

a Christian, plotted a large-scale insurrection. When news of the plan leaked, the authorities arrested 131 slaves, convicted sixty-seven, and executed thirty-five.[55] Furman saw the ordeal, coupled with a deadly hurricane—the other peril—as proof of the need for statewide repentance.

Furman offered the governor more than an argument for humiliation; he presented a Baptist treatise on slavery. He argued that the Bible prescribed slavery, though not necessarily in perpetuity. Moreover, he defended the importance of religious instruction. His argument was no casual aside. As Robert P. Forbes suggested, slavery needed no defense in South Carolina; Christianity among slaves did. Slaveholders must be disabused of the notion that the Christian faith is a "dangerous luxury in a slave society," as Forbes put it.[56] According to Furman, society depended upon vibrant religion in the upper and lower echelons. Furman's argument was radical. He declared that God demanded and the community needed slaves' religious and moral education, not simply to make them obedient, surely a common argument among Baptists, but because Furman knew that even slaves had certain, inalienable rights:

> I am brought to a part of the general subject, which, I confess
> to your Excellency, the Convention, from a sense of their duty,
> as a body of men, to whom important concerns of Religion are
> confided, have particularly at heart, and wish it may be seri-
> ously considered by all our Citizens: This is the religious interest
> of the Negroes. For though they are slaves, they are also men;
> and are with ourselves accountable creatures; having immortal
> souls, and being destined to future eternal award. Their religious
> interests claim a regard from their masters of the most serious
> nature; and it is indispensable. Nor can the community at large,
> in a right estimate of their duty and happiness, be indifferent on
> this subject.[57]

55. Lionel H. Kennedy and Thomas Parker, *An Official Report of the Trials of Sundry Negroes Charged with an Attempt to Raise an Insurrection in the State of South Carolina* (Charleston, SC: James R. Schenck, 1822) 47. See Douglas R. Egerton, *He Shall Go Out Free: The Lives of Denmark Vesey* (Lanham, MD: Rowman & Littlefield, 2004).

56. Robert P. Forbes, "Slavery and the Evangelical Enlightenment," in *Religion and the Antebellum Debate over Slavery*, ed. John R. McKivigan and Mitchell Snay (Athens: University of Georgia Press, 1998) 76.

57. Richard Furman, *Exposition of the Views of the Baptists Relative to the Coloured Population in the United States*, 2nd ed. (Charleston, SC: A. E. Milner, 1833) 13.

Furman's words were not without risk. Slaveholders considered religious instruction the seedbed of revolt. Weeks after the plot had been discovered, Charleston lawyers wrote that Vesey conspired in private church meetings, "held usually at night in some retired building, avowedly for religious instruction and worship, no white person attended." Religious instruction had become synonymous with conspiracy and rebellion: "That inflammatory and insurrectionary doctrines, without any direct proposal for such an attempt, were inculcated at these meetings of any kind to be held solely by slaves, and at such times and places, must forcibly strike every reflecting mind."[58] Every rumor of slave insurrection, made credible by the example of Haiti's successful rebellion in 1791, cast suspicion on white evangelical preachers.[59] Leading white southerners held that Christianity, if introduced to the slaves, would lead them to view themselves as the equals of whites and make them discontent with their own status. Such feelings gained new impetus in the wake of Nat Turner's 1831 slave rebellion.[60] That rebellion put Baptists, once again, on the defensive, arguing that evangelism among slaves would not tear apart society.

Defending and teaching Christianity to slaves at such a time put Baptists decidedly on the wrong side of white public opinion. This could be a dangerous place. In August 1833 John B. Pinney, a Presbyterian missionary, accepted an invitation to preach in Columbia, South Carolina, before a combined group of Presbyterians and black Baptists. His talk, which touched upon Pinney's recent visit to Liberia, outraged the citizens, and he barely escaped being tarred and feathered. Moreover, the very sight of the gathered black Baptists in the presence of a preacher was enough to incite the citizens to adopt the following resolution on August

58. Kennedy and Parker, *Official Report*, 23. On Southern white fears of slave Christianity, see Donald G. Mathews, *Religion in the Old South* (Chicago: University of Chicago Press, 1977) 204; Eugene D. Genovese, *From Rebellion to Revolution: Afro-American Slave Revolts in the Making of the Modern World* (Baton Rouge: Louisiana State University, 1979) 119.

59. Laurent Dubois, *Avengers of the New World: The Story of the Haitian Revolution* (Cambridge, MA: Belknap, 2005); Thomas O. Ott, *The Haitian Revolution, 1789–1804* (Knoxville: University of Tennessee Press, 1973).

60. "Humanitas" [pseud.], writing to the *Religious Herald* in 1832, approved of teaching slaves moral philosophy but not theology. "The first would make them more useful, the latter is too fruitful with prophetic signs, propelling them on to acts of insurrection and brutal rage." Humanitas [pseud.], "On Legislative Enactments," *Religious Herald*, 20 January 1832, 6.

26: "Resolved, that this meeting disapprove of the teaching of negroes, in any manner, to read or write, or of the holding of any unlawful assembly for any purpose."[61] The secrets of the Christian faith, available through study, were off-limits to many blacks, and in select cases like this, Christian preachers took considerable risk ignoring the will of the majority.

The religious instruction of slaves was not an example of pure philanthropy. How could it be in a culture imbued with racism? But nor was the promotion of religious instruction always only a means of social control. This tension is apparent in statements made by certain northern Baptists who promoted both abolition and religious instruction. The salvation of souls came first. Changing the social order could come later, if at all. The editors of the *Christian Watchman* in February 1835, for example, encouraged evangelism among the blacks promising it would not destroy the fabric of society: "Let the gospel, we say, be imparted to the colored man, because the gospel was designed for all men. Let it be imparted, because it is a safe measure. The gospel, in its influences upon human character, does not disturb any of those just relations among mankind, which are essential to human society; nay, it establishes and confirms all these relations."[62] The gospel, they argued, undergirds all that is best about America; it will not destroy it. Those who opposed religious instruction had no need to fear that the gospel would incite rebellion. These northern Baptists, though opposed to slavery, made the evangelistic ministry of religious education their first priority.

The next month, the same editors were explicit, condemning slavery, pleading for religious education, and defending their motive as religious, not political:

> We did not advocate the religious instruction of slaves as a means of accomplishing some favorite scheme of emancipation, but for the gospel's sake, as being just what the slaves need, just what is adapted to their condition; and, as being just what all Christians are under the most solemn obligation to give them. By so doing, we supposed that we were concurring with our excellent brethren at the South. Our intention was to reciprocate our kindest sympathies with our brethren in their noble undertaking, to give the gospel to the poor of their plantations.
>
> We say explicitly, that we believe the system of domestic slavery in this country to be wrong, that it cannot be justified

---

61. "Liberia and African Missionary," *Columbia Telescope*, 3 September 1833, 3.
62. "Religious Instruction of Slaves," *Christian Watchman*, 20 February 1835, 30.

by the Word of God. But even upon this subject, he might not find us altogether so extravagant as he now supposes us to be. But this is no reason why we should feel unkindly towards each other, and speak angrily of each other. There is enough sin and human weakness in the best of men to make them modest, and to render them sparing of their reproaches.[63]

The editors valued evangelism over emancipation. Not because they secretly opposed abolition, but because they advocated the spiritual welfare of the slaves and hoped to convince southern slaveholders of their moral responsibility to care religiously for them. Northern Baptist editors prepared their readers for the existence of a biracial community that depended upon republican virtues, which could only be found in religious teaching and practice. Whites and blacks ignored such teaching at society's peril.

Many Baptists, northern and southern, realized the potential for slave revolts but they rejected the notion that the gospel would breed it. They agreed that slaves, like whites, were made in the image of God, and this image demanded compassion in the form of evangelism. Many, moreover, Furman included, allowed that the slaves might one day be free. When that day came, two to three million impious and uneducated blacks would not serve society. The well-being of America depended upon the education of its captive blacks. Baptist advocates of religious instruction placed evangelism and social reform together. Though social reform in the context of slavery did not always mean for Baptists immediate abolition of the slaves, sometimes it did.

Abolition and Reform

A minority of Baptists in the upper South and a large percentage in the North promoted a form of emancipation rooted in Christian conviction and republican sentimentality.[64] In the South, these convictions ran into a proslavery movement that urged the church to be silent. In the North, religious abolitionists often quarreled with a political antislavery move-

---

63. "Religious Instruction of Slaves," *Christian Watchman*, 27 March 1835, 50.

64. Vivien Sandlund, "'A Devilish and Unnatural Usurpation': Baptist Evangelical Ministers and Antislavery in the Early Nineteenth Century, a Study of the Ideas and Activism of David Barrow," *American Baptist Quarterly* 8 (September 1994) 262–77; Monica Najar, "'Meddling with Emancipation': Baptists, Authority, and the Rift over Slavery in the Upper South," *Journal of the Early Republic* 25 (Summer 2005) 157–86.

ment. Antislavery, Christian social reformers were a marginalized but important force.

Northern Baptist abolitionists saw their religion as a motivating factor in ending slavery. They bemoaned those abolitionists who refused to rely upon biblical arguments for emancipation. Religious abolitionists, Baptists included, used their denomination as a platform for social reform. To understand their work, an earlier antislavery movement must first be examined, one that took place south of the Mason-Dixon line.

Prior to 1830 a number of southern Baptists advocated emancipation.[65] John Leland was a paramount example. In 1790 he offered a resolution that the Virginia Baptist General committee adopted: "Resolved, That slavery is a violent deprivation of the rights of nature, and inconsistent with a republican government; and therefore we recommend it to our Brethren to make use of every legal measure, to extirpate from the land, and pray Almighty God, that our Honourable Legislature may

---

65. Robert G. Torbet noted that Baptists "were beginning to question the validity of slavery as a practice among Christians" after the Revolution. The Ketocton Association in Virginia described hereditary slavery to be "a breach of the divine law." Torbet mentioned the formation of several emancipation societies that formed in Kentucky in the early years of the nineteenth century but in the end, he concluded that even given these sparks of interest, Baptists were generally cautious about engaging in antislavery activity. He gave three reasons. First, their preference for unity. Second, their desire not to engage in civil affairs. Third, membership of slaveholders in Baptist churches. Robert G. Torbet, *A History of the Baptists*, 3rd ed. (Valley Forge: Judson, 1963) 282–84. Jesse L. Boyd acknowledged the antislavery sentiments of some southern Baptists: "In 1828 there were three hundred abolitionist societies south of the Mason and Dixon Line; less than a decade thereafter not a single emancipation society remained in the South." Boyd credited the change to the dependency on the cotton in the South and radical abolitionism in the North. See Jesse L. Boyd, *A History of Baptists in America Prior to 1845* (New York: American Press, 1957) 158. Bill J. Leonard acknowledged the activism and limited success of David Barrow in Kentucky and the prominence of Baptists as antislavery reformers in New-England but concluded that "abolitionist sentiments were not extensive in the Deep South, where evangelization of slaves and continuation of slavery were dominant social attitudes, often supported with religious underpinnings." See Bill J. Leonard, *Baptist Ways: A History* (Valley Forge, PA: Judson, 2003) 186. Ann C. Loveland used the General Committee's decision to dismiss the subject of slavery as evidence that antislavery activity had disappeared among Virginia Baptists by the late 1800s. See Ann C. Loveland, *Southern Evangelicals and the Social Order, 1800–1860* (Baton Rouge: Louisiana State University Press, 1980) 191. For Lawrence Neale Jones, the highwater mark in Baptist life was John Leland's 1790 resolution before the General Committee decrying slavery: "The significance of these actions so far as blacks were concerned, lay in the fact that they were clear evidence that many whites in the churches were opposed to slavery." See Lawrence Neale Jones, *African Americans and Christian Churches, 1619–1860* (Cleveland: Pilgrim, 2007) 49–50.

have it in their power, to proclaim the general Jubilee, consistent with the principles of good policy."[66] The Baptists who accepted Leland's wording came from associations throughout Virginia. They believed that God's justice demanded the freedom of slaves and, at the time, they had no qualms with its politicization. However, in five years the General Committee reversed its course.[67]

The most famous Baptist emancipationist from the South also mixed republicanism and biblicism, though much more clearly: David Barrow, a Virginian who settled in Kentucky. Barrow was born in 1751, became a preacher at sixteen, an ordained minister at nineteen, and fought in the Revolution at twenty-five. In 1778, while Barrow was preaching, a mob attacked and nearly drowned him for being a Baptist. By his thirtieth year, Barrow had experienced conversion, pastoral ministry, war, and persecution. Twenty years later in 1798, he moved to Kentucky where he came to pastor Mount Sterling church, a member of the North District Baptist Association.[68] Here his antislavery views reached their height. On October 5, 1805, at a meeting of the North District Association, the neighboring Bracken Baptist Association accused Barrow of meddling with emancipation. The North District Association agreed that Barrow "gave cause of hurt to the Bracken Association," but Barrow apologized and the matter was temporarily put to rest.[69] However the next year the association unseated Barrow on the basis of his continued antislavery preaching and formed a committee to investigate his church activity.[70] In 1807 the association withdrew fellowship from Mount Sterling for countenancing its pastor.[71] In response Barrow and ten other ministers formed the antislavery Baptized Licking-Locust Association, Friends to Humanity. For a few years, it remained a small but vocal body.

David Barrow considered the Peculiar Institution to be both un-biblical and un-American.[72] In 1808 he published a pamphlet entitled,

66. *Minutes*, Virginia Baptist General Committee, 1790, 7.

67. Robert B. Semple, *A History of the Rise and Progress of the Baptists in Virginia* (Richmond, VA: Pitt & Dickinson, 1894) 105.

68. J. H. Spencer, *A History of Kentucky Baptists, from 1769–1885* (Cincinnati: J. R. Baumes, 1885; reprint, Lafayette, TN: Church History Research & Archives, 1976) 1:193–96.

69. *Minutes*, North District Association, 1805, 2.

70. *Minutes*, North District Association, 1806, 3.

71. *Minutes*, North District Association, 1807, 2.

72. Sandlund, "'A Devilish and Unnatural Usurpation,'" 263

Involuntary, Unmerited, Perpetual, Absolute, Hereditary Slavery Examined; On the Principles of Nature, Reason, Justice, Policy, and Scripture.
He argued, first, that by allowing slavery society perverted nature as God created it. It fell into a trap laid by the devil: "We have learned to enslave one another, from satan's conduct toward ourselves."[73] Second, slavery is both unreasonable and unjust because it is an institution founded on cruelty and deceit.[74] Third, Barrow questioned the policy of slavery on the grounds that it compromised society's well-being:

> I believe it is acknowledged by all men of understanding that the strength and riches of a civil community, principally consists in the number of its free, virtuous and industrious inhabitants. And that which gives men the strongest attachment to any country, is their having permanent interest in it, and an unmolested privilege in common with other good citizens, of acquiring, holding and enjoying property. That therefore, appears to be a foolish policy, that not only deprives vast numbers of the inhabitants of these states of a natural right, viz. of acquiring and possessing property; but contrary to the law of nature, converts men themselves into property:—thereby rendering them, not only in a manner useless, but really dangerous to the community:—at the same time, injuring their present owners and successors, by giving them an opportunity of living in idleness and extravagancy, to the injury of civil society.[75]

These were not new ideas for Barrow. When he began his travels through Kentucky, he noted how those regions which relied less on slaves supported a populace whom Barrow described as "consequently industrious."[76]

Slaveholders contended that republicanism depended upon slavery. Barrow argued the opposite. The principles of the Revolution could not support the enslavement of Africans on American soil. While slaveowners argued that slaves were immoral, Barrow argued slavery compromised the virtues of the masters and diluted the righteousness of the nation.

73. David Barrow, *Involuntary, Unmerited, Perpetual, Absolute, Hereditary Slavery, Examined; On the Principles of Nature, Reason, Justice, Policy, and Scripture* (Lexington, KY: D. & C. Bradford, 1808) 11.

74. Ibid., 13.

75. Ibid., 18–19.

76. "Diary of David Barrow, Pioneer Baptist Minister Virginia, Kentucky"; copied from original now in possession of descendent, 17 May 1795, 2. Archives and Special Collections, James P. Boyce Centennial Library, Southern Baptist Theological Seminary Archives, Louisville, Kentucky.

Barrow criticized slavery's racism. He warned Americans not to root their liberty in "the sandy foundation of the colour of your skins."[77] Barrow contended that the white tyrant who will have a child with a slave and then enslave that child, even if the slave "were seven eights white (which is sometimes the case) would not spare you, if he had you legally in his power."[78] Barrow judged that beneath the racial prejudice, slavery was fundamentally rooted in humanity's desire to oppress. "Upon the whole I find the depravity of human nature to be such, that it constantly seeks to aggrandize, raise and immortalize itself."[79]

Barrow closed his examination with a biblical treatment of slavery. He saved it for last, not because he thought it unimportant but in order to "cap the whole."[80] He began his argument by turning to several biblical texts and suggesting that they failed to prove either "unmerited," or "involuntary," or "perpetual," or "hereditary" slavery. For example, in 1 Samuel 8:10–19, Samuel conceded that the servants of Israel's king may in fact be slaves. However, such slavery was unlike America's chattel slavery: "I believe it cannot be proven from those accounts, that it was perpetual, hereditary bondage, servitude or slavery they were under, viz. such as is plead for by the despots of our day."[81] Chattel slaves could be bought and kept in perpetuity, whereas the slaves of the Old Testament were captured and would eventually be released.

His main biblical critique against slavery, however, was an implicit one. Enslaving one's fellow man contradicted the overall principles of scripture: "In pursuing the examination, I find the whole tenour of both law and gospel, is against unmerited, &c. slavery.—Oppression and extortion, which are synonymous terms, are held out in both Testaments, as highly offensive to God:—to quote passages, to prove this, would be needless, to those who are conversant with the Bible."[82]

It was finally the tenor of scripture, not a particular passage, which led Barrow to oppose slavery and take minority positions in his own denomination and the culture at large. He allowed, for example, that

77. Barrow, *Involuntary Slavery*, 21.

78. Ibid.

79. Barrow, "Diary," 11.

80. Barrow, *Involuntary Slavery*, vii. Surprisingly, Sandlund ended her summary of Barrow's pamphlet without commenting upon this scriptural section. Sandlund, "'A Devilish and Unnatural Usurpation,'" 272.

81. Barrow, *Involuntary Slavery*, 33.

82. Ibid., 37.

the abolition of slavery would eventually lead to interracial marriage. Though he stopped short of advocating such unions in 1808, he admitted it a better evil than the prevalent practice of white men taking blacks as mistresses: "It has long been my sentiment, that any woman, who is good enough to make a man a concubine, &c. ought to serve him for a wife."[83]

Carter Tarrant, a fellow emancipator on the Kentucky frontier and a member of "Friends to Humanity," shared Barrow's views. He rooted his antislavery message in biblical and republican principles. Tarrant's message failed to gain traction when he lost the respect of his peers and the support of his congregation. Barrow and Tarrant represented a small but vocal antislavery movement in the upper South whose dogma became the rallying cry of the northern abolitionist movement after 1830.

Tarrant labeled himself an "Emancipator in principle" and set out these principles on April 20, 1806, in Versailles, Kentucky, where he delivered an address in defiance of slaveholding. Prior to preaching this message, Tarrant had resigned as the pastor of the church at Hillsborough, Kentucky, because the congregation instructed him to refrain from espousing his emancipation views. A total of eighteen like-minded members left to form a congregation known as the Regular Baptist Church of Christ at Craig's Creek in Woodford County in May 1806.[84]

When told abolition was a topic best left to the state, he replied, "If we were under the government of a Despot, I should think their observations just; but in a government like ours; a redress of grievance must originate among the people." To the people, therefore, he declared slavery to be contrary to republican principles, good policy, and the word of God.[85]

He cited passages from the Virginia and federal constitutions that secured his freedom as proof of his right to advocate his antislavery principles: "What I am now about is no more than what every free citizen thinks himself entitled to under the benign influence of a republican government."[86] Tarrant believed republicanism necessitated the liberation of the slaves. The essence of hypocrisy, he insisted, was signing the Bill of Rights, only to consign blacks to bondage.[87]

---

83. Ibid., 45.

84. Carter Tarrant, *The Substance of a Discourse Delivered in the Town of Versailles* (Lexington, KY: D. Bradford, 1806) 25–27.

85. Ibid., 2, 8.

86. Ibid., 4.

87. Ibid., 9.

Like Barrow, Tarrant argued that slavery was bad public policy. It weakened the nation. The white population will constantly be in fear of the mutiny of the enslaved class while the slaves will live as a perpetual enemy. Moreover, as Barrow emphasized, the institution of slavery encouraged "pride, laziness, and avarice."[88]

Finally, the tenor of the gospel militated against slavery: "The exercise of moral justice, benevolence and humanity is enforced in the gospel."[89] The entire "Gospel system" condemned the institution as inhumane. He recognized his position was a minority one even among his fellow pastors:

> The clergy tell me I am wrong, and the reasons they assign for it are, First—Your doctrine does no good. Sirs, remember how long you have spoken against the iniquities of our land, and yet iniquity prevails. Have you in some instances reformed mankind? So have we. I think you are as unsuccessful in your declarations against pride, covetousness, and drunkenness, as we are in the doctrine of emancipation. Secondly—You say I am wrong, because my doctrine gives such offense, it renders families unhappy with each other.—When you talk thus you have lost sight of the doctrine of the cross.[90]

Tarrant told the clergy of his day that the validity of his movement could not be measured by its success nor its popularity. Other reform movements had not succeeded, but their reformers persisted in the knowledge that the social evils must still be addressed. More importantly, to stay the attack because it is offensive was to reject the very heart of the Christian call to deny the world and follow Christ. The cross separated families by forcing individuals to choose sides. One was either for Christ or against him. Likewise, one was for emancipation or against it. There was no middle ground.

Barrow and Tarrant saw themselves as moral activists, but they approved of the church pressing for political justice.[91] The Baptists around them were selective in the political movements they were willing to

88. Ibid., 10.

89. Ibid., 17.

90. Ibid., 23.

91. Monica Najar, "'Meddling with Emancipation': Baptists, Authority, and the Rift over Slavery in the Upper South," *Journal of the Early Republic* 25 (Summer 2005) 157–86.

support. The antislavery movement was not one of them.[92] The Friends of Humanity disbanded in 1820 and the antislavery movement in the upper South dissolved with it.[93] Eventually it moved to the North, where republicanism thrived.

The assault on slavery by northern Baptists began in the 1830s.[94] F. W. wrote to Boston's *Christian Watchman* to memorialize his support for immediate abolition, citing the "Golden Rule" as his defense:

> If some of our citizens should be condemned to slavery by barbarian masters, what a deep and universal interest would be manifest for their immediate liberation: but how calmly do we look upon the fact, that two million of our fellow beings,—flesh and blood, and immortal like ourselves, are consigned to perpetual ignominious bondage. 'As ye would that men should do to you, do ye also to them likewise.'

However, F. W. resisted legislative action. Emancipation was morally in the right but he acknowledged the slaveholder's legal right. Though slavery had become "of very great interest to benevolent men," it had to be approached cautiously. He appealed to another model, that of

92. Bertram Wyatt-Brown, "The Antimission Movement in the Jacksonian South: A Study in Regional Folk Culture," *The Journal of Southern History* 36 (November 1970) 501–29. Wyatt-Brown argued that Baptists in the South rejected benevolent causes in part because of a hostility against reform movements that seemed northern in origin and in politics.

93. Ibid., 184.

94. Scholars typically point to the 1830s as the beginning of the American abolitionist movement and often root it in the popularity of religious revivalism associated with Second Great Awakening. See "Introduction," in *Abolition and American Religion*, ed. John R. McKivigan (New York: Garland, 1999) vii. Barnes's now classic account of abolitionism, *The Antislavery Impulse*, begins with a chapter entitled, "The Great Revival," in which he described a transformation in theology: "As devotion to the common man increased, the dogmas of Calvinism lost authority. Though still the official creed of the Presbyterian and Congregational denominations, orthodox Calvinism had long been opposed in the east; and in the West—which, in 1830, was anywhere west of the Easter highlands—thousands were ripe for apostasy. It was among these that the Great Revival began, and it grew wherever belief in Calvinism declined." Barnes, *The Antislavery Impulse*, 3. John L. Hammond showed that religious revivals of the 1830s actually changed the way people voted, steering them toward antislavery activity. See John L. Hammond, "Revival Religion and Antislavery Politics," in *Abolitionism and American Religion*, ed. John R. McKivigan (New York: Garland, 1999) 379–90. However, these analyses fail to point out that another brand of activism took place during the same period, an activism that did not depend upon a gutted religious orthodoxy. For this, the Baptists of the North are helpful examples.

temperance: "I would go to Southern men as brethren, and warn, entreat, and exhort them as freemen, and Christians. . . . My views on this subject, coincide exactly with my views on Temperance. Let men talk, and write, and preach, and act immediate universal emancipation as fast as they are convinced; just as men write, and preach, and act entire abstinence, until public opinion is brought to view the monster in his native ugliness."[95] The argument of this correspondent reflected the tactics of most abolitionists in the early 1830s who began their efforts utilizing moral suasion.

It is no surprise that northern Baptists tried to persuade their southern brethren. They were part of one denomination. They cooperated in the work of the Triennial Convention, which had been supporting missionary work since 1814. Moreover, northern Baptists had enough in common with the southern slaveholders to expect that they could win the debate. All it took, as F. W. put it, was for the South to see "the moral light which is arising on this subject."[96] Though such confidence proved to be ill-placed, northern Baptists continued to promote persuasion as a means of ending slavery. The Baptist Board of Foreign Missions in America wrote a letter to the *London Baptist Magazine* in 1835 explaining why slavery is so complicated in America and, thus, difficult to abolish. They noted the authority of individual states as one hindrance. The fact that state legislatures cannot be compelled by the federal government to abolish slavery meant abolitionists could only convince slave owners by argument. In short, persuasion seemed the best course of action.[97]

Some Baptists believed the godliest route to emancipation avoided coercion. The editors of the *Christian Watchman* pled with their readers to commit to holiness and unity and to flee zeal and division. True progress depended upon slaveowners first recognizing the heinousness of their sin: "In just so far as the souls of men are rescued from the dominion of sin, so far will the bands of slavery be loosed, and no farther. . . . What we desire to see, then, is an increase of holiness in the church— more love and union among Christians—and then a corresponding train of benevolent action, and slavery will cease, and all that is crooked will be made straight."[98] In the years after the Turner rebellion, as abolitionist zeal grew, Baptists continued to make the case that bloodshed could best

95. F. W., "Slavery," *Christian Watchman*, 4 July 1833, 105.

96. Ibid.

97. Lucius Bolles, "Slavery in America, *Christian Watchman*, 27 February 1835, 34.

98. "Abolition of Slavery," *Christian Watchman*, 8 April 1835, 58.

be avoided by applying the precepts of the gospel to the evil of the South's peculiar institution: "Many good men have honestly made, we believe, a great mistake upon this subject," wrote the *Watchman's* editors. "They have forsaken their appropriate work in the vineyard of the Lord, and have endeavored to correct an evil by other means; while the gospel was the only power which was adequate to remove it. They have been too much for taking slavery by the horns, and dispatching it at once."[99]

Baptists, however, did not limit their appeals for reform to gradual emancipation. Some northern churches decided that love required more decisive action. The Fall River Baptist Church in Rhode Island called for the excommunication of slaveholders: "We verily believe it to be the solemn and imperious duty of ministers and churches and associations in non-slaveholding states to remonstrate against slavery with a spirit of love, but in the language of truth and in the tone of Christian decision. We believe it their duty to withhold fellowship from slaveholding churches and slaveholding ministers." That same year, the nearby Valley Falls Baptist Church expressed its conviction to see slavery's "immediate and entire abandonment."[100] The delegates to New York's Oneida Baptist Association, in 1840, decried slavery as "both a civil and moral evil" as well as "a cause of much reproach to the churches of the Lord Jesus." They committed themselves to "labor and pray for its peaceful and speedy abolition."[101] In 1841 the Oneida Baptists resolved "to employ every moral means in their power" to end slavery.[102]

In order to defend immediate emancipation, the editors of the *Christian Watchman* at times sought to downplay its costs. First, they argued that immediate emancipation was reasonable. The differences between immediate and gradual emancipation were narrowing. When summarizing a pamphlet published by the New York Anti-Slavery society, the editors of the *Christian Watchman* noted that the gradual abolitionists were willing to entertain some immediate action while the immediate abolitionists were content to exercise patience.[103] Second, northern Baptists argued immediate emancipation is safe. In March 1835 the *Watch-*

99. "Abolition and Anti-Abolition," *Christian Watchman*, 18 September 1835, 150.

100. "Abstract of Letters," *Warren Baptist Association*, 1836, 14, 16.

101. *Minutes*, Oneida Baptist Association, 1840, 8.

102. *Minutes*, Oneida Baptist Association, 1841, 9.

103. "Address of the New York City Anti Slavery Society," *Christian Watchman*, 22 November 1833, 188.

man reported about a cargo of American slaves that originated from the District of Columbia and set sail for Charleston, South Carolina. Bad weather forced the ship to land on the tiny island of Bermuda. A British colony, the Bermudan legislature had abolished slavery in 1834, the same year Britain ended slavery in all its colonies. When the slaves landed, they were immediately brought to the chief justice of the island who gave each slave the opportunity to remain in Bermuda, free, or return to the United States, enslaved. Only one woman and five children chose to continue to Charleston. According to the *Bermuda National Gazette*, the chief justice exhorted those who remained to work, soberly and honestly, and to capitalize upon the "boon of freedom, which by divine providence, had been granted to them."[104] The safe transition from slavery to freedom could take place on American soil as well.

The *Watchman's* editors knew that it would be difficult to convince their readers that immediate emancipation was safe. This explains why they published in 1834 an excerpt from the letter of an "intelligent gentleman in Alabama" written to a friend in New York. Given the note's sympathy for abolition, the Alabaman may have been a transplanted northerner. Northern readers undoubtedly considered him a better source regarding the intricacies of slave labor. He explained that if slavery should end quickly there might be some "embarrassment in business" and a number of slaves would "suffer an increase in evils, from an incapacity to provide from themselves" but no "serious evils would result to whites."[105] Statements like this infuriated slaveholders in the South and contributed to the abolitionist movement in the North.

It is difficult to assess just how supportive Baptists were of the antislavery cause.[106] With the exception of refusing to appoint slaveholders

104. "Seizure of Slaves in Bermuda," *Christian Watchman*, 27 March 1835, 49. See also, William Jay, *Miscellaneous Writings on Slavery* (Boston: John P. Jewett, 1853) 253; John Randolph Spears, *The American Slave Trade: An Account of Its Origin, Growth, and Suppression* (Port Washington, NY: Kennikat, 1900) 177. For an account of the origin of slavery in Bermuda, see Virginia Bernhard, *Slaves and Slaveholders in Bermuda, 1616–1782* (Columbia: University of Missouri Press, 1999). For an account of the abolishment of slavery in Bermuda, see Henry C. Wilkinson, *Bermuda from Sail to Steam: The History of the Island from 1784 to 1801* (London: Oxford University Press, 1973) 2:514–15.

105. "Slavery," *Christian Watchman*, 16 May 1834, 80.

106. Francis Wayland was a representative example of this difficulty. He argued against slavery most publicly in a series of letters first published in the *Christian Reflector*. See *Domestic Slavery Considered as a Scriptural Institution: In a Correspondence Between the Rev. Richard Fuller, the Rev. Francis Wayland* (New York: Lewis Colby,

as missionaries, the northern body did little, practically, to set itself apart as an antislavery organization. It would be years before Baptist mission societies took a firm abolitionist stance.[107]

Northern Baptist opposition to slavery, however, was more than nominal. Efforts made by Baptists to cajole their southern friends to reject slavery in friendly and sometimes less-than-friendly terms should not be dismissed. When Baptists in the South refused, their decision to form a separate missionary convention represented more than southern intransigence. It represented the tension between a Christian spirituality that struggled to keep Baptists united in the cause of evangelism and a spirit of antislavery social reform that made the division possible. Northern Baptists had prioritized social reform by refusing the appointment of slaveholding missionaries and southern Baptists prioritized Christian spirituality thus enabling the division to take place.

It is true that northern Baptists were incompletely committed to the abolitionist movement. This can be explained, however, not by questioning the religious impulse of the antislavery movement but by noting the significance of the dual commitment to republicanism and Christianity

---

1845). However, Wayland refused to participate actively in the antislavery movement. As Deborah Bingham Van Broekhoven argued, "Wayland's behavior was ambiguous, his silences on slavery punctuated with occasional antislavery sentiments." See Deborah Bingham Van Broekhoven, "Suffering with the Slaveholders: The Limits of Francis Wayland's Antislavery Witness," in *Religion and the Antebellum Debate over Slavery*, 197. Wayland is generally representative of the northern Baptist abolitionist movement. Anne C. Loveland's summary of the northern evangelical approach to immediate abolition is not in accord with Wayland's and the prevailing Baptist view: "Oriented toward the individual rather than society, conservative evangelicals concerned themselves with personal moral reform rather than social and political evils. In their eyes, slavery was a social and political evil, not a personal sin, and abolition was therefore secondary to and derivative from the primary goal of moral and spiritual reformation." Anne C. Loveland, "Evangelicalism and 'Immediate Emancipation' in American Antislavery Thought," in *Abolitionism and American Religion*, ed. John R. McKivigan (New York: Garland, 1999) 8. Wayland saw slavery as a moral and a social evil. To the extent that it violated the law of God, it was a moral evil. However, he allowed that some slaveowners who sought to benefit the slave did not necessarily sin—they simply suffered the consequences of the social evil of slavery. See *Domestic Slavery*, 48, 43. Charles C. Cole Jr. argued that conservative theologians, which included most Baptists of the 1830s, were "more likely to resist abolition or to take a proslavery defense." See Charles C. Cole Jr., *The Social Ideas of the Northern Evangelists, 1826–1860* (New York: Columbia University Press, 1954) 217.

107. John R. McKivigan, "The Sectional Division of the Methodist and Baptist Denominations as Measures of Northern Antislavery Sentiment," in *Religion and the Antebellum Debate over Slavery*, 353, 357.

as the foundation of emancipation rhetoric. Many radical abolitionists rejected biblical virtues. This made Baptist reformers uneasy and, at times, hesitant to join the cause on the terms prescribed by more radical abolitionists.

From the American Anti-Slavery Society's inception, Baptists objected to the strategy of the radical abolitionists. In 1833 the *Watchman* printed the following comments from the *Vermont Chronicle*, criticizing the policies of Garrison:

> For our part, we think the present policy of the Anti Slavery Society leads naturally, we may almost say, unavoidably, to the cultivation of bad passions. Its leaders are under a continual temptation to make the Colored People think as well of the Society, and as ill of every body else, as possible; to persuade them that they are hated, despised, vilified, persecuted and abused, by every body but the Anti-Slavery Society; to keep alive in them, the memory of all their wrongs, real and fancied, and to keep up, in its full strength, all that feeling of resentment, which the memory of their wrongs can sustain; all which, virtually, amounts to keeping up and nourishing a spirit of jealousy and revenge. Such a course cannot fail to re-act injuriously on the Whites . . .. It has the double tendency, to keep both races in this country, and to make them hate each other permanently.[108]

Such reflections tended to moderate abolitionist rhetoric among Baptists. The editors of the *Watchman* made sure that their readers knew, a few months later, that Garrison had been indicted by a Connecticut court for statements he made against men in his periodical, the *Liberator*.[109] Without giving specifics, the editors of the *Religious Herald* criticized the society's annual meeting held in New York in 1839: "The absurdity of their acts must, in a little time, render this society ridiculous, and take away from it the influence it had previously exercised. The welfare of the Union would be promoted by its dissolution."[110] A year later, when the *Herald* reported that Arthur Tappan had withdrawn himself from the American Anti-Slavery Society to form a new one, the editors simply

---

108. "Colonization and Anti-Slavery Societies," *Christian Watchman*, 2 August 1833, 122.

109. "William Lloyd Garrison," *Christian Watchman*, 15 November 1833, 184.

110. "American Anti-Slavery Society," *Religious Herald*, 24 May 1839, 33.

remarked, "The society we should judge was on the wane."[111] Baptists did not appreciate the direction Garrison took the abolitionist movement.[112]

The editors of the *Watchman* disdained the Garrisonian abolitionists for their heavy-handed approach toward the church: "Ministers of the highest standing in their denominations were denounced by name for the crime of hesitating to open the doors of their churches at the demand of unknown lecturers whose avowed object was to destroy both the church and ministry."[113] As time went on, these Baptists admitted that the division between themselves and the Garrisonites worked against the antislavery movement, but they confessed the great difficulty they faced uniting with those who defied God. One correspondent satirized the Garrisonian methods in 1857, arguing that the antislavery movement ought to be more forthright in its attack on the church, perhaps by publishing inflammatory notices:

> In the _____ church this evening, at seven o'clock, Mr. Blowout will abuse the Boston church, or the church in general, for one hour. Mr. Blowout's long experience as an anti-slavery agent, will enable him to do this thing with great power and effect. The public are invited, and a collection will be taken, to defray the expenses of the gifted and amiable lecturer.[114]

This satire is evidence of the marginalization of the Baptist antislavery reformers. These Boston Baptists saw themselves as part of an explicitly religious antislavery movement that was out of step with the leading abolitionists who saw the church as an enemy of reform. The marginalization had grown since 1834, when an auxiliary antislavery society formed in Salem, Massachusetts, and met in the second Baptist church, thankful for its support.[115]

111. "American Anti-Slavery Society," *Religious Herald*, 28 May 1840, 87.

112. This contradicts Bruce Dahlberg's argument that Massachusetts Baptists had every reason to claim Garrison as their own: "So, was William Lloyd Garrison a Baptist? He was not baptized, which for Baptist purists rules him out. Was Garrison indelibly shaped by Baptist faith and nurture? That much, Baptists can surely claim." Bruce T. Dahlberg, "Before Emancipation: Massachusetts Baptists and the Nineteenth-century Antislavery Struggle," *American Baptist Quarterly* 21 (March 2002) 63. To the extent that Garrison and many northern Baptists advocated abolition, they shared a great deal. However, northern Baptists separated themselves from Garrisonian tactics.

113. "Anti-Slavery Meeting," *Christian Watchman*, 31 January 1845, 19.

114. J. [pseud.], "Anti-Slavery Lectures," *Christian Watchman and Reflector*, 8 January 1857, 1.

115. "New Anti-Slavery Society," *Christian Watchman*, 21 February 1834, 32.

Some northern Baptists expressed significant support for the cause of abolition. In the early years of the American Anti-Slavery Society, when Arthur Tappan presided, Baron Stow, editor of the *Watchman*, participated in the organization. During a meeting held at the Third Free Church in 1835, he offered the following resolution:

> That this Society records with unfeigned joy and gratitude to Almighty God, the triumph of Christian benevolence in the emancipation of 800,000 slaves in the British dependencies, and its happy results; and, animated by the prospect of a union between the philanthropists of Great Britain and America in Christian efforts to extinguish slavery and the slave trade throughout the world, most fervently hopes that the delegates sent from Christian bodies in England to those in this country, will be men of uncompromising integrity and ever willing to co-operate with the Immediate Abolitionists of this country.[116]

A few years later, the *Watchman* included a lengthy address prepared by a "meeting of Baptists, at Worcester" that appealed for Baptist churches to take a stand against slavery, first, because slavery was sinful: "When, therefore, one portion of mankind takes from another, those rights which God has given them and for the use of which he holds them accountable to him, they must be guilty of the greatest injustice which they can commit against their fellow men." Second, though each Baptist church was autonomous, each was responsible for its actions to other churches of similar faith. This is true should a church apostatize theologically or morally: "If a church or any number of churches reject the divinity and atonement of Christ, or if they reject the practice of baptism, do we not feel compelled to admonish them—and in case of their pertinacious continuance in error, do we not renounce connection with them." Baptist churches had an ecclesiastical duty to address the sin of slaveholding: "In the relation we sustain to the church of Christ, we believe that it is our duty in the spirit of kindness, to bear decided testimony against slavery." Speaking directly to slaveholding churches, the Worcester Baptists spoke of the consequence of unrepentance: "Unless you take efficient measures to put away this evil from among you, we cannot continue to hold you as brethren." Third, they explained why the issue of slavery was such a serious issue for the church. Primarily, because it is a great injustice in the sight of God; but also, slavery had a stultifying effect: "The whole tone

---

116. "American Anti-Slavery Society," *Christian Watchman*, 22 May 1835, 82.

of Christian morals is lowered down by it in the church as well as in the community."[117]

Boston Baptists largely agreed and in 1844 Baron Stow, also an officer of the Foreign Mission Board, led the way.[118] He offered a resolution at the Boston Baptist Association that named slavery "a system of aggravated wrong." Moreover, he requested "all professors of religion who are connected with the system, to separate themselves from it as speedily as possible." Stow's resolution passed with only one opposing vote.[119] After the two mission boards of the Baptist General Convention refused to appoint southern slaveholders as missionaries and the southern Baptists seceded, Stow helped put together a revised northern convention. By then, however, a forty thousand debt, not slavery, preoccupied the leadership. Stow attended to revising a constitution, committing the convention wholly to missionary endeavors and raising money to erase the shortfall. By November of 1845 both projects had been accomplished.[120]

The work of northern Baptists against slavery was not insignificant. They helped created a culture that reaffirmed the immorality of slavery and prepared the nation to accept the necessity of war. However, that Stow and other Baptists could devote their attention so hastily away from antislavery to matters of solvency proves how quickly the Baptist antislavery efforts became a secondary concern.

The topic of slavery provides an interesting test case when looking at Baptists and social reform because it highlights the tension between a commitment to a purely spiritual Christianity and a Christianity that included social reform. Sometimes the two stood in stark contrast; at other times they complemented each other. For Baptist colonizationists, a compassion for blacks coupled with a love for the lost spurred them to act. This was spiritual Christianity, social reform, and, sometimes, social control woven together.

For advocates of religious instruction, compassion often compelled them to defend preaching and evangelism among slaves even when slaveholders contended these activities incited rebellion. Once again, the tension between spiritual Christianity, social reform, and benevolence as social control became unusually tight. Baptists displayed an interest not

---

117. "Slavery," *Christian Watchman*, 27 December 1839, 205.

118. John C. Stockbridge, *A Memoir of Rev. Baron Stow* (Boston: Lee & Shepard, 1894) 198.

119. *Minutes*, Boston Baptist Association, 1844, 8.

120. Stockbridge, *A Memoir of Baron Stow*, 205–6.

simply in the souls of slaves but in the status quo and the economic success of their plantations. Baptists appealed to motives of both saving sinners and social control. Religious instruction served more than one goal.

Finally, antislavery Baptists fought for slaves by combining civic virtue with Christian zeal. Commitment to a purely spiritual Christianity informed their rhetoric and it led southern Baptists to secede. The southern church usually had no room for antislavery social reform. However this had more to do with their antipathy for the antislavery movement than their reluctance to engage in political activism. Meanwhile, in the North, Baptists who infused the antislavery cause with religious zeal found themselves on the opposite end of the radical abolitionists' criticism. As a result, in both the South and the North, Baptist emancipationists turned their attention elsewhere. By 1860 the two sides could not have been any further apart. The *Watchman* had resigned itself to praising the Christian roots of the antislavery movement while the Charleston Baptist Association resolved that scripture sanctioned slavery.[121] Slavery, more than any other issue, reflected the conflicted character of evangelicalism in nineteenth-century America.

---

121. "Church Anti-Slavery Society," *Christian Watchman and Reflector*, 5 January 1860, 2; *Minutes*, Charleston Baptist Association, 17–19 November 1860, 4.

5

Church, State, and the
Sabbath Mail Debate

IN 1830 THE BOSTON Baptist Association reaffirmed its commitment to honoring the Sabbath: "Let that day be sacred; let no servile work be done therein; let worldly cares, and toils, and gratifications, which may be lawful on other days, give place on this, that the Christian Sabbath may be wholly given to God, and heavenly things."[1] These Baptists treated Sunday as a sacred day, and they knew their position had both private and public implications. To deny the importance of the Sabbath could bring irreparable harm: "If we pronounce that day common and regard it as such, which God has pronounced holy, we profane that sacred day: as men, and as citizens, we trifle with our temporal and eternal interests."[2] That same year, Virginia Baptists took a similar stand for the Sabbath: "The nation that disowns the Sabbath is necessarily a nation of infidels and atheists."[3] It is no coincidence that Baptists in the North and South spoke out in defense of the Sabbath in 1830. They were convinced it was under attack, and numerous Baptists took up their pens in its defense, arguing for a national policy of Sabbath protection.

Such a policy made perfect sense if the very integrity of the nation required honoring the Sabbath day as holy. But the continuation of a federal law, established in 1810, requiring the delivery of mail on Sunday, jeopardized that integrity. Efforts to overturn the law in 1829 and 1830 failed. When two congressional committees defended Sabbath mail delivery, they put an end to the question and shattered the reformers'

1. "Circular Letter," *Minutes*, Boston Baptist Association, 1830, 23.

2. Ibid., 19.

3. "The Sabbath," *Religious Herald*, 30 July 1830, 118.

hopes. For many, Congress's refusal to overturn this prohibition called into question whether America was truly to be a "Christian" nation. After all, if the people of the United States could not protect the Sabbath, what hope did the nation have of bringing in the millennium?[4]

Though all Baptists agreed the Sabbath must be honored, not all were convinced the United States Congress had a role to play. Presbyterians and Congregationalists spearheaded the effort to petition Congress to prohibit delivery of Sunday mail, and many Baptists joined the fight.[5] However, two Baptists made sure those petitions would not succeed: Richard M. Johnson, a United States congressman and senator from Kentucky, and Obadiah B. Brown, a Washington pastor and post office clerk. On the surface, the division among Baptists is obvious: Baptists wrote the petitions to Washington and other Baptists in Washington rejected the petitions. The actions of Johnson and Brown represented a deep division among the Baptist ranks as to the role of the church in the public square.

Defending the Sabbath

The Sabbath mail controversy began in 1810 when the United States Congress and James Madison passed "An Act Regulating the Post-Office Establishment." Section nine instructed every post office to remain open on every day that mail arrived "to deliver, on demand, any letter, paper, or packet, to the person entitled to or authorized to receive the same."[6] Hugh Wylie, a Pennsylvania postmaster and Presbyterian elder, precipitated this congressional action when he felt that his duties obligated him to disobey his church's General Assembly and keep his post office open

---

4. For this reason historian Mark Hanley suggested 1830 as a starting point for a decline in "mainstream Protestant confidence in the spiritual yield of republican liberty and faith." Mark Y. Hanley, *Beyond a Christian Commonwealth: The Protestant Quarrel with the American Republic, 1830–1860* (Chapel Hill: University of North Carolina Press, 1994) 1.

5. Wayne E. Fuller, *Morality and Mail in Nineteenth-Century America* (Urbana: University of Illinois Press, 2003) 8. Bodo suggested, "It was Lyman Beecher who embraced the [Sabbath] cause most fervently." John R. Bodo, *The Public Clergy and Public Issues, 1812–1848* (Princeton, NJ: Princeton University Press, 1954) 39. John Paul Rossing, "A Cultural History of Nineteenth Century American Sabbath Reform Movements" (PhD diss., Emory University, 1994) 77.

6. "An Act Regulating the Post-Office Establishment," 11th Cong., 2nd sess., in William Addison Blakely, *American State Papers Bearing on Sunday Legislation* (Washington, DC: Religious Liberty Association, 1911) 176.

on Sunday. Congress took up the matter and agreed with Wylie's view. They made Sunday mail delivery the law of the land.[7]

Many evangelicals protested. The House of Representatives Committee on Post-offices and Post-roads received petitions from concerned citizens and religious synods throughout the states. The memorialists, those individuals who petitioned legislators to reverse the law, argued that when Congress, "the most powerful influence in the Union," defended the violation of the Sabbath for the delivery of mail, it resulted in an overarching decline in the observance of Sunday as a day "set apart by the command of God for his more immediate service."[8]

The Postmaster General, Gideon Granger, must have received his share of protests as well for on January 30, 1811, he sent a letter to the House of Representatives and announced that, though he doubted his interpretation accorded with the intent of section nine, he nonetheless would limit post office hours to one hour on Sunday and ensure their operations did not conflict with church services.[9]

John Rhea, chairman of the House Committee on Post-offices and Post-roads, temporarily ended the crisis when he argued that mail needed to be delivered on Sundays to allow the United States to prosecute the war with the British. In a report responding to the memorials he received, Rhea noted, "however desirable it would be to advise the adoption of such regulations, relative to the carrying and opening of the mail, as might meet the views of the venerable Synod of Pittsburg, and the other petitioners, your committee cannot, at this peculiar crisis of the United States, recommend any alterations in the law regulating the Post-office Establishment."[10] Rhea made a similar statement six months and then three years later.[11] Nonetheless, throughout the war, memorials

---

7. Richard R. John, *Spreading the News: The American Postal System from Franklin to Morse* (Cambridge, MA: Harvard University Press, 1995) 170–71. Wylie believed he had no choice but to obey Postmaster General Gideon Granger and sort the mail every day it arrived, even if it arrived on Sunday. By 1808 he opened up the post-office simply as a courtesy to townspeople.

8. James P. Wilson and others, "Memorial and Petition," *American State Papers*, 179.

9. "Remonstrance Against the Delivery of Letters, papers, and Packets, at the Post-Office on the Sabbath," 11th Cong., 3rd sess. in Blakely, *American State Papers*, 177–78.

10. "Sunday Mails," in Blakely, *American State Papers*, 180.

11. Ibid., 181.

would continue, fueled by the energetic leadership of Lyman Beecher, New England's religious Reformer-in-Chief.[12]

By 1815, just five years after section nine became law, the delivery of Sunday mail had become part of the fabric of the postal service. Though petitions still implored Congress to prohibit the transportation and delivery of mail on Sunday, Senator David Daggett of Connecticut, who received the petitions in 1815, had no intention of responding affirmatively. First, he noted the United States had always transported mail on Sundays. Second, he quoted with approbation Postmaster General Granger's decision to limit Sunday operations. Finally, he pointed out that the War of 1812 justified keeping post offices open every day: "it is inexpedient to interfere and pass any laws on the subject-matter of the several petitions praying the prohibition of the transportation and opening of mails on the Sabbath."[13] In short, Congress heard and summarily rejected the evangelical protests.

By 1816 Congress could no longer use the War of 1812 as an excuse for delivering mail on the Sabbath. Still, after Congress approved the Treaty of Ghent it continued to receive and oppose the evangelical petitions to end the transportation and delivery of mail on Sunday. The argument for ending Sabbath mail now turned to financial considerations. The government contracted with private stagecoach lines, which operated every day of the week. Canceling mail on Sunday forced these lines—or so the argument went—to forfeit or renegotiate their contracts, costing the government more money.[14] This may have explained why mail must be transported on Sundays, but it did not account for the necessity of post offices remaining open. A better explanation is found in the party politics of 1816.

The Federalists, concentrated especially in New England, opposed the War of 1812. The Democratic-Republican Party did not want to see the Federalists prosper in any way. When Congressman Benjamin Tallmadge, a Federalist from Connecticut and a friend of Lyman Beecher, proposed an amendment to end the transportation and delivery of mail on the Sabbath, it failed by a roll call vote of one hundred to thirty-five. Unsurprisingly, the vast majority of support for prohibiting Sabbath mail delivery came from the New England states. The Sabbath mail

12. Lyman Beecher, *Autobiography* (New York: Harper & Brothers, 1866) 1:269.

13. "Sunday Mails," in Blakely, *American State Papers*, 183–84.

14. Fuller, *Morality and the Mail*, 14.

controversy from its inception, at least from the legislative side, had as much to do with politics as with principle. Still, evangelicals did not give up the fight, and the controversy exploded a decade later.[15]

The reason for the re-explosion had much to do with the Second Great Awakening exerting itself, as it so often did, in an organized reform movement.[16] In this case, evangelicals consolidated their efforts to prohibit the delivery of mail on Sundays. The General Union for Promoting the Observance of the Christian Sabbath was just one spoke in the wheel of a movement that included organizations for the distribution of tracts, the encouragement of Sunday Schools, the education of ministers, and many other virtuous ventures.

Lewis and Arthur Tappan, Beecher, and other reformers began the General Union in 1828 to resist the erosion of Christian morals represented by the government's postal legislation. For Beecher the nation stood at a crisis of faith and morality.[17] In a sermon preached years earlier, he lamented the deterioration of religion in and beyond Connecticut:

15. For the influence of party politics on the Sabbath mail controversy, see Fuller, *Morality in the Mail*, 15–17. Fuller's analysis is especially helpful in light of what Oliver W. Holmes previously referred to as "an unexplained lull in the agitation after 1816." Oliver W. Holmes, "Sunday Travel and Sunday Mails: A Question Which Troubled Our Forefathers," *New York History* 20 (October 1939) 417. Of course, separating politics and religious principles, as many have argued, is not so easy. Daniel Walker Howe, for example, noted that in the antebellum North, party politics became an instrument exercised by evangelicals to shape society. In that sense, it is, perhaps, too imprecise to separate politics from religious principle. See Daniel Walker Howe, "Religion and Politics in the Antebellum North," in *Religion and American Culture: From the Colonial Period to the Present*, ed. Mark A. Noll and Luke E. Harlow, 2nd ed. (Oxford: Oxford University Press, 2007) 136. Moreover, as Robert P. Swierenga has argued in his summary of the research, one's religious affiliation appears to have had a significant impact on the political persuasion of antebellum northerners and southerners. See Robert P. Swierenga, "Ethnoreligious Political Behavior in the Mid-Nineteenth Century: Voting, Values, Cultures," in *Religion and American Culture*, 156.

16. Donald G. Mathews, "The Second Great Awakening as an Organizing Process," in *Religion in American History: Interpretive Essays*, ed. John M. Mulder and John F. Wilson (Englewood Cliffs, NJ: Prentice-Hall, 1978) 203. Mathews wrote, "The Awakening in it social aspects was an organizing process that helped to give meaning and direction to people suffering in various degrees from the social strains of a nation on the move into new political, economic and geographical areas." Such a thesis fits the Sabbath mail crisis well. As America grew geographically and economically it challenged the fledgling democracy's morality and challenged her to address the problem with a political solution.

17. Rossing, "A Cultural History," 81.

"The polluted page of infidelity every where met the eye, while its sneers and blasphemies assailed the ear."[18]

At the union's annual meeting in 1830, they elected Senator Theodore Frelinghuysen as president, and Thomas S. Grimke, vice president. Just days earlier, Frelinghuysen failed to convince the Senate to instruct the Committee on the Post-office and the Post-roads to report a bill repealing delivery of mail on Sunday and prohibiting its transportation. "The Sabbath," Frelinghuysen argued," is justly regarded as a divine institution, closely connected with individual and national prosperity—no legislature can rightfully reject its claims."[19]

The General Union looked forward to Frelinghuysen's speech on the Senate floor. Thousands of petitions engulfed congressional offices from patriotic Christians hoping to persuade their leaders, in accord with the stated principles of the General Union, that the national government must change its policies.[20] "Thousands of our constituents, who would abhor all religious tests and ecclesiastical domination, sent up their request that a profanation of the Sabbath, as destructive of our temporal prosperity as it was offensive to God, might be repressed."[21]

The senator hoped to convince his colleagues that the memorialists did not want to build a theocracy. They "would not have been charged with the design of uniting Church and State, in any dangerous alliance, had their motives been justly appreciated." Frelinghusyen made several important points to defend the memorialist cause. First, sensitive to criticism that the petitioners were simply well-to-do New Englanders anxious to score a political victory, he noted that the memorials found their source in citizens from every walk of life, every profession, and every denomination. Second, he argued that the majority of Americans believed "that the first day of the week should be the Sabbath of our Government" and, in the case of a dispute, the majority wins. Third, he noted that England had no such requirement that mail be delivered on Sunday even though it had significant postal routes as well. Fourth, he emphasized that, fundamentally, Congress was being asked to remain passive, "to leave the Sabbath

18. Beecher, *Autobiography*, 1:273.

19. Theodore Frelinghuysen, *Speech of Mr. Frelinghuysen on His Resolution Concerning Sabbath Mails in the Senate of the United States, May 8, 1830* (Washington, DC: Rothwell & Ustice, 1830) 3.

20. *First Annual Report of the General Union for Promoting the Observance of the Christian Sabbath* (New York: J. Collord, 1829) 3.

21. Frelinghusyen, *Speech of Mr. Frelinghuysen*, 3.

alone . . . Congress are not asked to legislate into existence the precepts of piety." He concluded by reminding the other senators that the welfare of the country quite literally depended upon instructing the Post-office Committee to take action: "Let us weigh the interesting truth—that a free people can only flourish under the control of moral causes; and it is the Sabbath which gives vigor, and energy, and stability to these causes. The nation expects that the standard of sound principles will be raised here."[22]

Given Frelinghuysen's impassioned plea, his friends at the General Union immediately elected him president. The General Union also adopted a resolution proposed by Presbyterian pastor William Wisner of Ithaca, New York, which asserted that the present policy on mail delivery was a "profanation of the Christian Sabbath." Still, the members of the General Union must have been discouraged. Their two years of labor had thus far proved unsuccessful.

Sabbath mail reform portended therefore great consequences. It allowed for no partial victories; either Congress rescinds the Sunday delivery requirement and prohibits the transportation of mail on Sundays or the evangelicals failed. Christians from almost every state impressed upon their congressional representatives the urgency of this request. Congress received a compendium of hundreds of petitions in 1829, assembled by Jeremiah Evarts, which sought to change the legislators' minds.[23] Citizens of Boston, sensitive to complaints they wanted to establish religion wrote, "This application, we trust, will not be misunderstood. We do not ask Congress to enforce any season, or form, of public worship. . . . We only pray, that Congress may not counteract by its measures, those institutions, which are cherished by the community, as the means of public and private virtue." Meanwhile, representatives of Rowan County, North Carolina, were not so nuanced in their opposition: "Your memorialists consider the practice of transporting and opening the mails on the Sabbath contrary to the fourth commandment in the decalogue; and that the continuance and increase of our happiness depend on our obedience to the laws of God." Residents of Tallmadge, Ohio, noted that the public

22. Ibid., 4, 5, 7, 13.

23. *An Account of Memorials Presented to Congress During its Last Session, By Numerous Friends of Their Country and Its Institutions* (New York: Published at the Request of Many Petitioners, 1829). Jeremiah Evarts (1781–1831) a Congregationalist moral and social reformer compiled *An Account of Memorials*. See John A. Andrew III, *From Revivals to Removal: Jeremiah Evarts, the Cherokee Nation, and the Search for the Soul of America* (Athens: University of Georgia Press, 1992) 171–76.

welfare depended on the national observance of the Sabbath, an impossibility so long as mail is delivered: "Your memorialists would beg leave to suggest, that the stability and prosperity of our happy government depend, in a great measure, on the intelligence, morality, and virtue of the people; that religion exalteth a nation; that sin is a reproach to any people; and that it is a direct way to call down the vengeance of heaven, when human laws are made to violate the laws of God." Meanwhile, those in Elkton, Kentucky, warned Congress that it served as an example to the rest of the nation and should it approve of Sunday mail delivery the rest of the nation would see it as a sanction to violate the Sabbath.[24]

Because Congress would have expected pastors to support the petitions, Evarts left ministers largely off it. Instead, he affixed the names of merchants, lawyers, and bankers to prove that those who knew the most about finance and trade supported the post office being closed one day a week. If those most likely to be affected by the closure of the mail routes still wanted to endure the inconvenience, the government ought not to demur. The petition closed with the reminder that much more than a postal clerk's Sunday was at stake:

> As the preservation of moral integrity, or a sense of responsibility to God, extensively among the people, is confessedly essential to the continuance of a republican government,—every enlightened patriot, as well as every true Christian, must cherish the institutions of religion, as the great means of perpetuating our free government; that the laws of the several States are disregarded, and the religious privileges of the people invaded, by the present regulations of the post office.[25]

In short, the memorialists considered the Sabbath mail controversy a test of "enlightened patriotism." Mail delivery threatened the foundation of America as a free, Christian nation. The religious privileges of a people who once fought for the right to worship as they saw fit now perceived themselves forfeiting these rights upon an altar of progress constructed by the very government their virtue was supposed to ensure. Daniel Dodge, a Baptist and one of the only ministers to sign the petition, sought to reclaim the Sabbath and, in turn, Christian morality.

Richard M. Johnson, a Baptist and the chairman of the Post-office and Post-roads Committee in the Senate and subsequently in the House

24. Ibid., 9, 15, 23.
25. Ibid., 31.

of Representatives, disagreed. His opinion won the day and highlighted the diversity of thought on the issue of public engagement in Baptist life. Many Baptists labored to reclaim Sunday from the requirement of Sabbath mail delivery, but other Baptists like Johnson and Washington pastor Obadiah Brown supported the law. These two Baptists had power and willingly exercised it. The response to Johnson underscored the differing opinions in Baptist thought concerning the legislation of virtue and the strategy of social reform. Some put themselves decidedly in the reformist camp by advocating political activism. Others believed such a strategy to be inconsistent with American and Baptist polity.

Defending Liberty

To Richard Johnson's critics he may have been an unenlightened patriot, but there could have been no doubt of his commitment to the public welfare. In 1804 Johnson won office to the Kentucky House of Representatives.[26] He became a U.S. congressman in 1807 and he won reelection handily in 1810. Days before the bill regulating the post office went into effect, Johnson's attention was on foreign affairs, namely, the crisis with England that Congress and the president, James Madison, hoped could be solved without recourse to war. Johnson lent his support to an import tariff against foreign goods: "So long as France and Great Britain believe that we are dependent upon them for a market, or their goods, so long will they insult the honor of our flag, and trample upon the rights of this nation."[27] A year later it became clear that neither Madison nor congressional Republicans wanted to continue economic sanctions against England, and the War of 1812 began with Johnson's full support. He left for Kentucky for two tours of duty where he led a cavalry unit in the service of Major General William Henry Harrison. When he returned to Washington bearing his battle scars, he was a renowned American patriot.[28]

In June 1815 Johnson confessed his repentance from sin and faith in Christ at his father's church and received baptism in June 1815.[29] How-

26. Leland Winfield Meyer, *The Life and Times of Colonel Richard M. Johnson of Kentucky* (New York: Columbia University Press, 1932) 49.

27. Ibid., 76. Quoted from *Annals of Congress*, 1810, part 2, 1909–12.

28. Jonathan Milner Jones, "'The Making of a Vice President: The National Political Career of Richard M. Johnson," PhD diss., University of Memphis, 1998, 12–47. On the extent of Johnson's injuries, see Meyer, *Life and Times*, 129, 301.

29. *Minutes 1813–1861*, Great Crossing Baptist Church, June 1815, 17.

ever, his participation left much to be desired. In 1820 the congregation rebuked him for neglecting his church duties and expressed the hope that "he will bee more attentive in coming to meeting."[30] Johnson's most famous transgression, however, was his relationship with a mulatto, Julia Chinn, who ran his Kentucky home and bore him two girls who eventually married white men and inherited a portion of Johnson's estate.[31] Johnson's personal morals may not have been exemplary, but his Baptists credentials cannot be doubted.

Johnson's experience with Baptist churches and preaching informed his outlook. He counted Jacob Creath Jr., a Kentucky Baptist pastor, a great friend. In a letter to Andrew Jackson, Johnson noted the minister's influence: "I am under more obligation [to Creath] for my political elevation than any other man on earth."[32] Johnson's religious convictions led him to introduce a federal bill to abolish imprisonment for debt. He noted to his colleagues the incongruity of a nation rooted in Christian principles that nevertheless gave "one citizen a control over the personal liberty of another." He argued that a nation that so vigorously advocated benevolence should not so easily be able to imprison its own for debt:

> The good and the virtuous throughout Christendom are employing all their energies; and Christians, of every denomination, are united in the mighty effort. Benevolent societies have been established in every region of the civilized world. . . . Missionaries of our holy religion are penetrating every country. Burmah and Hindostan are receiving lessons of Christian morality, and the worshippers of Juggernaut are learning the knowledge of the true God. Jerusalem is again becoming the field of gospel labour. Divine light begins to beam on Persia, where the sun has long been the idol of their devotion. The savages of our own country are recipients of the same benevolent

30. *Minutes 1813–1861*, Great Crossing Baptist Church, June 1820, 67.

31. Meyer, *Life and Times*, 317, 321. Meyer described Chinn as Johnson's mistress but left open the possibility that Johnson married Chinn. Meyer cited a *Lexington Observer and Kentucky Reporter* article from July 1835 which intimated the two were married. According to the minute book of Great Crossing Baptist Church, Chinn died in 1833, along with several others in Johnson's household. There is no record of his being disciplined by his church for his relationship with Chinn, which indicates the congregation may have accepted they were married. See *Minutes 1813–1861*, Great Crossing Baptist Church, 5 May 1833, 265.

32. Quoted by Meyer, *Life and Times*, 302. Johnson also included the prominent Kentucky pastor Silas Mercer Noel in his circle of close friends. See Meyer, *Life and Times*, 302.

efforts, and the wilderness of America begins to wear the aspect of gladness. It is not expected that we, as a government, should become members of these societies, and make appropriations of money to carry on their designs; but while we witness these interesting scenes, which, on every hand, are calculated to rejoice the heart of the philanthropist, it is our duty, and I trust we shall find it our pleasure, to remove every obstacle to the happiness of the human race, and to take from the hand of tyranny the rod of oppression.[33]

Johnson's public declaration of Christianity as "our holy religion" helped many Baptists to consider Johnson as one of their own. However, no Baptist was closer to the Kentucky politician than the Washington pastor, Obadiah Brown. Brown led Baptists in Washington. He was pastor of the First Baptist Church from 1807 to 1850.[34] In 1808 the Baltimore Baptist Association chose him to be their moderator. The following year he preached the introductory sermon and for several years remained very active in the association until his church joined the Columbia Baptist Association in 1820.[35] In 1822 he helped found the *Columbian Star* along with Luther Rice and William Staughton, a Philadelphia pastor who moved to Washington to become Columbian College's first president.[36]

Brown's life intertwined with politics from the beginning of his ministry at First Baptist Church. Because residents of Washington were relatively poor and the visitors supported churches in their home states, it was not uncommon for district pastors to find a clerkship in the federal government to supplement their salary. Brown rose quickly to one of the highest posts in the land, that of chief clerk to the postmaster general. It would be years until the establishment of the income tax during the Civil War necessitated the creation of the Internal Revenue Bureau and a large federal bureaucracy. For now, the federal government was small and its

33. "Imprisonment for Debt," *Columbian Star*, 1 March 1823, 36. Johnson lost this and subsequent debates on this issue. See Jones, "The Making of a Vice-President," 207–16. Imprisonment for debt ceased on July 14, 1832. See Meyer, *Life and Times*, 289.

34. Dorothy Clarke Winchcole, *The First Baptists in Washington, D. C., 1802–1952* (Washington, DC: First Baptist Church, 1952) 5.

35. Joseph H. Jones, *History of the Baltimore Association* (Baltimore: T. A. Rhoades, 1872) 9, 15.

36. Gaylord P. Albaugh, *History and Annotated Bibliography of American Religious Periodicals and Newspapers* (Worcester, MA: American Antiquarian Society, 1994) s.v. "Columbian Star."

chief domestic duty consisted in the delivery of mail. Thus, Brown served as an important cog in the small federal machine. He had profound influence on his Baptist friend, Johnson.

In 1828, when the Sabbath mail controversy became a national issue once again and no national crisis could be used as an excuse to extinguish it, Johnson found himself at the center of the melee as a member of the Senate Committee on the Post-office and Post-roads. Given his support for the abolition of imprisonment for debt and even his approbation of Christian societies to organize for that cause, it is easy to assume that evangelicals thought they had an ally in the Kentucky senator. However in 1829, when he delivered a report outlining the position of the committee supporting the delivery of mail on Sunday, he argued in its defense.

The authorship of the Johnson reports—one produced in the Senate, one in the House—is disputed. His biographer, Leland Meyer, argued Johnson produced the report with some help from Brown and even Postmaster Amos Kendall.[37] John Rossing took a middle ground, arguing that since "Johnson and Brown boarded together in the capital . . . it seems likely that they collaborated on the Sunday mail report."[38] Wayne Fuller concluded Brown to be the author: "Presumably it was Brown, a shrewd and calculating Baptist minister with a sharp pen, who composed Johnson's reports. But it must be supposed that Johnson fully agreed with the reports, the emotionally charged language of which was reminiscent of that he had used to castigate Federalists in Congress through the years."[39] Richard John defended Brown's authorship arguing that Johnson simply lacked the education to produce "such a learned exposition" and everyone in Washington knew it. Furthermore, according to John, "as a Baptist minister, Brown was familiar with the evangelical anticlericalism that was the Baptists' stock-in-trade and well equipped to prepare a vigorous, brief, and effective harangue that was sure to be reprinted in newspapers throughout the United States."[40]

37. Meyer, *Life and Times*, 262.

38. Rossing, "A Cultural History," 103.

39. Fuller, *Morality and the Mail*, 26. John A. Andrew also argued Brown wrote the report, "Although the report was prepared by a Baptist minister (who was also chief clerk of the Post Office Department) its major significance was not just this strict separation between the religious and the secular." The report was important for arguing that an industrialized society now required seven-day mail delivery. Andrew, *Revivals to Removal*, 172.

40. John, *Spreading the News*, 199.

Johnson may have been the author. He understood Baptist life well enough to pen the reports. He grew up in a Baptist home, joined a Baptist church, and remained close to some of the most prominent Baptists of the day as an adult. Johnson probably understood anticlericalism as well as Brown, who grew up Presbyterian. The report, at any rate, is hardly a philosophical treatise. Its greatness is in its pitch-perfect appeal to popular politics. Johnson had proved already his ability in this area. But even if Johnson wrote it, Brown's influence seems strong. Brown handled all of the day-to-day affairs of the post office department. More important, he hosted Johnson, the ranking member of Congress's post office committees in his spacious E Street home.[41] The Kentucky Baptist politician and the Washington Baptist pastor likely collaborated.

Johnson delivered his first response to evangelical petitions on January 19, 1829, reporting from the Senate Committee on the Post-office and Post-roads. He argued with the utmost brevity that the prohibition of Sunday mail delivery by Congress would be improper, impractical, and absurd.

The federal legislature had no business deciding for American citizens when they should observe the Sabbath. "We are aware," wrote Johnson, "that a variety of sentiment exists among the good citizens of this nation, on the subject of the Sabbath day; and our government is designed for the protection of one, as much as for the other."[42] To adjudicate between Jews and Christian sabbatarians who observe Saturday as the Sabbath and other Christians who observe Sunday would "willingly introduce a system of religious coercion in our civil institutions, the example of other nations should admonish us to watch carefully against its earliest indication."[43] Here Johnson's argument was the most incendiary—he charged the evangelicals with wanting to establish a state religion: "they assume a position better suited to an ecclesiastical than to a civil institution."[44] If one could be a faithful American and disagree as to the proper day to observe the Sabbath, then the government should take no action in this matter: "It would involve a legislature decision in a religious controversy; and on a point in which good citizens may honestly

41. Winchcole, *The First Baptists*, 5.

42. Richard M. Johnson, "In Senate of the United States," 20th Congress (19 January 1829) 1.

43. Ibid., 2.

44. Ibid.

differ in opinion, without disturbing the peace of society, or endangering its liberties."[45]

Johnson also condemned the proposals of the memorialists on the grounds they were simply impractical. Unhindered mail delivery, he argued, is an essential governmental service. "One important object of the mail establishment is, to furnish the greatest and most economical facilities for such intercourse."[46] Forcing carriages to stop, and delaying the works one day will increase the expenses of the system. Moreover, adding to the inconvenience, "passengers in the mail stages, if the mails are not permitted to proceed on Sunday, will be expected to spend that day at a tavern upon the road, generally under circumstances not friendly to devotion, and at an expense which many are but poorly able to encounter."[47]

Finally, Johnson pointed out the absurdity of the request. Logic and consistency require the government to cease and desist any and all action on Sunday: "Nor can the committee discover where the system could consistently end. If the observance of a holyday becomes incorporated in our institutions, shall we not forbid the movement of an army; prohibit an assault in time of war; and lay an injunction upon our naval officers to lie in the wind while upon the ocean on that day."[48]

The real interest of the nation, Johnson said, depended on private virtue encouraged by private means. Instead of trying to influence the legislature, evangelicals should be minding their own souls for society's sake:

> Let the professors of Christianity recommend their religion by deeds of benevolence—by Christian meekness—by lives of temperance and holiness. Let them combine their efforts to instruct the ignorant—to relieve the widow and the orphan—to promulgate to the world the gospel of their Saviour, recommending its precepts by their habitual example: government will find its legitimate object in protecting them. . . . Their moral influence will then do infinitely more to advance the true interests of religion, than any measures which they may call on Congress to enact.[49]

45. Ibid.
46. Ibid., 3.
47. Ibid.
48. Ibid., 4.
49. Ibid.

Just over a year later, after Johnson had left the Senate and been elected again to the House of Representatives, he issued another report on the controversy. This time, he pressed even further the point that prohibiting the transportation and delivery of mail on Sunday put Congress in the position of establishing a state religion:

> In our representative character our individual character is lost. The individual acts for himself; the representative for his constituents. He is chosen to represent their political, and not their religious views—to guard the rights of man; not to restrict the rights of conscience. Despots may regard their subjects as their property, and usurp the Divine prerogative of prescribing their religious faith. But the history of the world furnishes the melancholy demonstration, that the disposition of one man to coerce the religious homage of another, springs from an unchastened ambition rather than a sincere devotion to any religion.[50]

Once again, according to Johnson, government ought not to infringe in a religious controversy. Effectively, Johnson applauded the existence of a republic of Christians, but he refused to promote a Christian nation.

The congressman also censured the memorialists for missing the point. Like a pastor rebuking his congregation for hypocrisy, Johnson reproved these evangelicals for holding the government to a standard they themselves were unwilling to meet: "If it be sinful for the mail to carry letters on Sunday, it must be equally sinful for individuals to write, carry, receive, or read them."[51]

In one of the great ironies of the nineteenth century, Jefferson's famous letter to the Danbury Association hardly made a splash in 1802 but is common knowledge today while the Johnson reports gained immediate notoriety but are unknown now.[52] The reports made Johnson instantly famous.[53] In a few short pages, Johnson articulated a commonsense

50. Richard M. Johnson, *Sunday Mail*, 21st Congress (Washington, DC: House of Representatives, 1830) 2.

51. Ibid., 5.

52. Philip Hamburger, *Separation of Church and State* (Cambridge, MA: Harvard University Press, 2002) 163–65. Hamburger noted that though the Danbury Baptists wrote to Jefferson asking for help from the Connecticut government that required them to certify their status as separatists, the Baptists did not embrace Jefferson's response that a wall of separation be erected between church and state. These Baptists wanted the state to cease interfering in their affairs while retaining the right to influence the state but they saw in Jefferson's letter, a movement toward overcompensation.

53. John, *Spreading the News*, 201–2.

doctrine of the separation of church and state that catapulted the patriot into even further heights of national prominence. In 1833, in remarks that paved the way for Johnson's 1836 nomination to become Martin Van Buren's vice president, Ely Moore, a New York congressman, said of Johnson, "I will hazard the declaration that Col. Johnson has done more for liberal principles, for freedom of opinion, and for pure and unadulterated democracy, than any man in our country—by arresting the schemes of an ambitious irreligious priesthood."[54] Not all Baptists, however, could affirm Moore's conclusion. Their piety demanded a political solution.

Debating Reform

Baptists knew they wanted the nation to honor the Sabbath. They never reached an agreement however on how to address the action taken by Congress. They divided into two groups. The first group, accomodationists, insisted the state should accommodate or protect their view of the Sabbath. They sided with the memorialists and lobbied Congress through various petitions while encouraging others to do likewise. A second group, separationists, either affiliated themselves with Johnson or simply objected to interference. They believed their distinct duties as citizens and Christians made petitioning Congress inappropriate; loyalty both to faith and country prohibited legislated social reform. Baptist accomodationists and separationists both wanted to see the Sabbath honored. They conceived of themselves as social reformers but they had a different conception of their political role.[55]

On February 6, 1829 the *Christian Watchman* in Boston reprinted and criticized the Johnson Senate report. The accomodationist Baptist editors defended the memorialist position: "Those who, from a conscientious regard for the Lord's-day, have subscribed the Memorials against the running of the Mails on this portion of the week, must feel satisfied, whatever may be the final result of their petitions, that the evil is not chargeable on them."[56] By "evil" the editor meant the very destruction

54. Cited by Meyer, *Life and Times*, 405–6. See William Emmons, Ashel Langworthy, and Ely Moore, *Authentic Biography of Col. Richard M. Johnson, of Kentucky* (New York: H. Mason, 1833).

55. For a discussion of accomodationism and separationsim as the two basic interpretations of the Establishment Clause, see Derek H. Davis, *Religion and the Continental Congress, 1774–1789* (Oxford: Oxford University Press, 2000) 10–14.

56. "Report on Sabbath Mails," *Christian Watchman*, 6 February 1829, 22.

of America's civil institutions, which depended upon religion for their stability. When Congress chose to permit the delivery of mail on the Sabbath it implied that morality no longer needed a religious undergirding. Sunday mail delivery meant that the foundation of the republic was set to crumble. Washington argued in his Farewell Address that morality needed religion. They took that to mean that the separation of church and state could never be so comprehensive as to deny America is a Christian nation.

Accomodationists spent most of their time defending themselves from the accusation they wanted to unite church and state. To Johnson, who insisted that outlawing Sunday mail delivery implied the legislation of one religion over another, the *Watchman* editor replied there stood a stark difference between calling upon Congress to legislate and calling upon it "only to abandon a course, believed to be a flagrant violation, under his sanction, of a day sacred to religious worship."[57] Accomodationists who insisted Congress must end the delivery of Sunday mail believed they were simply asking Congress to reverse course, not to enter unchartered territory.

Broad appeal for the prohibition of Sabbath mail delivery made the church and state criticism ridiculous, the accomodationists argued. After all, even the *Christian Register*, a Unitarian periodical, lent its support to their cause. The Unitarians, hardly militant in their theology, had no interest in seeing Protestant Christianity established as the national religion and yet they saw the merits of a day of rest recognized by the postal service. Baptists and Presbyterians joined ranks with Unitarians proving how foolish the charge that "orthodox Christians were endeavouring, by Memorials to Congress, to unite Church and State!"[58]

The accomodationists continued to defend themselves by pointing out that before the petitions ever flooded the halls of Congress, Senator Martin Van Buren encouraged the Post Master General to discontinue mail delivery. Printing a piece originally published in the *Philadelphian*, the *Watchman* noted that Van Buren shared the reformers' view on Sabbath mail without being known as a churchman: "Was he ever accused of being too fond of the Church?" the piece asked. "Men whose religion is of no denomination, but *sui generis*, can see that Christians ought not to be excluded from every office in the Post office department, by requiring

---

57. Ibid.
58. "Church and State!" *Christian Watchman*, 13 March 1829, 41.

of them an oath to violate the rest of the Sabbath. How comes it, then, that all the infidels and universalists, with not a few cunning politicians, are charging all the petitions against Sunday mails to ecclesiastical and especially Presbyterian ambition?"[59]

The accomodationists claimed their position as being fully in line with historical Baptist views. When James Staughton, a British medical doctor, commented to Baptist pastor Joseph Ivimey that the Johnson Senate report was essentially a Baptist document, the *Watchman* protested: "We regret that the above unguarded sentence should have escaped the Doctor's pen; for we believe, in so far as his remarks apply to the Baptists in New-England, that they are not correct."[60] Staughton argued Johnson's views were thoroughly Baptist and once again the activists had to explain how Baptists could advocate religious liberty while lobbying Congress to change its policy. The *Watchman* explained:

> The Baptists in our section of the country are as decidedly opposed to every measure, which would have a favourable aspect to a religious establishment, or to any interference of the government in matters of conscience, as are the citizens of any portion of our United States. They therefore consider that part of the Report, which suggests the danger of an 'extensive religious combination to effect a political object,' and applies this contemptible motive to the Memorialists against Sabbath Mails, as an intimation unfounded in fact, and unworthy of being presented before an enlightened Committee of so dignified a body as the Senate of the United States.[61]

Baptists in New England generally did not share the same political views as Baptists in the South, which explains, at least in part, why they took the side of the accomodationists against the Democratic separationists. Baptists in New England were part of a larger social and political movement that sought to make public policies reflect private evangelical concern.[62] Robert P. Swierenga described this type of activism as "Yankee pietism." Such evangelicals, Baptists included, "did not compartmentalize

59. Ibid.

60. "Sabbath Mails," *Christian Watchman*, 16 October 1829, 166.

61. Ibid.

62. See Anne Norton, *Alternative Americas: A Reading of Antebellum Political Culture* (Chicago: University of Chicago Press, 1986); Daniel Walker Howe, *The Political Culture of the American Whigs* (Chicago: University of Chicago Press, 1979); and Howe, "Religion and Politics in the Antebellum North," 135.

religion and civil government. Right belief and right behavior were two sides of the same spiritual coin." They launched "a crusade to Christianize America." The crusade began with the spread of the gospel in the 1810s, Swierenga argued, but by the 1830s it included the formation of the Whig party in formal opposition to the Jacksonian Democrats who fought against anything that looked like state interference with religious life.[63]

Though accomodationists came under fire for blurring the line between church and state, they believed their petitions actually prevented a *de facto* religious establishment. Requiring the delivery of mail on the Sabbath effectively excluded devout men from civil office. The *New York Observer* summarized their position accurately: submitting to the status quo "is to sanction a principle which may be used to rob religious men of all their rights, and to convert our happy republic into an infidel despotism. The principal Baptists, we repeat it, see this as clearly as intelligent men of other denominations, and we believe are firmly resolved to unite with them in all proper measures for the protection of their common rights and privileges."[64] The law in fact drove some evangelicals to resign. Thomas Shove of Petersburg, Virginia, quit his office as a local postmaster, a position he held for thirty years due to "the necessity imposed upon him by the laws of Congress to devote the Sabbath-day to purposes wholly secular."[65] The memorialists were accomodationists who disclaimed aspiration for a union between church and state.

Baptist accomodationists saw themselves as social reformers willing to leverage the power of the state for the good of its citizens. They rejected a state church but embraced a state supportive of a holy day. Accomodationists carefully framed the debate in terms of government withdrawal and not government engagement. They knew they would lose the debate if Johnson could convince the country the memorialists were asking the government to legislate in the realm of religion. Accomodationists argued just the opposite; the state had imposed itself in the realm of religion when it started delivering mail on Sunday, and they wanted Congress to extricate itself from this unsettling alliance. They argued that Sabbath mail proved to be a religious test in violation of the Constitution since it effectively excluded men of principle from serving in certain federal positions on Sunday. Sabbath mail delivery left a minority of Americans

63. Swierenga, "Ethnoreligious Political Behavior," 150–51.

64. "Sabbath Mails," 166.

65. "Sabbath Mails," *Christian Watchman*, 21 October 1842, 167.

disenfranchised. Finally, civil society needed a healthy church to succeed, and a pure Sabbath was critical to this pious goal. When Congress chose to deliver mail on Sunday it shot an arrow in the heart of the church and, in turn, threatened the well-being of society. Advocates of Sunday mail delivery appeared willing to gamble with the morality and prosperity of the nation. Accommodationism was more than a philosophy of church-state relations. To supporters, it was the republic's best hope. Piety and politics met in the accomodationist effort.

Obadiah Brown's close relationship with the editors of the *Columbian Star* may explain why the *Star* and, later, the *Christian Index* chose to oppose lobbying Congress to abolish Sunday mail delivery. The Baptist paper published relatively little information on the controversy, even after it made national news. In March 1830 the paper reprinted a copy of Johnson's most recent report leaving its readers "to judge of its logic and morality."[66] Separationists refused to remain silent however and fought back against those who insisted the sanctity of the Sabbath depended upon the federal government's intercession.

In May of 1830 the editor of the *Star* called, "reprehensible," a resolution submitted at the General Union for Promoting the Observance of the Sabbath meeting in New York. Presbyterian pastor, William Wisner, introduced the motion that read:

> *Resolved*, That the law of this land requiring the profanation of the christian Sabbath, and its violation by so many of the people, calls loudly upon the friends of civil and religious liberty to humble themselves before God, and by prayer and supplication, to seek the aid of the Holy Spirit, to turn the hearts of our citizens to the religion of their fathers, that the deserved wrath of the Almighty might be averted, and our country continue to enjoy its inestimable privileges.[67]

The editor took offense at the notion that the current law required "the profanation of the christian Sabbath." By requiring Sunday mail delivery, the government treated all religions equally. The editor asked, "Must Congress pass laws making exceptions in favor of Christianity, or else be subjected to the imputation of 'requiring its profanation?'" Thus, the separationists concluded that promoting legislation to end the delivery of

---

66. "Sabbath Mail Report," *The Columbian Star and Christian Index*, 13 March 1830, 175.

67. "Reprehensible," *The Columbian Star and Christian Index*, 22 May 1830, 339.

Sunday mail, "however desirable to many pious, good people, is a thing at war with the character of good government."[68]

The first year of the controversy, the separationists failed to take a clear stand respecting their position on Sabbath mail delivery. However in February of 1831 the *Christian Index* spelled out its opinion: "The ground which we took respecting the petitions to Congress for the suspension of Sabbath Mails, was not that it was undesirable to have such mails discontinued, but that such means as the petitioners proposed for the accomplishment of their object, were not wise nor seasonable."[69] Government must not be impressed upon to honor the Sabbath. The petitioners instead should follow the example of the early Christians: "They fasted, and prayed, and preached, and reasoned. They went forth with all meekness and submission of obedient subjects, but at the same time with boldness, confidence, and untiring perseverance of men persuaded that the Omnipotent Governor of the world was on their side; and, that, in his own time, he would crown their honest labors in his cause with a blessing."[70]

Some separationists could be found in New England. Barnabas Bates, a Baptist pastor, addressed the Committee for Protecting the Equal Rights of Conscience at Tammany Hall in New York in December 1829.[71] He knew he risked scorn by rejecting political engagement: "It has become fashionable, in these canting times, to brand every man as impious and heretical, who will not pronounce the shibboleth, nor bow down to the Baal of 'National Institutions!'"[72] Bates, like Johnson, saw the movement to petition Congress to end Sunday mails as "the stepping stone to a union of Church and State."[73]

Bates envisioned a grand conspiracy contrived by evangelicals to end the transportation and delivery of mail on the Sabbath. If the memorialists could not attain their goal in the short-run they would wait, educate youth through the Sunday schools, and slowly but effectually "prevent the election of men to our state and national legislatures, except

---

68. Ibid.

69. "As We Judged at First," *The Christian Index*, 12 February 1831, 108.

70. Ibid., 109.

71. Barnabas Bates, *An Address Delivered at a General Meeting of the Citizens of the City of New-York to Express Their Sentiments on the Memorials to Congress* (New York: Office of the Gospel Herald, 1830) 3.

72. Ibid., 4–5.

73. Ibid., 6.

they are friendly to their views, they then be able to obtain all they may ask."[74] Bates warned that some accomodationists wanted a quicker solution. The Presbyterian minister, Ezra Stiles Ely, for example, proposed a Christian political party to be established immediately in order to, according to Ely, "elect men who dare to acknowledge the Lord Jesus Christ for their Lord in their public documents."[75] This proposal infringed upon the civil and religious liberties of scores of Americans whose spiritual credentials failed to live up to Ely's standards, argued Bates. The Baptist pastor espoused separationism because he saw in American history, from Roger Williams to William Penn, a spirit of toleration that the prohibition of Sunday mail delivery undermined: "And shall it finally come to this, that a system of proscription, more intolerant than that of the Inquisition, shall be avowed and maintained, without a single effort to arrest its baneful progress? I trust not."[76]

The most famous Baptist separationist was the preacher John Leland, who described the Johnson report as "replete with candour and strength of argument; the radical parts of which never have been confuted."[77] Leland remained unconvinced by the accomodationist arguments. For example, the Virginia Society for Promoting the Observance of the Christian Sabbath argued for the end of Sunday mail delivery because Christians represent a majority of the American population and had a right to allow the Bible to guide civil affairs: "Had this been a nation of Mohometans, the Koran would undoubtedly have been selected for this purpose."[78] Leland disagreed: "It amounts to nothing to say 'there is a majority that prefer the observance of Sunday to any other day,' for minorities have unalienable rights, which ought not, and cannot, be surrendered to Government."[79] Leland believed, with the other separationists, that prohibiting the delivery of mail on Sunday effectively made religion a matter of public policy, circumscribed religious liberty, and in

---

74. Ibid., 8–9.

75. Ibid., 10.

76. Ibid., 12.

77. "A Subscriber, Elder John Leland," *Religious Herald*, 20 January 1830, 16. For a detailed description of Leland's view of the Sabbath mail controversy see Brad Creed, "John Leland and Sunday Mail Delivery: Religious Liberty, Evangelical Piety, and the Problem of a Christian Nation," *Fides et Historia* 33 (Summer–Fall 2002) 1–12.

78. "To the People of the United States," Virginia Society for Promoting the Observance of the Christian Sabbath (n.p., n.d.).

79. A Subscriber [pseud.], *Religious Herald*, 20 January 1830, 16.

words that hearkened back to those of Bates, called for war: "Admit of the principle, and you approve of that which has reared an inquisition and drenched the earth with blood."[80]

Separationists considered themselves social reformers but they rejected the notion that federal legislation would help an immoral people: "Let it not be said," wrote J. A. James, a Virginia Baptist, "that virtue would do all this without religion; for where did natural virtue ever exist, in the absence of religion?"[81] The fate of communities, and the fate of the nation depended on people eager to observe the Sabbath: "When Sunday comes, let the weary be at rest . . . Nor let him think it too hard, if in the mean time his letter remain unread in the Post-Office. They will not grow stale before correspondence with his agent or consignee."[82] One way to encourage Sabbath observance was to support the efforts of the Society for Promoting the Sanctification of the Sabbath. Even though others objected to the creation of such societies on the basis that there was no express warrant outside the New Testament, the editors of the *Religious Herald* concluded this particular "object is good and important."[83] Legislation to end the delivery of mail would not inculcate the virtue necessary to change the common man.

These southern separationists considered themselves to be social reformers because they advocated Sabbath observance for the good not only of the church but of society at large. They disdained the federal government allowing the delivery of mail on Sundays but they refused to interfere. When the Virginia Society for Promoting the Observance of the Christian Sabbath first met, it chose not to address the federal action:

> With regard to the national violation of the Sabbath, in the transportation of the mails, and the transaction of Post Office business on that day, consecrated by the Creator to religion and to rest—it was distinctly avowed, that *as a body*, we should never exercise the right of remonstration with our legislations against this crime. This declaration which was made at the time of the

80. Ibid.

81. J. A. James, "The Intimate Connection Between Religion and National Prosperity," *Religious Herald*, 18 December 1828, 297.

82. "The Day of Rest," *Religious Herald*, 13 August 1830, 138, first published in *North American Review*.

83. "Society for Promoting the Sanctification of the Christian Sabbath," *Religious Herald*, 3 December 1830, 190.

organization of the society has to be construed into a pledge to observe silence on that subject in our public communications.[84]

The meeting took place at a Baptist church and had James B. Taylor, a prominent Virginia Baptist, as a member. The society called upon the church, not Congress, to act: "It is the duty of all ministers and members of the Church of Christ, to labor—to expose the enormity of the sin of Sabbath breaking."[85] The separationists repeatedly displayed their belief that the government could neither profane nor redeem the Sabbath— such power rested in the actions of the people: "We have all found out, or we all ought to know, that there is one thing in our great, free country, stronger than the Laws.—It is public opinion. It is of no more use to make laws which are not in accordance with public opinion, than it would be to oppose our feeble breath to the blast of a hurricane."[86] Public opinion, they argued, was forged in the pew. By marshalling the forces of congregations throughout the nation they hoped "to effect the greatest moral revolution that ever occurred on these Western shores."[87]

By increasing the number of souls who truly obeyed the Sabbath, a social reformation was within reach: "With such a number of true Sabbath friends, we ask for no laws—no human legislation on the subject. We will thank our fellow citizens—our government and other nations, not to disturb us in our holy and joyful hours set apart for God."[88] The movement to honor the Sabbath had no hope of succeeding if the people disregarded it: "So long as ministers of the gospel, officers of the churches, and professed disciples of Jesus Christ, travel, and in other ways, violate, the holy Sabbath, it is in vain to appeal to government, or to hearts and consciences of the community at large."[89] However, should the churches obey the Sabbath, the country will change: "Let the Christian community free itself from this wide spread evil—let ministers and churches be exempt from the great transgression, and they will be masses of living fire illuminating the land and inculcating with irresistible energy the precept,

84. "First Annual Meeting of the Virginia Society for Promoting the Observance of the Christian Sabbath," *Religious Herald*, 15 April 1831, 68.

85. Ibid. James Barnett Taylor authored *Virginia Baptist Ministers* (Philadelphia: J. B. Lippincott, 1859)

86. "The General Union for Promoting the Observance of the Sabbath," *Religious Herald*, 27 May 1831, 78.

87. Ibid.

88. Ibid.

89. "General Sabbath Union," *Religious Herald*, 25 May 1832, 78.

Remember the Sabbath day and keep it holy."[90] Baptist separationists embraced social reform but rejected political activism.

Accomodationists and separationists rested on opposite ends of the spectrum. Each group believed the Sabbath should be honored, each group believed church and state ought to be separate and each group believed their view toward petitioning congress protected the civil and religious rights of American citizens. The accomodationists, however, contended that the rights of the orthodox to civil posts was at stake and feared a state that would, even indirectly, deny a pious American such a position. The separationists, on the other hand, were convinced that a government which legislated in favor of the Sabbath crippled religious liberty. Compromise seemed impossible.

For historians of church and state, the divide between accomodationists and separationists is further evidence that America wrestled with the meaning of the First Amendment throughout the nineteenth century, paving the way for further debate today. Derek H. Davis, a staunch defender of the founders' original intent to create a government that espoused separationism, argued that accomodationism is both wise and necessary. Traditions ranging from the congressional chaplaincy to the observance of Thanksgiving as a national holiday evidence a nation that started and remains "pervasively religious."[91] The Continental Congress moved the fledgling nation sharply in the direction of neutrality in matters of religion. Davis argued that civil religion—the state's adherence to and promotion of a transcendent faith—did not become popular until after the Civil War.[92] Davis, however, did not give enough credit to the battle for civil religion that took place before the Civil War. Civil religion gained traction because Americans grew accustomed to debating the merits and perils of living as citizens under God. The Sabbath mail controversy shows this. Neither side publicly advocated a civil religion—both rejected it. But both sides defended the public acknowledgement of the Sabbath's importance. The accomodationists, moreover, were quite willing for the state to recognize Sunday as the Sabbath. Nonetheless both sides implicitly advocated a civil religion to the extent that they all agreed—from Wayland to Manly, and from Johnson to Taylor—that a country which failed to recognize the value of the Sabbath would subsequently fail to

90. Ibid.

91. Davis, *Religion and the Continental Congress*, 228.

92. Ibid., 215.

prosper. Separationists won the Sabbath mail debate but the battle for accommodation was far from over. The call for a congressional end to Sunday mail delivery by the accomodationists, long before the Civil War, proved that the demand for civil religion ran deep.[93]

Defeating the Sabbath

Winton Solberg insightfully described Sabbath observance as "the palladium of religion" in early New England.[94] This religious holiday became a social establishment that shaped the nation, instilling "in the American character a strength and simplicity dependent on the severity of an unwavering religious discipline."[95] By the nineteenth century, Solberg argued, "Americans viewed the Sabbath as a safeguard of the republic, believing that a nation founded on a substratum of infidelity has but a short existence."[96] Baptists perpetuated this Sabbath-centric morality. According to Baptist missionary John Mason Peck, the spread of strict Sabbath observance, from New England to St. Louis marked the work of God sanctifying the nation. He noted that by 1817, for example, St. Louis could

> vie with many New England towns in the observance of that holy day. The Presbyterians and Methodists have commodious houses of worship, neatly finished, and which are usually filled with worshippers every Sabbath. The Baptists have a publick worship unfinished, but in which worship is well attended, when

93. Philip Hamburger critiqued the notion that the founders intimated a separation of church and state. The evangelical dissenters who fought for an establishment cause always wanted accommodation to account for items that blurred the line between church and state such as government sanction of Christian marriage. The "wall of separation" came to be interpreted so strictly in part because Jefferson responded strongly to the Congregationalists of Connecticut, because nativists wanted a principle to fend off what they perceived to be the threat of the Roman Catholic hierarchy to the church, and because theological liberals of the nineteenth-century rallied for a more secular state. However, Hamburger missed the conservative impulse that also advocated separation. Though Baptists in New England fit in the accomodationist camp, conservative Baptists in Washington also fit nicely into the separationist camp. In other words, the movement for separation was more diverse than Hamburger seemed to allow. See Hamburger, *Separation of Church and State*, 107.

94. Winton U. Solberg, *Redeem the Time: The Puritan Sabbath in Early America* (Cambridge, MA: Harvard University Press, 1977) 299.

95. Ibid., 301.

96. Ibid.

preaching is enjoyed, which is usually once each month; and the Episcopalians are about organizing a Society. All the stores and shops are shut, business is entirely suspended, two flourishing Sabbath Schools for whites, and one for blacks are in operation, many other flattering indications of an increase in virtue and religion are discovered."[97]

To ignore or disdain the Sabbath, was considered disastrous for the nation.

It is tempting to argue that Baptists were like-minded when it came to inculcating virtue in the young nation. They were not. Baptist spirituality did not always lead in the same political direction. William McLoughlin thus incorrectly lumped all Baptists together when he argued they shared a reforming impulse with other nineteenth-century evangelicals: "The Baptists . . . nevertheless insisted as much as the Trinitarian or evangelical 'theocrats' like Jedediah Morse, Timothy Dwight, and later Lyman Beecher, upon the necessity for strict enforcement of the Puritan blue laws and Sabbatarian restrictions."[98] Likewise, Robert Handy pointed to an evangelical consensus that Baptists shared: "Protestant forces across a wide sweep of denominational and theological opinion struggled for the Sabbath as a day apart—a day that would characterize American civilization as Christian. For them, this was a distinctive symbol of the kind of Protestant culture they were laboring to maintain and extend."[99] To the extent that Baptists wanted the Sabbath honored, McLoughlin and Handy are correct. To the extent Baptists wanted Sabbath observance enforced, Baptists were divided. When it came to the Sabbath mail controversy, there was no consensus. Some Baptists certainly followed in the footsteps of Beecher but others resonated with the principles of Johnson and Brown. Each cared about the Sabbath and society, virtue and reform, but they disagreed over the role of the federal government. They were all sympathetic to social reform. They were not all amenable to political action—at least when it came to relying on Congress to spread virtue.

Historians of the Sabbath mail controversy recognize the existence of an antisabbatarian movement. However the dissent tends to

97. John Mason Peck, "Letters from the West, No. II," *Christian Watchman*, 6 January 1826, 18.

98. William G. McLoughlin, *Isaac Backus and the American Pietistic Tradition* (Boston: Little, Brown, 1967) 212.

99. Robert T. Handy, *A Christian America: Protestant Hopes and Historical Realities* (New York: Oxford University Press, 1971) 51.

be described as coming from either non-Christian camps or from the fringes of evangelicalism as in the case of the bombastic Leland or the anticlerical sects like the Disciples of Christ.[100] However, separationists were neither antisabbatarian, theologically liberal, nor anticlerical. They simply rejected the notion that virtue required any political propping up from the state. Richard John helpfully expressed the antisabbatarian impulse as a mainstream, religious movement.[101]

Among Baptists at least, John is right. The Sabbath mail controversy proved to be "a debate among evangelicals over the proper relationship of church and state."[102] The controversy centered in Washington: Johnson and Brown shared evangelical convictions and yet authored the report that put efforts to rescind Sabbath mail laws to death. Other separationists were Baptist newspaper editors who agreed with Johnson and Brown that the loss of religious liberty was too high a price to pay to secure congressional interference on this topic. The debate took place in the South as well. Separationists in Richmond, Virginia, like J. A. James and James Taylor rejected the political fight and urged Baptists to sew seeds of virtue in their lives. In so doing they called Americans away from the halls of power and into the prayer closets. Accomodationists and separationists were both social reformers. Each group wanted a society blessed by the principle of Sabbath observance. They disagreed regarding how this principle ought to be regulated.

When Congress refused to prohibit the transportation and delivery of mail on the Sabbath it effectively forced Baptists and other evangelicals to accept Johnson's view of separation. Even if they disagreed in principle, in practice the accomodationists lost and, except for a brief try a decade later, evangelicals did not make another attempt, on explicitly religious grounds to legislate against Sabbath mail.[103]

This is typically considered a defeat for evangelicals. However, given the popularity of Johnson and the wide reading given to the separationist position, it is possible that more evangelicals supported non-interference than is commonly thought. Either way this much is certain: the debate over church and state in the nineteenth century represented differences near the center of Baptist life. Accomodationists demanded their

100. Hamburger, *Separation of Church and State*, 14–15; John, "Taking Sabbatarianism Seriously," 554.

101. Ibid., 555.

102. Ibid.

103. Fuller, *Morality and Mail*, 42.

Christian nation live up to its calling while separationists insisted that Christians best served their country by serving their own souls. Politics and piety were related, but they did not always mix.

6

Poverty and a Baptist Social Conscience

NINETEENTH-CENTURY BAPTISTS POSSESSED A social conscience, however imperfect that conscience may have been. Pastors of the antebellum North and South took it to be the responsibility of both the church corporately and Christians individually to care for the dispossessed. Rank and file Baptists followed, committing themselves to the spiritual and physical relief of the poor. Southern Baptist pastor and educator Basil Manly Sr. expounded on these commitments in the "Duty of Benevolence" based upon Galatians 6:10, "As we have, therefore, opportunity, let us do good unto all men, especially to them who are of the household of faith." Faithfulness to Christ demanded generosity, Manly argued, and benevolence ought not to be restricted to the church. Just as "the Lord is good to all mankind in general," so all "should share in our good will." Manly urged his listeners to extend themselves for others: "A man that loves to be good, will be good in all times and places." Manly exhorted them to follow Jesus in the practice of self-denial: "Christ was sensible as we are . . . for thirst, cold, pain, poverty . . . benevolence which calls for self-denial is richest and best." Nonetheless, special attention should be paid to those within the "household of faith," the church. Furthermore, the most important benevolence aimed for the restoration of the human spirit. As Christ attended to the souls of the needy, so should Christians. Jesus could have organized a political revolution, but he did not. He

> might have taught science and the arts—hastened forward institutions, and have antedated by many centuries the origin of the great improvements . . . this he leaves to men. On the same principles as he said, "Let the dead bury their own dead," more important business engages Him. He gives them the gospel. This only can do the sinner good. He opposes the corrupt passions

and false principles of men, gives just notions of God, his Law,
the soul, way of salvation, practical religion, and a future state,
and applied his instruction and benefits to men suitably, season-
ably, impartially, simply so that to show that his object was to
do good.

Manly believed the primary means of doing "good unto all men" was
attending to their spiritual needs. But he did not discount their temporal
needs either, and he expected the Christian faithful to change the world.
"Benevolence fulfills our destiny," he asserted. "What were we made for?
We should accomplish some things. We should not be willing to live in
the world, and have it not better for our being in it. And how much good
a plain man may do!" For all his focus on the salvation of the individual
soul, Manly assumed benevolent acts would change society: "Society is
[the] gainer, even considered individually, by benevolence. What would
be the condition of the world, if every one should be selfish!"[1]

Baptists in the nineteenth century shared Manly's view. They committed themselves to poverty relief. Spurred on by the example of Christ
and the principles of the Bible they saw in the benevolence toward the
poor another opportunity to link their piety, evangelism, and social
reform.[2] Many are familiar with Walter Rauschenbusch and the Social
Gospel movement. Advocates equated the Good News of Christianity
with social concerns such as the alleviation of poverty.[3] Yet long before

1. Basil Manly Sr., "Duties of Benevolence," 21 May 1837. Basil Manly Sr. Papers,
Archives and Special Collections, James P. Boyce Centennial Library, Southern Baptist
Theological Seminary, Louisville, Kentucky. Manly preached this sermon at least three
times. The first time in Charleston, South Carolina, on May 21, 1837. The second time
in in Charleston April 24, 1859, and a third time in Montgomery, Alabama, June 9,
1861.

2. Some representative works on Christian approaches to poverty include Kelly
S. Johnson, *The Fear of Beggars: Stewardship and Poverty in Christian Ethics* (Grand
Rapids: Eerdmans, 2007); Ronald J. Sider, *Just Generosity: A New Vision for Overcom-
ing Poverty in America*, 2nd ed. (Grand Rapids: Baker, 2007); Kent A. Van Till, *Less
Than Two Dollars a Day: A Christian View of Poverty and the Free Market* (Grand
Rapids: Eerdmans, 2007); *The Option for the Poor in Christian Theology*, ed. Daniel
G. Groody (Notre Dame, IN: University of Notre Dame Press, 2007); Leslie J. Hoppe,
There Shall Be No Poverty Among You: Poverty in the Bible (Nashville, TN: Abingdon,
2004); *Toward a Just and Caring Society: Christian Responses to Poverty in America*, ed.
David Gushee (Grand Rapids: Baker, 1999).

3. Walter Rauschenbusch, *A Theology for the Social Gospel* (New York: Macmillan, 1917; reprint, Nashville: Abingdon, 1945); Walter Rauschenbusch, *Christianity
and the Social Crisis in the 21st Century: The Classic that Woke up the Church* (New
York: HarperCollins, 2007); *The Social Gospel in America, 1870–1920*, ed. Robert T.

Rauschenbusch, and without equating the Gospel with social reform, Baptists churches expressed their concern for the poor. Christians took it as their duty to meet the spiritual and physical needs of the disaffected. Timothy L. Smith, who began his classic study of social reform around 1840, argued that "distinctions between piety and moralism, spiritual and social service" declined as Christians rallied to meet the needs of the poor in the mid-nineteenth century.[4] Smith was correct, but the social concern goes back even further, into the eighteenth century. Baptists considered it their responsibility not only to preach to the poor but also to feed them, not only to evangelize society but also to address the disparity between the wealthy and dispossessed.

It is not always easy to discern which was more important in Baptist life, benevolence as a Christian virtue or benevolence as a means of evangelism. In the former case, Baptists aided the poor directly, financing and sometimes organizing relief. In the latter case, the aid was indirect. Baptists "laid the axe to the root of the tree," addressing the spiritual needs of the poor while believing that the transformed character of the repentant sinner would strongly tend to ameliorate poverty. Both forms of relief explain the nineteenth-century Baptist concern for the immediate and eternal well being of humanity. Both forms of relief proved that antebellum Baptists were social reformers.

Poverty and Benevolence

Baptists gave to the poor to improve their faith and society. In 1785 Baptist pastor Samuel Stillman of Boston preached a sermon on charity before the masons of Charleston, Massachusetts. He chose the first few verses of 1 Corinthians 13 for his text, including verse three: "though I bestow all my goods to feed the poor, and though I give my body to be burned, and have not charity, it profiteth me nothing."[5] He described charity as love to God and man, and he exhorted his audience to exercise both: "The

---

Handy (New York: Oxford University Press, 1966) remains one of the best introductions to Rauschenbusch and the Social Gospel. See also Gary J. Dorrien, *The Making of American Liberal Theology: Idealism, Realism, and Modernity, 1900–1950* (Louisville, KY: John Knox, 2003).

4. Timothy L. Smith, *Revivalism and Social Reform in Mid-Nineteenth-Century America* (New York: Abingdon, 1957) 176.

5. Samuel Stillman, *Charity Considered in a Sermon Preached at Charleston* (Boston: T. & J. Fleet, 1785) 5.

ever blessed God not only commands us to love him with all our heart, but to love our neighbor as ourselves."[6] "Our neighbor," Stillman argued, includes anyone in need: "We shall quickly feel for objects in distress, and chearfully contribute to their relief, without stopping a moment to ask, of what nation they are, or to what religious society they belong? The only question is, Are they proper objects of our charity? Thus, charity urges us to obey that divine injunction, Do good to all men."[7] Stillman reminded his audience that relieving the needy is the "duty of religion and humanity" and precious in God's sight: "He that hath pity on the poor, lendeth to the Lord: and that which he hath given him, will he pay him again."[8] Stillman advocated service to the poor out of personal conviction. He did not address the state's obligation, focusing instead on private Christian responsibility.

The responsibility to care for the poor also found congregational expressions in the earliest days of the American republic. On September 11, 1793, the Warren Baptist Association of Rhode Island received a query from the Providence church asking what should be done if a member refused to help meet "his proportion of the expenses that necessarily arise from the existence of that Church." The expenses included "supporting the poor, maintaining the ministry, keeping the house of worship decent, &c." In other words, the church understood "supporting the poor" to be a regular part of its divine commission. The association responded that if it can be proved the individual failed to give, he should be admonished.[9]

6. Ibid., 9.

7. Ibid., 14. By preaching against asking from "what nation" a potential recipient of charity may originate, Stillman is condemning the public custom of "warning out" whereby community leaders protected themselves (and their coffers) against giving charity to individuals who did not belong, legally, to their township. See Ruth Wallis Herndon, "'Who Died an Expence to This Town': Poor Relief in Eighteenth-Century Rhode Island," in *Down and Out in Early America*, ed. Billy G. Smith (University Park: Pennsylvania State University Press, 2004) 136–37.

8. Stillman, *Charity Considered*, 17.

9. *Minutes*, Warren Baptist Association, 1793, 6. Ruth Wallis Herndon noted that in cities throughout Rhode Island, poor relief involved more than the church, it "involved an entire network of people, at the center of which sat five or six elected town councilmen." These leaders sought to establish residency and need before providing assistance. Furthermore, public assistance became available only when "other private and public resources had been exhausted." See Herndon, "'Who Died an Expence to This Town': Poor Relief in Eighteenth Century Rhode Island," in *Down and Out*, 136, 139. Thus, town leaders would surely have calculated the churches' role in the care of the poor.

Benevolence, for these early Baptists, meant more than simply a disposition to aid another person or an affection of goodwill; benevolence implied a physical act of compassion. Henry Holcombe, editor of the *Analytical Repository*, described another congregational display of such kindness, this one clearly organized by the church and directed to those outside its walls. A Savannah, Georgia, Baptist church, constituted in 1802, chose as one of its first actions to take "into consideration the necessity of a permanent plan for the relief of the poor."[10] The church created a standing committee, instituted deacons and "two judicious female members" as agents to do the work of the church committee, and resolved to keep careful records of all income and expenses. The church felt a special responsibility to meet the needs of the poor, in part because Savannah had no organized means of providing for the indigent:

> A plan of the above form, appeared to the church the more necessary, as there is no poorhouse in this city, nor any other effectual means of relieving helpless sufferers, who are ready to perish in the streets. Indeed, a man, with all the marks of the deepest poverty, and distress about him, lately died, alone, in one of the public markets! Individuals, who have been unoccupied in providing, and enlarging the sphere of diversions for the community, have done much for their perishing fellow-men; but, notwithstanding, much remains to be done.[11]

Statements like this indicate that Baptists did not take complete responsibility for the social welfare of their communities. Should the city have erected a poorhouse, the church may have found it "less necessary" to devote as much of its time and energy to the alleviation of poverty. The church saw a need and met it. Gary B. Nash has argued that poverty could be found "in small and large communities, North and South, by the mid-eighteenth century."[12] The needs in Savannah only proved his point. Assistance was offered "by family members, friends, and church-centered private charity," all which grew in the eighteenth century.[13] As

---

10. Henry Holcombe, "A Sketch of the Baptist Church in Savannah," *Georgia Analytical Repository* (November–December, 1802) 183.

11. Ibid., 184.

12. Gary B. Nash, "Poverty and Politics in Early American History," in *Down and Out*, 3.

13. Ibid.

Holcombe insisted, prior to the action of the Savannah Baptist Church, the poor of Savannah had been "shamefully neglected."[14]

As the century wore on Baptists throughout America showed that "pure religion" included a tangible display of compassion to the poor. Writing to the member churches of the Charleston Baptist Association in November 1804, Richard Furman, longtime moderator of the association, asked the question, "By what means may a Christian secure to his own Soul the Consolations of pure Religion, rise to real eminence in the Christian Character, and become most useful in the cause of God?"[15] He offered several particulars, ranging from following the example of Christ, valuing justice, and not withholding the payment of a debt. And he did not ignore the needy: "Compassion to the poor and afflicted, justly ranks among the most amiable of dispositions; and relief to them in their distresses, among the best actions."[16]

William Staughton, a Baptist pastor and college president, in a sermon published for the benefit of a Female Benevolent Society, implored his audience to give. He saw benevolence as a unique act of Christian kindness. Like Furman, he considered it to be an implication of biblical Christianity and thus he quoted from James 1:27 in defense of benevolence: "Never forget that attention to 'the fatherless and widows in their affliction' is an important branch of 'pure religion undefiled before God and the Father.'"[17] He left his listeners with a firm, impassioned call to action: "Come, my brethren, discharge your duty, adorn the gospel, disappoint the devil, gratify angels, and revere a present God."[18]

In a circular letter to the churches of the Elkhorn Baptist Association of Kentucky, the author charged his readers to be zealous in Christian activities including evangelism, Sabbath observance, church attendance, and, not to be overlooked, benevolence: "God has enjoined on us in his word, to honor him with our substance, to take care of the poor, to support the ministry, to maintain his worship in decency and good order."[19] Poverty relief did not have special prominence in the Christian life, but its casual mention belied its importance.

14. Holcombe, "A Sketch," 185.

15. *Minutes*, Charleston Baptist Association, 1804, 3.

16. Ibid., 7.

17. William Staughton, *Compassion to the Poor Recommended* (Philadelphia: Bartholomew Graves, 1810) 13, 17.

18. Ibid., 27.

19. *Minutes*, Elkhorn Baptist Association, 1823, 6.

These Baptists assumed that faithful Christian living required relief of the impoverished. Whether speaking to congregations or individual believers, they urged attention to the poor. They refused to speak of the Christian life only in terms of evangelism, a point made sharply by the nation's leading Baptist newspaper.

Washington's *Columbian Star*, in a three-part series entitled, "Christian Efforts," written in 1822, drove home to its readers the point that Christian living required action. Christians had a responsibility to serve by "according prompt countenance and liberal contributions to every project of good."[20] The editors expressed a concern for the betterment of society, an improvement that depended upon the concerted and cooperative efforts of believers: "It is a happy trait of the present times, that by the extensive combination of various Societies, provision is made for an actual investigation into the wants of the community, and for a prompt application of requisite relief."[21] Christian compassion must be tangible.

They obeyed the injunction. They gave to the needy. Often the poor belonged to the church. Thomas Meredith, editor of the *Biblical Recorder*, took it to be a matter of principle that local churches ought to take care of their own. Members in need must not be required to "go to the county poor-house, nor to become, in any way, an object of public charity. Such was not the usage of the primitive churches."[22] Examples of relief abounded. The Kiokee Baptist Church of Columbia County, Georgia, in 1805, agreed to give five dollars above its collection of $6.50 to meet the needs of Old Sister McDaniel.[23] Similarly, the members of Bethesda Baptist Church in Greene County, Georgia, were urged in 1819 to come to a gathering prepared to financially support Sister Agnes Hunt.[24] Baptists followed the admonitions to care of the needy in their midst, encouraged by the admonitions of pastors like R. Babcock of the Philadelphia Baptist Association who urged each local church to care for "all its members" and asked all these members to "devote themselves to visiting the sick, the bereaved, the poor and the imprisoned, ministering to the wants of the

---

20. "Christian Efforts, Continued," *Columbian Star*, 25 May 1822, 3.

21. "Christian Efforts, Continued," *Columbian Star*, 1 June 1822, 3.

22. Thomas Meredith, "Query," *Biblical Recorder*, 13 June 1846, 2.

23. *Church Book*, Kiokee Baptist Church, Colombia County, Georgia, 1 February 1805.

24. *Church Book*, Bethesda Baptist Church, Greene County, Georgia, 16 February, 1819, 7.

body and the soul."[25] Care for church members did not exclude a commitment to care for needy in the community. Like the church in Savannah, Baptists understood they had a responsibility for those outside their own congregations. The *Christian Watchman* argued, "the population of every parish in which a church exists is a vineyard for its benevolent labors."[26]

As the century progressed, and as the disparity of incomes increased for the first time dramatically, Baptists articulated a doctrine of poverty and wealth that demanded the rich to act. In 1829 the *Star* published an address first delivered in Philadelphia that argued the rich had an obligation to serve the poor: "It is the duty of the rich, and in proportion of their means, ought to be their pride and pleasure, to meliorate the condition and relieve the distresses of the deserving and suffering poor."[27] Likewise in Boston the editors of the *Christian Watchman* cited the prayer of Agur from Proverbs 30, "Give me neither poverty nor riches," and lamented that "by the mere accidents of fortune, if we may so speak, a few become immensely rich, and many extremely poor. Now this tendency is undesirable; and it is one which Christianity is admirably adapted to counteract." The editors did not call for socialism, but they did demand charity. The wealthy ought "to look upon the whole race of mankind as one common family, and by a just estimate of moral responsibility, to labor for the benefit of all. The rich are required to befriend the poor, the strong are required to protect the weak."[28]

The editors of the *Religious Herald* printed a letter with a similar theme in 1844, reminding their readers that "it is obligatory upon the rich to minister to the wants of him who is in distress, either in mind or body." The author cited Paul's words in Romans, "weep with them that weep," as well as Proverbs 3:7, "Withhold no good from him to whom it is due, when it is in the power of thy hand to do it," to encourage generosity and, moreover, make the case that benevolence from the rich to the poor is, in fact, a biblical requirement.[29]

25. Circular letter published as R. Babcock, "The Duty of Churches to Their Individual Members," *Christian Watchman*, 3 November 1837, 173.

26. "The Neglected Class," *Christian Watchman*, 17 November 1837, 181.

27. "Society for Bettering the Condition of the Poor," *The Columbian Star, and Christian Index*, 10 October 1829, 232.

28. "The Influence of Christianity on National Wealth," *Christian Watchman*, 2 March 1838, 34.

29. Tiro [pseud.], "The Obligations of the Rich to the Poor," *Religious Herald*, 29 February 1844, 34.

Though the obligations of the rich to the poor stand out, every Christian was obliged to give. Pharcellus Church, pastor of Second Providence Baptist Church in Rhode Island, reminded the churches of the Warren Baptist Association in 1831 that the responsibility to ease the physical burdens of others was universal: "Every man, therefore, should make himself so well acquainted with the duty of devoting a portion of his worldly income to the purposes of religion, and with the claims of different objects of benevolence, as to be able to act with judgment and propriety in this matter." The use of property, he insisted, was a religious act: "The alms we bestow upon the physical, intellectual or moral necessities of the poor, are given without hope of remuneration. By devoting property in this way, we perform an act of worship to God."[30] D. H., in a letter published by the *Christian Index*, censured the "church as a body" for failing to do all it could to meet the needs of the day: "Let the church as a body come up to this standard, and she can adopt an intelligent and systematic course of benevolent action, which will result in unspeakable blessings to themselves and the world."[31]

In 1844 James Smith wrote in the *Religious Herald* that the church should be busy, "every member should be a working member; and if this was the case, how much good would be done; and be done with ease and comfort, too."[32] Similarly, the Home Missionary Society of Baltimore urged all the members of its churches to "not forget the duty which devolves upon them, as followers of Christ, of visiting such needy ones, and ministering to their wants, both spiritual and temporal."[33]

The editors of the *Religious Herald* in 1848 made the case that social progress, which included benevolence, depended upon Christianity: "In all ages Christianity has concerned itself actively with the social condition of man, and the Church has never utterly forgotten to enjoin mercy upon the powerful, and offer comfort to the feeble." The editors proceeded to list the accomplishments of the church: "the rebuke of oppression—the emancipation of the slave,—the elevation of the laborer,—the defence of the feeble,—the protection of woman,—the abolition of polygamy,—the care of the poor,—the religious education of the people." Each individual church, the editors noted, bore the obligation of benevolence: "We have

30. *Minutes*, Warren Baptist Association, 1831, 9, 10.

31. D. H., "The Church Must Act as Well as Pray," *Christian Index*, 4 August 1832, 73.

32. James Smith, "The Church at Work," *Religious Herald*, 12 September 1844, 145.

33. "Visit the Destitute," *Christian Watchman*, 26 June 1846, 101.

never yet seen the church that did not . . . extend to the poor relief in sickness." In short, the *Herald* argued that by modeling mercy, the church had become the hope of civilization: "If any thing like a true Christian heart prevail throughout Christendom, we should have very little fear for the civilization of the nineteenth century, with all its wealth, science, art and enterprise."[34]

All these examples indicate that, for Baptists, benevolence included the physical, or as the Home Missionary Society of Baltimore put it, "temporal" relief of the needy. Baptist churches understood it to be a part of their mission, and individual Christians recognized it as part of their personal discipleship. By the mid-nineteenth century, the relief of the poor was not merely a duty but a Christian badge of honor.

Poverty and Virtue

Baptists expected their faith to be seen. John R. Bodo, in his classic *The Protestant Clergy and Public Issues*, argued that patriotic Christians, "theocrats" as he called them, believed societal reformation came out only through individual regeneration.[35] The motivation of nineteenth-century social reformers has created controversy among historians. Bodo and a few others advanced the social control thesis, the idea that conservative church leaders sponsored social reform movements mainly to preserve their class privileges in society.[36] Other historians disagreed and argued

34. "Christianity and Social Progress," *Religious Herald*, 30 November 1848, 189.

35. John R. Bodo, *The Protestant Clergy and Public Issues, 1812–1848* (Princeton, NJ: Princeton University Press, 1954) 176. "The theocrats who thought in terms of society as a whole and specifically in terms of American society from a patriotic stand-point, rejected every suggestion of reforming society except by means of regenerating individuals."

36. See Bodo, *The Protestant Clergy*; Charles C. Cole Jr, *The Social Ideas of Northern Evangelists, 1820–1860* (New York: Columbia University Press, 1954); Charles I. Foster, *An Errand of Mercy: The Evangelical United Front, 1790–1837* (Chapel Hill: University of North Carolina Press, 1960); Clifford S. Griffin, *Their Brothers' Keeper: Moral Stewardship in the United States, 1800–1865* (New Brunswick, NJ: Rutgers University Press, 1960); Steven Berk, *Calvinism versus Democracy; Timothy Dwight and the Origins of American Evangelical Orthodoxy* (Hamden, CT: Archon, 1974). Daniel Walker Howe pointed out that the social control theory has undergone a significant change. Newer advocates such as Paul Johnson and David Brion Davis argue that the reformers had an unconsciously deleterious effect on society. For example, while northerners advocated against slavery, they "provided a moral sanction for new capitalist methods of exploitation." Howe, "The Evangelical Movement and Political

instead that the reformers had a genuinely religious motivation.[37] The social control theory wrongly denigrates the validity of religious motivation. The spirituality of these reformers spurred them to social action.

Baptists regularly explained that benevolence is a Christian virtue. It reflected their theology. In 1801 Samuel Stillman spoke before the Boston Female Asylum. His address provided a snapshot of the benevolent enterprises of the day. He described the Boston Marine Society, established in 1742 and charged with relieving "distressed mariners, their widows and children." He praised the denominational charities operated by the Episcopal and Congregational Charitable Societies. The Boston Humane Society served as an early paramedic service, recovering "persons from apparent death by suffocation and drowning." The Massachusetts Charitable Fire Society and the Boston Dispensary also provided invaluable aid. Likewise, he described the Boston Almshouse as "another excellent provision for the poor; and which reflects great honor on the benevolence and liberality of the metropolis." All of these institutions, including the Boston Female Asylum, a home for poor orphan girls, deserved the attention of Christians who are obligated to reflect God's benevolence. For Stillman, the equation was simple. God gave his own son, therefore, "let us, my friends, not only admire, but as far as possible imitate, Divine Benevolence."[38] The Boston Female Asylum heard a similar message, a

---

Culture in the North and During the Second Party System," *The Journal of American History* (March 1991) 1219. See also Paul Johnson, *A Shopkeeper's Millennium* (New York: Hill & Wang, 1978); idem, *The Early American Republic, 1789–1829* (New York: Oxford University Press, 2007) and David Brion Davis, *The Problem of Slavery in the Age of Revolution, 1770–1823* (Ithaca, NY: Cornell University Press, 1975).

37. Thus, Timothy L. Smith in *Revivalism and Social Reform* argued that the impetus to change society found its origin in the holiness movement within revivalist Christianity. Lois Banner suggested that by 1800 Protestants had abandoned Jonathan Edwards's postmillennial eschatology and now a millennial expectation shaped all their activities, explaining their reformist zeal. See Banner, "Religious Benevolence as Social Control: A Critique of an Interpretation," *The Journal of American History* 60 (June 1973) 35–36. James H. Moorhead disagreed with the social control thesis as well, arguing along the lines of Smith that Charles Finney's theology led him into the field of social reform. See Moorhead, "Social Reform and the Divided Conscience of Antebellum Protestantism," *Church History* 48 (December 1979) 416–430. Dietrich Buss agreed with Banner that the social control theorists ignore the millennial vision that captivated the reformers, according to his examination of Congregationalists. See Buss, "The Millennial Vision as Motive for Religious Benevolence and Reform: Timothy Dwight and the New England Evangelicals Reconsidered," *Fides et Historia* 16 (Fall-Winter 1983) 18–34.

38. Samuel Stillman, *A Discourse Delivered Before the Boston Female Asylum*

few years later, from Boston's other preeminent pastor, Thomas Baldwin. He wondered whether divine love dwells in the heart of the individual who refused to help the fatherless.[39]

Baptists did not only look backward, toward the cross, they looked to the future as well, with the expectation that benevolence would usher in the last days:

> So also Christians believe at the present day; but that belief ani-
> mates them to vigorous exertions, and they read the fulfillment
> of the promises in the moral impulse which those exertions are
> giving to the world. The present inquiry is: Do they read the
> signs of the time aright? Or, in other words: Are the benevolent
> efforts of the present day the means which Providence is using
> to introduce the millennial dispensation? . . . I shall attempt to
> maintain . . . that the benevolent efforts of our day are entirely
> different from those of any former age; and that the peculiar
> characteristics of these efforts warrant the belief that they will
> be finally successful.[40]

However, references to the millennium in Baptist periodicals are the exception, not the rule. Much more common is the simple explanation that when the gospel takes root in the believer's life, society changes. As "Wilson," who wrote to the *Religious Herald*, argued in 1829, the acknowledgement of "the one true God, and Jesus Christ, whom he hath sent" is powerful and effective: "The minister of religion is the father and friend of all. Disease and vice and misery begin to be lessened and disappear. Virtue, peace, industry, social order, are the lovely fruits of the Christian faith."[41] Likewise, reminiscent of Stillman's and Baldwin's reflections on divine love in the North, the editors of the *Herald* offered similar conclusions on the motivation for benevolence: "We hold it as an incontrovertible axiom, that whenever genuine Christianity is felt, the heart of its possessor in a greater or less degree becomes the seat of benevolence, philanthropy, and good will towards all the human family. The heart that glows with love to God will look with regard [not] with complacency

---

(Boston: Russell & Cutler, 1801) 3–9.

39. Thomas Baldwin, *A Discourse Delivered Before the Boston Female Asylum* (Boston: Russell & Cutler, 1806) 11.

40. "On the Peculiar Characteristics of the Benevolent Efforts of Our Age," *Columbian Star*, 20 July 1822, 3.

41. Wilson [pseud.], "Benign Influence of Christianity," *Religious Herald*, 30 October 1829, 169.

on his fellow man; will be eager to minister not only to his spiritual but to his temporal necessities."[42] That same year, 1831, the Warren Baptist Association urged its churches to carefully consider the motives behind almsgiving: "On this point our Saviour is very explicit. 'Take heed that ye do not your alms before men, to be seen of them, otherwise ye have no reward of your Father, which is in heaven.'"[43] Manly urged his audience to exercise benevolence out of "gratitude due to Christ, 'who was rich, yet became poor.'"[44]

Baptists throughout the century urged each other to recognize that philanthropy could be executed for the wrong reasons. Benevolence might simply be vanity or pride. Thus the *Religious Herald* in 1849 commended a sermon by the Reverend John Olin, president of Middletown Wesleyan Seminary, on the danger of works. Olin noted a church may contribute to the cause of benevolence but not in accordance with Jesus' words in Matthew: "Let your light so shine before men, that they may see your good works, and glorify your Father which is in heaven." Olin preached that benevolence is futile without sincerity of heart: "Show me a Church of poor, illiterate, unknown, obscure, unnoticed, but praying people, they shall be families that do not know one week where they are to get their bread for the next . . . but with them is the hiding of God's power."[45] Likewise, the Boston South Baptist Association warned its churches in 1851 of the danger of benevolence without godliness:

> This is emphatically an age of action. Many things tend to excite a love for humanity that do not excite love to God. And as a consequence, there is by far more philanthropy than piety among us. And yet many do not discriminate between the two,—do not perceive that it is one thing to be actively engaged in religious things, and another thing to cultivate true personal religion. Both are necessary. While Christians are active they should also be pious.[46]

The Elkhorn Baptist Association shared the concerns expressed by their Boston Baptist brethren. Decades of benevolent activity had left the association with the impression that Christian virtue and obedience were

---

42. "Charity," *Religious Herald*, 4 March 1831, 34.

43. *Minutes*, Warren Baptist Association, 1831, 11.

44. Basil Manly Sr., "Duties of Benevolence."

45. "The Power of the Church," *Religious Herald*, 1 November 1849, 173.

46. *Minutes*, Boston South Baptist Association, 1851, 8.

actually and ironically being divorced: "We may become great philanthropists in the sight of man," the association told its churches, "by be-
stowing our goods to feed and clothe the poor, but we can not be good
Christians without love to God also."[47]

Nonetheless, the danger of hypocrisy did not diminish the call to
serve physically. Heman Lincoln urged the pastors of the Boston South
Baptist Association to philanthropy on the basis of the doctrine of the
incarnation. However, unlike Stillman, who rooted philanthropy in
Christ's propitiatory sacrifice, Lincoln grounded benevolence in Christ's
example: "Christ Jesus came to save the lost, and only as we imitate His
example can we imitate His beneficence."[48] W. S. McKenzie, in a circular
letter to the churches of the Warren Baptist Association in 1864, urged
the churches to remember what should have been a familiar theme, "the
gift and sacrifice of the Son of God for human Redemption." As a result,
he argued, "it delights to wipe away tears of sorrow, to feed the hungry, to
clothe the naked, to smooth the rough path of the children of want, and
to reach forth a helping hand on every field where the cause of God is
struggling against the antagonisms of sin."[49]

Though no one can know the motivations of these Baptists for
certain, it is most likely the case, as Beth Barton Schweiger described
in her work on southern Protestantism, that they intended to see "the
gospel working up."[50] Churches and Christians linked religion and progress, the gospel and social concern. Even their millennial expectations
found their origin in an incarnate, crucified, resurrected, and returning
savior. Moreover, they took this divine storyline as evidence of cosmic
love that demanded human emulation. They pointed repeatedly to the
covetousness in their own hearts that needed to be rooted out so that
philanthropy could blossom.[51] Sin in the heart of the philanthropist was

47. *Minutes*, Elkhorn Baptist Association, 1862, 7.

48. *Minutes*, Boston South Baptist Association, 1859, 20.

49. *Minutes*, Warren Baptist Association, 1864, 17.

50. Beth Barton Schweiger, *The Gospel Working Up: Progress and the Pulpit in
Nineteenth-Century Virginia* (New York: Oxford University Press, 2000).

51. Baptists saw the sin of covetousness as the main obstacle to benevolent giving
and wrote against it consistently throughout the century. See Richard Furman's circular letter on the theme of covetousness: *Minutes*, Charleston Baptist Association, 1808,
6–9; Barnabas Bates's circular letter on covetousness: *Minutes*, Warren Baptist Association, 1816, 10–16; "Circular Letter," *Minutes*, Elkhorn Baptist Association, 1823,
3, which warns that "covetousness is idolatry"; William Hooper's circular letter on
covetousness: *Minutes*, Sandy Creek Baptist Association, 1835, 12–15; "Benevolence,"

not the only, or even the most important problem. Baptists argued that sin caused poverty. For this reason they concluded that benevolence as an act of physical relief may be to no avail. To succeed, social reformers had to attack vice.

Poverty and Vice

Evangelicals considered vice the root of poverty and this shaped their approach to social reform. For much of the seventeenth century ministers lived under the assumption that a sovereign God directly caused poverty, an assumption that went unchallenged until a series of catastrophes increased the number of widows and orphans. Eventually, poverty among able-bodied men increased as well and "ministers by the 1750s had completely abandoned the idea that God caused poverty, believing instead that people were poor because they were unwilling to work."[52] By the nineteenth century Baptists largely agreed. Though they sympathized with the notion that all their lives, finances included, rested in the hands of God, more often than not they placed the blame for poverty squarely on the shoulders of the impoverished themselves. This complicated their approach to benevolence. Baptists did not simply give; they gave discriminately.

The link between poverty and vice in the minds of nineteenth-century Baptists was strong. After Stillman spoke to the Boston Female Asylum about the need to support orphan girls, another minister reminded the audience that these girls were "defenceless, wretched, poor; Snatch'd from the haunts of vice and care."[53] He understood poverty and vice to be two sides of the same coin, even when an adult's vice caused a child's poverty, as in the case of the distressed orphans. It is no surprise then that in the asylum, Stillman promised the girls would be instructed in "the great principles of religion and morality."[54] They needed a reformation of character to be freed from the moral destitution of poverty.

Christian Watchman, 17 March 1837, 42; and "Church Poverty, What is It?" *Religious Herald*, 9 September 1852, 145.

52. J. Richard Olivas, "'God Helps Those Who Help Themselves': Religious Explanations of Poverty in Colonial Massachusetts, 1630–1776," in *Down and Out*, 265.

53. Stillman, *Discourse*, 17.

54. Ibid., 10.

Similarly, in 1820 the editors of Boston's *Christian Watchman* considered the birth of another benevolent society designed "for the relief of the indigent." The architects of this organization aimed to solve not just the physical but also the moral problems associated with poverty, asserting that "the virtue and comfort of this less fortunate part of the community is a subject of deep and universal interest."[55] Vice bred poverty. Intemperance was the chief but not the only culprit.[56] Presbyterian Gardiner Spring argued that poverty was less likely to be found among those who honored the Sabbath, to the apparent approval of the *Columbian Star.*[57]

The editors of the *Christian Watchman* averred a few years later that the poor have the ability to provide for themselves. They minced no words:

> There are, comparatively few people in this country, who have not sufficient physical ability to earn their own subsistence. There are infants, the aged and infirm, but these could easily be provided for. The great majority of those who are found in the wretchedness of poverty, have been brought there by idleness, intemperance and other vices. Means, therefore, should be provided in every community, by which all who possess requisite physical energy, should be made to earn their own subsistence. In fact, all efforts for the benefit of the poor, should be directed, not so much to provide for them, as to enable them to provide for themselves.[58]

The poor were locked into vice. They possessed a corrupt character. Critics often described them as "vicious" or addicted to vice to emphasize their need for a renovation of the inner man. For the editors of the *Religious Herald,* an acknowledgment of the spiritual need of the poor spurred them to greater zeal: "Oh! Let us not fold up our hands, while so much may be done for the relief of the distressed and for the reformation of the vicious."[59] This perspective affected the Baptist approach to be-

55. "Employment for the Poor," *Christian Watchman & Baptist Register*, 22 January 1820, 3.

56. "Intemperance and Pauperism," *Christian Watchman*, 2 August 1823, 135.

57. "The Sabbath," *Columbian Star*, 27 September 1823, 156.

58. "New Benevolent Society," *Christian Watchman*, 2 October 1835, 158.

59. "Christian Charity," *Religious Herald*, 28 October 1847, 169. The "vicious" poor was a term common in the nineteenth century to describe someone who lacked virtue. However, it could also be used, more particularly, to modify "poor" leaving the reader

nevolence, in part by leading them to give discriminately. "Discriminate giving" became a mantra Baptists were loath to ignore lest their aid to the poor be wasted. Not every individual mired in poverty could be trusted to use assistance well.

In one sense, discriminate giving always existed among nineteenth-century, Baptist philanthropic enterprises. For example, when Stillman listed those charitable institutions in 1801, he noted how they chose to serve only certain classes of the poor, ranging from widows and orphans, to the sick, to fire victims.[60] Charitable institutions naturally gravitated toward the most needy individuals. However, as the century progressed and the number of benevolent institutions increased, discriminate giving on the part of philanthropists rose as well.

The editors of the *Christian Watchman* were convinced mere benevolence was insufficient: "Among the numerous Societies, which have been established for the relief of the indigent, none appears calculated to produce a permanent change" in the situation of the poor. "Gratuitous aid, while it affords but a transient support, offers no stimulus to exertion, and when the temporary supply is exhausted, the unhappy sufferer is again reduced to want, or to the degradation of beggary." Simply providing financial assistance had proven ineffective. The poor needed benevolence of a different kind: "The best means, no doubt, of affording that class a regular subsistence is to give them employment."[61] These criticisms were rooted in the view that vice caused poverty. The poor required a "stimulus to exertion" because their depravity kept them from helping themselves. True benevolence, philanthropists began to argue more forcefully in the 1820s, must discern between the truly needy and the "vicious." It did so by forcing the able poor to work—something the vicious refused to do.

One of the most publicized and supported benevolent societies of the nineteenth century, the Howard Benevolent Society, became known for its commitment to discriminate giving. In the winter of 1820 the Boston chapter reported expenditures of approximately $1300 and noted

---

to understand the poor were impoverished due to their sin. See "Charity vs Pauperism," *Christian Watchman*, 5 March 1841, 38; "City Missions," *Christian Watchman*, 6 November 1846, 177; "City Missions in Providence," *Christian Watchman*, 3 December 1847, 194; "Duty of Christians Toward Cities," *Religious Herald*, 4 January 1855, 205.

60. Stillman, *Discourse*, 3–7.

61. "Employment for the Poor," *Christian Watchman & Baptist Register*, 22 January 1820, 3.

"this has been distributed in small sums, frequently repeated, accordingly as circumstances in each individual case, carefully ascertained by personal attention, seemed justly to require."[62] A few years later, in a report authored by Josiah F. Bumstead, the same committee announced that it had spent $2045, once again conscious of the need to give carefully:

> Your Committee are fully aware of the importance of contributing to the relief of the poor and destitute in that way which is least likely to offer them any inducements to look to charitable aid as a source of support; and they have taken every occasion to make it known, that the object of this Society is not to assist in *maintaining* the poor, but simply to aid in relieving casual sickness and distress. They have not failed, in the course of frequent visits, to set forth the advantages and importance of industry, temperance and prudence; nor have they neglected to impress upon the minds of those whom they have visited, by serious and affectionate advice, the necessity of living sober, righteous and godly lives.

Bumstead addressed the issue of discriminate giving to respond to critics of the Howard Benevolent Society who argued it actually increased pauperism "by leading the poor to depend upon the aid which they may thence expect to receive, and consequently to neglect the proper means of support, and thus become idle and intemperate."[63] Financial aid, they argued, could not make the vicious poor any less vicious. Bumstead therefore took great pains to respond that his organization carefully and discriminately dispersed its funds among the deserving poor. He sought only to relieve those willing to work their way out of poverty. A correspondent came to the defense of the society: "No relief is given without a personal investigation into the necessities of the sufferer, and in no case is money given. The discriminatory eye of charity can easily detect the many 'loop holes,' at which misery enters the habitation of the poor, and renders aid, where its calls are most pressing."[64]

Other cities felt the pressure to give discriminately. During the proposal of a new benevolent society in Philadelphia in 1829, those charged to give assistance also had the responsibility to "discern where pecuniary

---

62. "Howard Benevolent Society," *Christian Watchman*, 2 June 1821, 2.

63. "Howard Benevolent Society," *Christian Watchman*, 6 November 1824, 190.

64. S [pseud.], "Howard Benevolent Society," *Christian Watchman*, 13 January 1826, 190.

assistance is truly needed."[65] When Jeremiah Bell Jeter preached on benevolence before the Baptist General Association of Virginia at Second Baptist Church in 1843, he took as his text Acts 20:35, "It is more blessed to give than to receive" and argued not only that true Christian beneficence requires giving liberally, cheerfully, systematically, and prayerfully, he also insisted it included giving "with discrimination."[66] For Baptist social reformers the reality of sin shaped their approach to benevolence. "Discriminate giving" became the byword of evangelical poverty relief.

Poverty and Evangelism

Baptists gave discriminately because they took moral depravity seriously. This ultimately led them to conclude that discriminate giving alone was insufficient. The "vicious" must be more than fed, however carefully. Their souls must be reclaimed.[67] Even on the coldest winter night, Baptists argued, the poor needed more than a blanket; they needed "good lessons of morality and religion."[68] The Baptist view of vice shaped their role as social reformers. It required they place evangelism at the heart of poverty relief. The poor needed an inward, effective work of the Spirit of God:

> If, then, we would exercise the most enlightened and effective benevolence, let us impart that knowledge and influence by which the hearts of men may become purified by faith in Christ, and by the Spirit of our God. Thus we shall lay the axe at the root of the tree of evil, and thus secure present and lasting blessings to our fellow-men.[69]

This explains why, throughout the nineteenth century, Baptists saw evangelism of the individual as a means of bringing reform to society.[70]

65. "Society for Bettering the Condition of the Poor," *Columbian Star*, 10 October 1829, 233.

66. J. B. Jeter, "The Nature and Reward of Christian Beneficence," *Religious Herald*, 14 September 1843, 145.

67. "Christian Charity," *Religious Herald*, 28 October 1847, 169.

68. "Society for Bettering the Condition of the Poor," *Columbian Star*, 10 October 1829, 233.

69. "The True Benevolence," *Christian Watchman*, 17 January 1840, 10.

70. Timothy L. Smith, on the other hand, seems to argue that by the 1850s, Christians in America began marrying "spiritual to social service." That marriage, in fact, happened much earlier. See Smith, *Revivalism*, 173. Kathryn Teresa Long, contra

For many concerned with the temporal affairs of their neighbors, evangelism was key. The editors of the *Columbian Star* saw a link between earthly and spiritual interests: "Christian benevolence has organized and put in motion a most extensive system of operations, for the benefit of mankind; regarding as well their temporal as their eternal interests."[71] However, what made benevolence unique, in the present age, argued the *Star's* editors, was not the focus on meeting temporal needs, but the focus on the gospel. The public "is forming a habit of benevolent exertion . . . from year to year, the public is doing more and more for the propagation of the gospel."[72]

Though Christianity joined physical and spiritual succor, Baptists knew that Christianity stood alone as the only faith that truly offered the latter: "The fact, therefore, that Christianity is, in the broadest sense of the terms, glad tidings to the poor, is perfectly original. It stands without rival or comparison."[73] For this reason, Baptists painted the portrait of a faithful pastor as one who ministered to the poor: "When a minister is not only willing to preach in great assemblies, but also to small; when he habitually instructs his people in spiritual things at their firesides; when he often enters the dwelling of the poor and obscure to warn or console . . . then he is a good pastor."[74]

Baptists expressed their conviction that the church had a unique responsibility of delivering the gospel to the poor. When the Association of Delegates from the Benevolent Societies of Boston first reported on its activities in 1835, it argued the necessity of reaching out the poor for the sake of their souls:

> We are strongly impressed with the duty, on the part of the prosperous, and of those in circumstances of competency, in Churches,—by which we mean congregations which assemble

Smith, argued that the revival of 1857–58 marked a different kind of turning point where the church moved away from social concern and toward a stress on "evangelism and shared devotional piety." However, 1857, as remarkable as that year certainly was, did not mark "a more socially conservative view of revivalism" as Long suggested. For decades prior the church had evangelized the poor and emphasized poverty relief. See Long, *The Revival of 1857–58: Interpreting an American Religious Awakening* (New York: Oxford, 1998) 124–25.

71. "Christian Efforts," *Columbian Star*, 1 June 1822, 5.

72. "On the Peculiar Characteristics of the Benevolent Efforts of Our Age, Continued," *Columbian Star*, 27 July 1822, 3.

73. "The Gospel Preached to the Poor," *Christian Watchman*, 9 June 1826, 105.

74. "Preachers and Pastors," *Christian Watchman*, 4 July 1833, 108.

for worship,—to make it an object of especial care, and watch-
fulness and exertion, to do what they may, in their capacity as
Churches, to bring the poor and the poorest, and even the out-
casts of the earth into their number; and thus to the preaching,
and under the influence of the Gospel. Let the avowed believers
in Christianity, as individuals and as Churches, thus feel and
carry out their obligations to Christianity and the Poor, and not
only will multitudes be saved from falling into pauperism; but
the poor of every Church, taken as they should be, in respect
to their temporal necessities, into the charge of the Christian
Society with which they shall worship, will be doubly blessed
in the alms they will receive,—for they will then be the alms of
Christian and fraternal sympathy, interest and respect.[75]

They took as exemplary Jesus' claim in Luke 4:18 that the Spirit of the
Lord had anointed him to preach good news to the poor. They expected
their churches, evangelists, and missionaries to follow Christ's lead. Full
of the love of God, they, too, ought to have a heart for the dispossessed:
"It is certain that a religion that has nothing to do with the feelings, is not
the religion of the Bible. . . . It is this that prompts Christians to action.
. . . This stirs the soul of the missionary and constrains him to leave his
friends, to go and preach the gospel to the poor, the benighted, and the
lost."[76] With Christ's own ministry firmly established, they understood
true benevolence to be, as the editors of the *Watchman* articulated, "directed towards the eternal interests of man; which, while it forgets not
that he has a body, most earnestly remembers that he has a soul."[77] Here
again, in 1841, they pointed to Christ as an evangelist: "He laid the axe at
the root of the tree. He reproved individual sins to individual faces. He
presented the pure, holy, philanthropic principles of that gospel which
bringeth salvation to individual minds and hearts, accompanied with awful sanctions of God's eternal law."[78]

Baptists committed themselves and their churches to poverty relief
as an act of Christian discipleship. It may be the case that other reformers,
Charles G. Finney, for example, spurred himself and others on toward
the benevolent enterprises in an effort to attain evangelical perfection.[79]

75. "Gospel to the Poor," *Christian Watchman*, 20 November 1835, 185.

76. "Feelings Prompt to Action," *Religious Herald*, 11 January 1839, 5.

77. "True Benevolence," *Christian Watchman*, 17 January 1840, 10.

78. "The Gospel as Reformer," *Christian Watchman*, 22 January 1841, 14.

79. William G. McLoughlin, *Revivals, Awakenings, and Reform: An Essay on Religion and Social Change in America, 1607–1977* (Chicago: The University of Chicago

However, well into the nineteenth century, Baptists did not have perfectionism in mind when they articulated their responsibility to serve the poor, physically and spiritually. They fed the needy because the biblical message challenged them to seek and save the lost.

Evangelism and social reform easily mixed. Missions agencies with spiritual duties readily accepted social outreach as an extension of their gospel ministry. The Home Missionary Board of the Charleston Baptist Association, reporting to its overseeing churches in 1850, assumed that the members of their churches would meet the physical needs of the impoverished: "What, brethren, if one were to enter your dwellings, and tell you of a settlement with the bounds of your loved Association, where the people were destitute of food, where starvation was staring the inhabitants in the face, and multitudes daily dying from hunger and want; how would you act? . . . We cannot doubt the course of action you would pursue in such a case."[80] The missionary board, charged with sharing the gospel, stirred the churches to relieve the impoverished.

Nonetheless, salvation remained the preeminent concern and the poor remained a unique field to be harvested. This sentiment rested at the heart of a message preached by Baltimore pastor, Richard Fuller, at Madison University in Hamilton, New York, in 1848. The poor needed more than food, they needed the gospel:

> We shall at once see, amidst all the multiform changes and inequalities of society, there is but one event which can really alter anything in a man's condition, but one difference which separates man from man. We shall discover only one broad unbending line of discrimination passing through all the population of the earth, throwing on the right hand those who are converted to God and therefore saved, and on the left hand, the impenitent, the unconverted, who dying thus must forever be lost. Ah yes, let the rich approach the Cross, and contemplate its glories, and they will forget their riches, and 'weep and howl' for the poverty which shall come upon them if they pass unrenewed into eternity. And ye poor people, come here! Hard is your lot, but come here!—Behold this love, this priceless sacrifice for you, and you will no longer feel your poverty and humiliation. You will rise to a just sense of what you are, and what you are destined to be.[81]

Press, 1978) 128.

80. *Minutes*, Charleston Baptist Association, 1850, 16.

81. Richard Fuller, *The Benevolence of the Gospel Toward the Poor* (Baltimore:

In the face of poverty, preacher and reformer merged. The poor needed the spiritual gospel to realize physical change. The ultimate solution to poverty required the intervention of the preacher not the reformer. Though everyone was a sinner, the Baptist view of the "vicious" poor necessitated evangelism. Poverty was the result of poor choices that could only be rectified by a miraculous conversion.

Ultimately, Baptists saw no disjunction between evangelism and poverty relief. Christians never had the option of ignoring the poor because scripture commanded their attention to poverty. The debates that took place in the following decades centered on the question, how should the poor be helped, through individual or social regeneration? Baptists may have agreed with later proponents of the Social Gospel that the church had an obligation to help the poor, but they were skeptical of the effectiveness of means that denied the significance of individual conversion: "The Saviour . . . though the greatest of all philanthropists and reformers, said very little about the existing relations of men, and forms of society; fruitful in evil as they were. He did not attack institutions, nor laws, nor masses of men. He adopted a more excellent way. He laid the axe at the root of the tree."[82]

Baptists committed themselves to social reform. They neither cloistered themselves in congregations nor committed themselves solely to private prayer. They aided the needy within and without the church. Baptists united evangelism and social reform in their efforts to relieve the impoverished. Though in his benevolence sermon, Manly did not close by appealing to his audience to make use of the gospel, he charged them to make good use of their money. For all its spiritual components, the benevolence demanded by Galatians 6:10 required a practical outlay of time and resources:

> How many fair opportunities have we missed! And how much good we might have done with our means . . . gone never to return. Other and similar opportunities may come; but these too, are liable to slip away unimproved. If times are hard, and our money is leaving us, we should make deposit of a portion in the Lord's bank—it will not fail but will be returned with interest.[83]

George F. Adams, 1848) 19.

82. "The Gospel as Reformer," *Christian Watchman*, 22 January 1841, 14.

83. Basil Manly Sr., "Duties of Benevolence."

Baptists identified the gospel as motivation for social reform. Piety and evangelism were part and parcel of the Christian life, but so was serving the poor for these nineteenth-century reformers.

7

Temperance and a Divided Baptist Social Conscience

ON MAY 15, 1888, at the First Baptist Church in Richmond, Virginia, the recently elected president of the Southern Baptist Convention, James P. Boyce, ruled out of order two resolutions on temperance made individually by representatives from Virginia. After appeal, the convention sustained both rulings, barely, the first by a vote of 130 to 100, the second, 115 to 110.[1] William Barnes gathered from an eyewitness that the convention favored taking a public stand in support of the temperance movement, but it chose to muster support for the ailing and revered Boyce who died a few months later.[2]

John E. Massey, who offered one of the resolutions Boyce dismissed, served as lieutenant governor of Virginia and as a convention messenger of his church. Upon his return he wrote to the *Religious Herald*, voicing his dissatisfaction with Boyce's decision. Massey argued that Boyce had misinterpreted Article II of the convention's constitution which stated that the design of the convention was "to promote foreign and domestic missions, and other important objects connected with the Redeemer's kingdom." Massey heard from Boyce that though he supported temperance as a social movement it stood outside the purview of the convention's mission. Massey responded that a previous president, P. H. Mell, did not think so, since in 1886 the convention approved a resolution protesting the manufacture, sale, and consumption of intoxicating liquors.

1. *Proceedings of the Southern Baptist Convention, May 11–15, 1888* (Atlanta: Jas. P. Harrison, 1888) 33–34.

2. William Wright Barnes, *The Southern Baptist Convention, 1845–1953* (Nashville: Broadman, 1954) 246.

Moreover, Massey argued, as temperance reformers had for decades, that even the moderate drinking of alcohol was dangerous and, thus, a topic worthy of the convention's interest.[3]

The fight for temperance was more than a reformation in manners for Baptists; it was a sacred and secular mission to change society. Baptists merged politics and piety in their battle against drunkenness. From the beginning of the temperance movement and well into the age of prohibition, Baptists waged war against alcohol. Moral suasion was certainly their weapon of choice but, even in the early years, political action remained in their arsenal. Baptists spent most of the nineteenth century vigorously fighting for temperance.[4] Antebellum Baptists typically fought the temperance reform on the evangelistic front, but they were willing to petition for political change as well. Primarily concerned about the salvation of souls, Baptists saw intemperance as a stumbling block to conversion. The intemperate needed to repent of their addiction to the bottle and submit to the lordship of Christ. For many Baptist preachers, a temperance sermon was an opportunity to call sinners to Jesus. The goal was conversion and the means was the church and the temperance society. Both were an integral part of the Baptist commitment to the cause. Nor did Baptists shy away from political activism as a means of securing victory over drunkenness. Legal measures complemented moral suasion as Baptists sought every available method to end intemperance. This level of political engagement may appear to contradict the notion of an apolitical church, especially in the South. Yet many believed that politics was a necessary means to achieve the noble ends of a temperate nation.

Of course, Baptists did not speak univocally on temperance. As the Boyce – Massey controversy already showed, division existed among them. While they agreed that the temperance reformation needed to

3. "Hon. John E. Massey, Lieutenant-Governor of Virginia, Speaks," *Religious Herald*, 12 July 1888, 109.

4. For Rufus Spain, who explored the social interests of Southern Baptists from 1865–1900, Boyce's opposition to temperance reform in 1888 was but a footnote of restraint in a narrative of rapidly expanding Baptist moral reform efforts. In the late 1880s Baptists "awakened to the seriousness of the liquor problem and assumed a share of the responsibility for it solution." Rufus B. Spain, *At Ease in Zion: Social History of Southern Baptists, 1865–1900* (Nashville: Vanderbilt University Press, 1967) 196. Spain emphasized the ambivalence toward reform that existed well into the 1880s as Baptists like Boyce questioned the appropriateness of church involvement in the temperance crusade. Such ambivalence existed long before the 1880s though the majority of Baptists, as this chapter will argue, pushed the church to fight drunkenness.

move forward for the sake of the gospel, Baptists did not always agree how the movement ought to progress. They divided over the scriptural foundation of the temperance reformation and they argued especially about the role the church played. These controversies indicate that there was not one Baptist approach to social reform.[5]

Temperance and Religion

The nineteenth-century temperance movement was a religious crusade that involved Baptists from the beginning. The particulars are still not widely known, especially the involvement of individual denominations.[6]

5. Historians assume but rarely explore in depth the evangelical nature of the nineteenth-century temperance movement, and this is especially true of its origins. They prefer to shed light on the social factors that stimulated society's interest in reducing and ultimately eliminating the consumption of alcoholic beverages: factory owners wanted sober employees; politicians promoted virtuous voters; citizens hoped to reform the political process; farmers found outlets for grain other than distilleries. Indeed, the movement owed much gratitude to profound economic, commercial, and political changes. As Rumbarger argued, the temperance movement rested at the heart of industrialization, as "wealthy capitalists regarded temperance reform as integral and necessary to establishing a capitalist, industrial social order." John J. Rumbarger, *Profits, Power, and Prohibition: Alcohol Reform and the Industrializing of America, 1800–1930* (New York: State University of New York Press, 1989) xix. Furthermore, social and economic factors seemed to explain a difference in attitude between northerners and southerners when it came to temperance. Southerners, who came to depend on the revenue from the grain sold to distilleries, had a real incentive to keep away from abstinence pledges. Ian R. Tyrrell, "Drink and Temperance in the Antebellum South: An Overview and Interpretation," *Journal of Southern History* 48 (Fall 1982) 485–510. The first comprehensive work on temperance to treat the religious origins of temperance, John Allen Krout, *The Origins of Prohibition* (New York: Russell & Russell, 1953) is widely dismissed for focusing too much on the religious roots and generally failing to provide an interpretation of temperance reform. It was followed by Joseph Gusfield, *Symbolic Crusade: Status Politics and the American Temperance Movement* (Urbana: University of Illinois Press 1963) which had a similar emphasis on the religious underpinnings of the movement. However, more recently, temperance historians have moved away from the religious backdrop and emphasized the social origins. See Ian R. Tyrrell, *Sobering Up: From Temperance to Prohibition in Antebellum America, 1800–1860* (Westport, CT: Greenwood, 1979); Robert L. Hampel, *Temperance and Prohibition in Massachusetts, 1813–1852* (Ann Arbor, MI: UMI Research Press, 1982); Jack S. Blocher Jr., *American Temperance Movements: Cycles of Reform* (Boston: Twayne, 1989); Rumbarger, *Profits, Power, and Prohibition*; and Thomas R. Pegram, *Battling Demon Rum: The Struggle for a Dry America, 1800–1933* (Chicago: Ivan R. Dee, 1998).

6. Tyrrell described the identification of the temperance movement with

Pastors delivered messages that stirred the temperance troops. Church buildings housed the temperance societies in which they gathered. Denominational papers printed the constitutions that articulated the pledges stating the terms of the fight. Baptists believed that drunkenness was a national crisis. Its severity demanded a swift and determined response. Evangelicalism's greatest leaders waged a war against the physical and moral damage left in the wake of intemperance. The scope of the problem, the activity of other reformers, and the religious roots of the movement underscored the point that Baptists were motivated to join the crusade to save souls and the nation.[7] They felt compelled early on to fight drunkenness on all fronts: spiritual and political.

The temperance movement in the North and the South started independently though practically simultaneously. Massachusetts reformers initiated the northern movement with the Massachusetts Society for the Suppression of Intemperance (MSSI) which officially organized in 1813. It tolerated the moderate consumption of alcohol and focused

---

evangelicals as one of its important legacies. Tyrrell, *Sobering Up*, 318. More recently, McKenna associated the temperance reform with American Puritanism, with not even a reference to economics. George McKenna, *The Puritan Origins of American Patriotism* (New Haven, CT: Yale University Press, 2007) 218–22. For studies that address the religious aspect of the movement, see Joe L. Coker, *Liquor in the Land of the Lost Cause: Southern White Evangelicals and the Prohibition Movement* (Lexington: University of Kentucky Press, 2007); Charles A. Israel, *Before Scopes: Evangelicalism, Education, and Evolution in Tennessee, 1870–1925* (Athens: University of Georgia Press, 2004); Hampel, *Temperance and Prohibition in Massachusetts*; John J. Coffey, "A Political History of the Temperance Movement in New York State, 1808–1920," PhD diss., Pennsylvania State University, 1976; C. C. Pearson and J. Edwin Hendricks, *Liquor and Anti-Liquor in Virginia, 1619–1919* (Durham, NC: Duke University Press, 1967); Daniel Jay Whitener, *Prohibition in North Carolina, 1715–1945* (Chapel Hill: University of North Carolina Press, 1945).

7. Francis Wayland, one of the first members of the American Temperance Society, described in 1832 what ought to motivate someone to join the temperance cause. He painted the individual, social, and economic effects of intemperance. Alcohol's corruption of individual morals brought social misery: "And if you would mark the misery which this vice infuses into the cup of domestic happiness, go with me to one of those nurseries of crime, a common tippling shop; and there behold collected till midnight, the Fathers, the Husbands, the Sons, and the Brothers of a neighborhood." Francis Wayland, *An Address Delivered before the Providence Association* (Boston: Lincoln & Edwards, 1832) 10. Christians shared a concern for the virtue of individuals and the effect intemperance had on society at large. Boston's *Christian Watchman* worried that even religious parents raised intemperate children, "In this way, temperate and even pious people are peopling the world with a generation of future drunkards." "Ardent Spirits," *Christian Watchman*, 16 February 1822, 40. By linking temperance and virtue, Baptists easily linked intemperance and sin—just as Massey did decades later.

on curbing excessive drinking. The MSSI had religious, though not evangelical roots—forty percent of its founding members affiliated with Unitarianism, including Abiel Abbot, pastor of First Church in Beverly, Massachusetts. By its third year, when Abbot delivered the anniversary address, the MSSI had organized over thirty auxiliary societies. Some were influential in their communities. The Concord Society, for example, reported that the custom of "giving and receiving of ardent spirits and wines at funerals" had ceased due to its efforts. Meanwhile, the Gorham Society announced its plan to fight intemperance by "example, advice, persuasion, reproof, and, (when necessary,) executing the laws of the Commonwealth."[8]

For the next several years, Massachusetts Baptists, through their most prominent periodical, the *Christian Watchman*, remained apprised of the dangers of intemperance. The paper served as a clearinghouse of national temperance news, publishing accounts of murders "undoubt- edly" caused by drunkenness, such as an Indian who killed his grand- mother on Thanksgiving day by knocking her into the fire.[9] All sins however came under Baptist judgment—a strategy in line with the mis- sion of the MSSI to address intemperance and its "kindred vices." Thus, in 1825 the editors of the *Christian Watchman* reminded their readers that "intemperate eating" ought not to be countenanced since it too could lead to "instantaneous death."[10]

The MSSI may signify, technically, the beginning of the temperance movement in America, but 1826 marks its symbolic start. This is the year that Lyman Beecher published for a national audience his six sermons on intemperance. The Connecticut Congregationalist had already earned a name for himself as a warrior for virtue, but these sermons changed the face of the temperance movement. No longer would societies be content with temperance addresses like that given by Abiel Abbot in 1815 where he spoke sweetly and gently about the possibility of a drunkard's reform. From now on sermons, pamphlets, tracts, and newspapers would be re- plete with the apocalyptic danger of drunkenness and the necessity of

8. In 1815, Abbot's anniversary sermon and the third annual report of the MSSI with an account of auxiliary society activity were published together. Abiel Abbot, *An Address Delivered before the Massachusetts Society for Suppressing Intemperance* (Cam- bridge, MA: Hilliard & Metcalf, 1815) 8, 20. For a history of the MSSI see Hanley, *Temperance and Prohibition*, 2–24.

9. "Effects of Intoxication," *Christian Watchman*, 22 December 1821, 5.

10. "Intemperance," *Christian Watchman*, 16 July 1825, 128.

entire abstinence from ardent spirits. Never before had anyone spoken of intemperance in such forceful terms: "Our foundations rest on the heaving sides of a burning mountain, through which, in thousands of places, the fire has burst out, and is blazing around us."[11] America's only hope was the "banishment of ardent spirits," not by force of law but by a renovation of "public sentiment."[12] Herein lay the genius of Beecher's plan. He appealed to the conscience of the consumer, uniting Christians in the noble mission of changing the affections of the nation: "Let the temperate cease to buy—and the demand for ardent spirits will fall in the market three fourths, and ultimately will fall wholly, as the generation of drunkards shall hasten out of time."[13]

The same year Beecher preached about giving up ardent spirits entirely, the American Temperance Society formed. The tone of the debate had changed and, as Ian Tyrrell noted, "the hesitant, tentative efforts of the Massachusetts Society for the Suppression of Intemperance faded before the confident campaign launched by the American Temperance Society (ATS) after its creation in 1826."[14] The new society, led by evangelical clergy, committed itself to moral suasion, to persuading citizens to abstain from alcohol and encouraging them to memorialize their decision by signing an abstinence pledge.[15] ATS leaders, who included

11. Lyman Beecher, *Six Sermons on the Nature, Occasions, Signs, Evils, and Remedy of Intemperance*, 10th ed. (Boston: Perkins & Marvin, 1829) 59. Many credited Beecher's leading role. For example, the *Cyclopedia of Temperance, Prohibition and Public Morals* (Cincinnati: Methodist Book Concern, 1917) s.v. "Beecher, Lyman": "Perhaps no man in America has done more to mould public opinion on the temperance question than Lyman Beecher. He was first aroused to a realization of the magnitude of the drink evil in 1808, while pastor at East Hampton, by observing how a conscienceless grogseller corrupted the Montauk Indians. . . . "Dr. Beecher's celebrated 'Six Sermons on Intemperance,' . . . did more than any other agency to create a distinct and practical temperance sentiment, and were recognized as the standard authority on the temperance question for many years. In them he indicated the necessity for the absolute Prohibition of the liquor traffic."

12. Ibid., 64. The Massachusetts Society for the Suppression of Intemperance had not taken the step of outright banning the use of ardent spirits. Hampel, *Temperance and Prohibition*, 25.

13. Beecher, *Six Sermons*, 65.

14. Tyrrell, *Sobering Up*, 54.

15. "Temperance leaders believed so strongly in the power of influence that they refused (until the early 1830s) to consider law enforcement or legal revision, tactics endorsed earlier by the M.S.S.I. The only coercion they sanctioned was a promise not to offer liquor to others at any time. Even that provision, which reflected a desire to change custom and fashion, offended some abstainers who otherwise supported the

Andover pastor, Justin Edwards, Andover Seminary professor, Leonard Woods, and Baptist Francis Wayland, combined their efforts to wage war against intemperance.

Northern Baptists led the temperance cause, rallying their churches to join the crusade. Just before the publication of Beecher's sermons and the formation of the ATS, Baptists in Boston had been exhorted to take temperance reform seriously. On January 20, 1826, the editor of the *Christian Watchman*, Benjamin Franklin, lamented intemperance and vice: "The disregard of the christian Sabbath in every part of the United States is notorious; and intemperance in the use of ardent spirits is, in fact, a growing and truly alarming evil."[16] He urged all churches to insert into their covenants a requirement that members abstain from drinking:

> The Churches of the various religious denominations may be regarded as forming one grand moral community, which is ready for every good work. In this cause let them, for once, be unanimous. Let it be introduced, as an article, into their respective covenants, that they bind themselves totally to relinquish the use of this article, which is so destructive a natural, as well as moral poison to multitudes; and, that they will, by every means in their power, seek its annihilation in the respective societies, with which they are connected. Here is a moral influence absolutely within human control.[17]

With grass roots support and powerful preachers like Beecher a mainstay at temperance meetings and conventions for years, the ATS and affiliated groups multiplied dramatically and spread nationwide.

The southern branch of the temperance movement started simultaneously, independently, and based on the same principles. It began in Virginia and, like its Massachusetts counterpart, grew beyond its own borders. Unlike the northern movement, this one originated as a Baptist endeavor. The Virginia Temperance Society (VTS) formed in the Ash Camp Meetinghouse in Charlotte County, Virginia, under the leadership of Abner W. Clopton, doctor turned preacher. Baptist pastor and newspaper editor, Jeremiah Bell Jeter, signed the abstinence pledge as one of the first members. Like its counterpart in the North, the VTS quickly gave birth to five societies in 1827 that swelled to fifty in 1829

---

drink reform." Hampel, *Temperance and Prohibition*, 27.

16. Benjamin Franklin, *Christian Watchman*, 20 January 1826, 26.

17. Ibid.

with membership in each society ranging from a dozen to one hundred, though membership in a city like Richmond soon reached to upwards of 1,000. By 1836 250 societies had formed.[18]

Clopton called on pastors to lead the organizing effort. He placed his hope more in the commitment of ministers than in the efficiency of the societies: "Let the ministers of the Gospel endeavour to realize their awful responsibility. For upon a sober, temperate, faithful ministry—upon a pure preached Gospel, and strict Apostolic discipline, the cause of temperance—the cause of Truth and of God, depends, more than upon detached Societies, which, at best, can only operate as useful auxiliaries."[19] Clopton's address epitomized the religious nature of the movement. It depended upon a committed ministry. He did not oppose benevolent societies, as some of his Baptist brethren did, but he emphasized the importance of the minister and his congregation. The temperance reformation required congregations to preach the gospel and to discipline members who refused to live in accordance with the gospel's precepts. Without churches committed to such basic evangelical tenets, temperance reform had no hope of gaining traction.

The religious motivation for temperance reform, in the North and the South, proved too compelling for evangelicals to ignore. Starting in 1826 temperance societies radiated outward from Massachusetts and Virginia.[20] If the gospel demanded they wage a battle against drunkenness, then they concluded the battle must be fought on all fronts, the spiritual and the political. Though the movement began largely with the goal of individual conversions in mind, it grew to espouse political activism. Individual transformation and political influence both had a part to play in the Baptist approach to antebellum temperance reform. The emphasis however was always on evangelism.

18. Pearson and Hendricks, *Liquor and Anti-Liquor*, 59–60.

19. Abner W. Clopton and Eli Ball, eds., *Wisdom's Voice to the Rising Generation: Being a Selection of the Best Addresses and Sermons on Intemperance* (Philadelphia: n.p., c. 1828) 152.

20. Not all temperance societies began in these two centers. According to Whitener, North Carolina formed its own temperance societies before 1826, as early as 1822. Whitener, *Prohibition in North Carolina*, 23.

Temperance and Evangelism

To Baptists, the temperance reformation was more than a religious movement; it was an evangelistic mission. Christians believed in the primacy
of individual transformation by personal faith in Jesus. Baptists contended that temperance reform, to be truly successful, required a spiritual
change in the subject. For this reason, local churches stood at the heart
of the movement even while temperance societies served helpful, even
necessary roles, augmenting but rarely replacing the work of the local
church. The primacy of evangelism for the sake of regeneration formed a
rallying cry that enabled most Baptists to promote and embrace the temperance movement from the beginning. They viewed temperance reform
as both a spiritual endeavor and as a social cause. It was part of their work
as evangelical social reformers.

Social transformation, according to Baptist reformers, started with
individual change. The *Columbian Star* published a circular letter of the
Virginia Temperance Society which challenged ministers to lay before
the drunkards in their congregations the need for conversion: "Let each
minister then ask his own conscience . . . whether he hath again pointed
the drunkard to the fiery doom that awaits his soul."[21] They remained
largely uninterested in systemic factors contributing to drunkenness.
The Dover Baptist Association, likewise, in 1827 urged pastors to preach
on the topic and exhorted private members of its associated churches
to confront individuals: "Seize every opportunity to warn saint and sinner against the evils of this destructive vice."[22] In New York the Oneida
Baptist Association impressed upon its members a similar challenge in
1831: "Resolved, that in our opinion it is the duty of every disciple of the
Lord Jesus Christ, to unite with a Temperance Society; and where this is
impracticable, to put in practice the principle of entire abstinence from
distilled spirit, and adopt this motto, 'Touch not, taste not, handle not,
the accursed thing which the Lord hateth.'"[23] Ministers from Virginia to
New York identified drunkenness with reprobation and temperance with
spiritual deliverance. The Oneida Baptist Association made membership with temperance societies a matter of Christian "duty" because they

21. "Virginia Society for the Promotion of Temperance," *Columbian Star*, 23 December 1826, 201.

22. *Minutes*, Dover Baptist Association, 1827, 7.

23. *Minutes*, Oneida Baptist Association, 1831, 7.

believed the salvation of souls depended upon church member participation in the temperance cause.

The emphatic link between temperance reform and spiritual regeneration led some to denigrate the movement as the brainchild of Calvinists. Certainly many reformers espoused Calvinism. Some leading Methodists noticed this, in fact, and chose not to cooperate with the temperance cause.[24] In October 1829 the editor of the *Columbian Star* noted that the Methodist *Christian Advocate and Journal* and *Zion's Herald* refused to support the temperance society movement, arguing the societies were "mere Calvinist coalitions." The *Star* responded: "Now, we love a good argument though it be against us; but in the present case we really think our Wesleyan friends are a little too sensitive. Their olfactories are surely very keen, if they can smell out Calvinism in the temperance institutions, composed as they are, of men of all churches, and of no churches." The Methodist editor in question must have been Nathan Bangs, infamous for his refusal to support the temperance cause.[25] His opposition illustrates that the temperance reformation was a Calvinistic movement. However, as the *Star's* response indicates, even if Calvinists

---

24. "Temperance Societies and the Methodists," *Columbian Star and Christian Index*, 3 October 1829, 219. In his introduction to *The American Evangelicals*, McLoughlin argued that the perfectionist impulse that grew out of the Second Great Awakening and matured in the doctrine of perfectionism that Charles G. Finney borrowed from the Wesleyan Methodists undergirded the benevolent reform movements of the nineteenth century. There are two ironies here. One, Methodists were not united in their support of benevolent reform, and, two, Calvinists, who rejected the perfectionism of Methodism are still closely identified with benevolent reform. The perfectionist impulse is simply not a sufficient explanatory factor for the benevolent empire. See William G. McLoughlin, ed., *The American Evangelicals, 1800–1900* (New York: Harper & Row, 1968) 10–12. Since Timothy L. Smith, *Revivalism and Social Reform in Mid-Nineteenth-Century America* (New York: Abingdon, 1957) and McLoughlin, the idea that the perfectionist impulse explains social reform has been taken for granted. For example, when Jack S. Blocker Jr. sought to explain why the temperance movement moved from prohibiting the drinking of ardent spirits to all intoxicating beverages, he appealed, without any evidence, to the perfectionist impulse: "What made the reformers think they could expect more from the movement? Contributing to this hope was the perfectionist impulse that emerged from the revivals of the Second Great Awakening (1800–35) a belief that, with God's grace, human beings could speed the coming of the millennium by improving themselves and their society on earth. The perfectionist vision appeared to be confirmed by the success of the temperance movement in mobilizing its army of reform." Jack S. Blocker Jr., *American Temperance Movements*, 22.

25. Douglas J. Williamson, "The Rise of the New England Methodist Temperance Movement," *Methodist History* 21 (October 1982) 18–20.

comprised the core of the movement, it quickly grew much larger.[26]
Its leadership was Calvinistic buts its rank-and-file support was much
broader.

Baptists targeted individuals because they felt sure that intemperance had the power to kill the soul, and only the gospel could save it. In
other words, even if Ian Tyrrell was correct that the temperance movement received "much of its support" from businessmen looking to better
their workforce and "improve" nineteenth-century America, Baptists
early on had a different agenda: personal salvation.[27] This is why the
Charleston Baptist Association formed a temperance society in 1826 that
prohibited its members from "the use of Ardent Spirits." These southern
Baptists called on Christians to present an "unsullied example of sobriety
and temperance" because drunkenness "destroys the soul."[28]

Second Great Awakening Baptists naturally promoted temperance
with revivalism because they equated temperance with repentance, a
necessary precondition for salvation. A letter written to the *Columbian
Star* in June 1829, told of a revival near Sumter, South Carolina, between
November and June of that year in which five churches saw 167 baptisms.
The conversions came like a breath of fresh air to a community in the

26. Francis Wayland believed the temperance movement provided a platform for
personal encounter. His biographer summarized his view, "If Christian men would go
personally to the drunkard and to the rum-seller, and would converse with them, appealing to their consciences, and pleading with them to abandon their ruinous courses,
accompanying every effort with prayer for the aid of the Holy Ghost, he believed that
it could not fail to receive the divine blessing." Francis Wayland and H. L. Wayland, *A
Memoir of the Life and Labors of Francis Wayland* (New York: Sheldon, 1867) 2:333.

27. Tyrrell would not object. In fact, after noting the economic motivation for
temperance reform he turned to the evangelicals: "Evangelical clergy, in particular,
supported temperance as a means of promoting morality and saving souls. These
churchmen hoped to build a temperate and Christian nation on the firm basis of the
material improvement of society which they witnessed in the Jacksonian era." Tyrell,
Sobering Up, 7. When it comes to Baptist life and rhetoric, he may be right and, in
fact, Baptists did not ignore the "material improvement of society," they did, however,
emphasize the salvation of souls.

28. "Anti-Intemperance Society," *Columbian Star*, 24 June 1826, 98. The level of
Calvinist support for societal reformation through individuals has too often been dismissed. So Noll wrote, "Many Calvinist Baptists . . . remained fundamentally distrust-
ful of aggressive personal striving both in theology and society; to them this kind of
activism meant a sinful replacement of dependency upon God with idolatrous reliance
upon the self." Certainly, as shown below, many Baptists did not support the temperance movement, but there is little evidence that this is because they hesitated to display
personal effort. Mark Noll, *America's God: From Jonathan Edwards to Abraham Lincoln*
(Oxford: Oxford University Press, 2002) 312.

grip of intemperance: "Thousands and tens of thousands of gallons of ardent spirits have been sold, and thousands of persons have been made demoniacs by its exhilarating, debasing influence." Change came when reformers preached the anti-temperance gospel. According to this eye-witness, the gospel changed the town and the proof was in the bottle:

> The consequence is, men met, transact their business, and retire in good season, without any brawls, fightings, bloody eyes and mangled visages. Thus a change, a mighty change is effected in this place. Drunkenness, which before might be witnessed at any hour of day or night, is entirely banished, and good order and quietness succeeded, to the no small gratification of those who have been thus active in securing this change.[29]

The fact that men gave up drinking, with its attendant evils, proved that the Holy Spirit was at work in Sumter. Moreover it validated for Baptist readers, early on in the movement, not only that God's hand was on the temperance cause, but that the movement benefited society at large.

The decision to link temperance and evangelism spurred revivals. Preachers exhorted drunkards to personal righteousness and divine reliance. They called on believers to abstain from alcohol for the glory of God. The *Religious Herald* published a temperance sermon by a Mr. Gillet. He insisted that embracing temperance blessed society: "The Church was instituted to shine as a light to the world. Awaken then, I entreat you, from your apathy . . . so shine so that others may take knowledge of your good works, and glorify your Father who is in heaven." The work, Gillet argued, belonged to God and secured eternal deliverance: "The battle is the Lord's and the prize that awaits you—immortal life."[30] Abner Clopton maintained that revivalism and temperance reform worked together. Not only did communities that experienced revivals better receive the temperance message, but temperance tilled the soil for revival: "As Temperance Societies, in some cases, seem to be harbingers of revivals, so revivals are admirable preparatives for Temperance Societies. And the late wonderful revivals have opened far more extended fields for renewed and unwearied effort to bring the whole rising generation under Temperance influence."[31] The Charleston Baptist Association also saw temperance as

29. "Revivals and Intemperance," *The Columbian Star and Christian Index*, 18 July 1829, 34, 35.

30. "Extract from an Address to a Temperance Society, by Mr. Gillet," *Religious Herald*, 14 May 1830, 76.

31. "Temperance Record," *Christian Index*, 30 June 1832, 405.

a means to spread the gospel. The association agreed that meetings devoted to the temperance cause led to the edification of the saints and the salvation of sinners: "Among most of these churches the subject of the Temperance reformation has excited more or less attention and support. And the whole review affords abundant evidence, if any were needed that protracted meetings judiciously conducted, are an important link in the chain of means now used by the Lord for the building up of his church, and the conversion of souls."[32] The gospel, revivalism, and temperance reform went hand in hand.

Faithful Baptists, therefore, could not countenance intemperance for it was the enemy of the gospel and the bane of the nation. As the *Christian Index* reported: "We have endeavored to give this subject a calm and deliberate investigation, and our examination has irresistibly led us to the conclusion, that the use of ardent spirit for any other purpose than as medicine, is at war with the spirit, the doctrines, and precepts of the gospel."[33] In Boston, where reformers labored more vigorously than in the South, the editors of the *Christian Watchman* warned that should the temperance cause lose the gospel as the motivating factor, its effect would be certainly diminished. For these men, the Second Great Awakening meant saved souls and a renovated society. The antislavery and peace movement, American republicanism, temperance, and civilization itself depended upon the gospel of Christ:

> Whatever has been done in the civilization of the world, or in lessening the Slave Trade, the cruelties of war, or the devastations of intemperance, has been accomplished under the influence of men who have deeply imbibed the spirit of the gospel of Christ. It is Christian principle that is now sending the Bible and the messengers of salvation to the lands of heathenism; and should Christianity cease to exert its salutary power in our States, our Temperance movement, and our free institutions would desert our land, and every vice in grossest form would curse our now happy community.[34]

Though these Baptists acknowledged that social reform might persist without the gospel, they held that its true power for lasting reform derived from the gospel. They believed both that God worked in the lives

32. "A Summary View of the State of the Churches," *Minutes*, Charleston Baptist Association, 1832, 16.

33. "Churches and Ardent Spirits," *Christian Index*, 16 March 1833, 171.

34. "Another Temperance Meeting," *Christian Watchman*, 8 March 1833, 38.

of sinners, bringing them to a saving knowledge of their creator, and that God ordained temperance reform as the means not only of making the United States a more congenial place to live, but as the means to convert the lost. Evangelism as a means of social reform became an essential component of the Baptist ministry.

Temperance and the Clergy

Temperance societies allowed reformers to spread the movement beyond the churches, but most Baptists associated the reform with the churches. Congregations and ministers proved to be the heartbeat of the temperance crusade. With few exceptions Baptists used their church buildings, associations, and even their services to further the temperance mission. Reformers asked pastors to take center stage and, from their pulpits, to lead their churches in the fight against drunkenness. As "A Lover of Temperance" suggested, "it should be the minister's part, then, to lay the axe at the root of the tree, by constantly and fearlessly proclaiming the enormity of the transgression, and its tremendous penalty." He considered the pastor to be the ultimate agent of social reform: "By his godly and faithful warnings, feelings of disgust towards intemperance may be implanted, which society may feel in succeeding ages."[35] Likewise, the Virginia Temperance Society urged its first members to see in its pastors the backbone of the movement: "The cure for this disease—the balm of these wounds, must commence with the ministry."[36]

Most churches and pastors, consequently, embraced temperance societies. On July 4, 1829, at the Baptist Church at Walnut Fork, Jackson County, Georgia, the congregation gathered to celebrate the holiday "in some religious way." At the day's end, the church resolved to form a temperance society.[37] Many other Baptist churches followed suit.[38] Bap-

35. A Lover of Temperance [pseud.], "Reformation of Society," *Columbian Star*, 26 August 1826, 135.

36. "Virginia Society for the Promotion of Temperance," *Columbian Star*, 23 December 1826, 201.

37. "Abstinence from Ardent Spirits," *Columbian Star and Christian Index*, 8 August 1829, 90.

38. "Proceedings and Constitution of the Edgefield Village Temperance Society," *Columbian Star and Christian Index*, 17 October 1829, 250. "Temperance in Boston," *Christian Index*, 31 March 1832, 199. In Boston, Justin Edwards addressed fourteen Congregations, Baptist and Methodist, "and assisted in forming a Temperance

tists urged their churches to support temperance. The Charleston Baptist Association in South Carolina expressed thanksgiving that its churches defended the temperance cause: "Among most of these churches the subject of the Temperance reformation has excited more or less attention and support."[39] The association resolved to promote the progress of temperance, including entire abstinence, among its member churches.[40] Even when not actually sponsored by a particular congregation, temperance societies often gathered together in churches. In 1833 W. B. Johnson chaired a meeting of temperance societies that met at a Baptist meeting house in the District of Edgefield in Edgefield, South Carolina.[41] At other times, the influence was more direct. Such as in November of the same year when the Baptist church of Parma, Virginia, voted to invite the different Christian societies to gather together to conspire how best to "purify the church of God from the contaminating influence of ardent spirits."[42] Justin Edwards, preaching at the Federal Street Baptist Meeting House, used the pulpit to promote the cause. At the start of the temperance movement in 1826 "it was believed, that a prevalence of intemperance constitutes one of the greatest barriers to the spread of the gospel." Almost ten years later, Edwards could cite 7,000 temperance societies, 23 state societies, and 3,000 who have stopped manufacturing ardent spirits.[43] It was gospel work and ministers responded to the call.

Baptist churches in Kentucky had organized into the Elkhorn Baptist Association in 1787, adopting as their doctrinal standard the Philadelphia Confession of Faith.[44] At their meeting in 1831, these Calvinistic Baptists turned their attention to temperance reform: "Look around you, and see what this foul destroyer of morals, and of civil society has been doing, and is yet doing." The association agreed that intemperance caused poverty, crime, sickness, insanity—every social ill worth fighting made

---

Association in connexion with each."

39. "A Summary View of the State of the Churches," *Minutes*, Charleston Baptist Association, 1832, 16.

40. *Minutes*, Charleston Baptist Association, 1832, 7.

41. "Temperance Record," *Christian Index*, 25 May 1833, 330.

42. "Temperance in the Churches," *Religious Herald*, 8 November 1833, 174.

43. "Temperance Lecture," *Christian Watchman*, 2 January 1835, 2. See William A. Hallock, *"Light and Love": A Sketch of the Life and Labors of Rev. Justin Edwards* (New York: American Tract Society, 1855).

44. Ira Birdwhistell, *The Baptists of the Bluegrass: A History of the Elkhorn Association, 1785–1985* (Berea, KY: Berea College Press, 1985) 20.

the temperance cause worth supporting: "Charity would hold our pen, but faithfulness says move on though unpleasant the task."[45] They urged their churches to change society. When Virginia's Dover Baptist Association met in 1840, this gathering, largely of pastors, also committed themselves to the movement:

> Let every church see to it, that she is purified from the pollution of intemperance by the exercise of a wholesome, efficient discipline. Let sermons and lectures be delivered, and Tracts distributed, on the enormous evils of intemperance; and all the influence of self-denying example, convincing argument, kind persuasion, and faithful warning, be employed to induce all men to forsake at once, and forever, the habitual use of a beverage, which produces evil, evil only, and evil continually.[46]

By the 1850s, the call to fight the evil had reached a fevered pitch. A convention of pastors gathered in Boston to lament intemperance and lay out a plan of attack. Lyman Beecher addressed the crowd full of men undoubtedly thrilled to hear the figurehead of their crusade. One attendee could not suppress his enthusiasm: "we felt in retiring from that meeting, that the hold of true religion, as well as that of its ministers upon the community, had received strength."[47] He became convinced that a true pastor did more then deliver the gospel. Every preacher must understand

> that the Gospel comprehends precepts of morality and virtue, that it sends out its currents of influence to reach society, in all its corruption, and pours its waters of healing upon man, wherever sick, bruised, or wounded. This it has always done; and in an age in which the human mind has awoke to perceive and realize the claims of brotherhood, and of the race, as these have not been perceived or realized since the dawn of Christianity, we may conclude that the Gospel, in its direct tendency, will more and more take cognizance of the ills which appetite, cupidity, love of power, and wickedness in general, have fastened upon the multitude.

These comments suggest that the clergy were an integral part of the temperance reform movement. They defended their activity in the temperance cause by refusing to separate the preaching of the gospel from the

45. *Minutes*, Elkhorn Baptist Association, 1831, 8.

46. J. B. Jeter, "Report of the Committee on Temperance," *Minutes*, Dover Baptist Association, 1840, 12.

47. "The Ministry and Reform," *Christian Watchman*, 24 March 1853, 46.

promotion of social virtue. With the gospel in one hand and holiness in the other they led their churches into the temperance crusade.[48]

Temperance and Division

Not all Baptists condoned the church using temperance to win the lost and improve the country. In fact, some even objected to the benevolent societies because they seemed to unite church and state. By promoting evangelism and social reform as two sides of the same coin, they sent a mixed message, undermining earlier victories for freedom of conscience. Religious liberty for Baptists in Virginia had been won in 1785 when the legislature approved the "Bill for Establishing Religious Freedom." Connecticut citizens lived under an established church until 1818. They remembered the kind of persecution that took place when the state became too aligned with the church. The temperance reformation, which aimed to convert sinners and change public policy, represented a misguided direction.

In many ways, disestablishment spurred the early American reformers into action. Activists like Lyman Beecher expected the state and the church to help each other. He went so far, as one historian put it, to describe government as "the legislative will of God."[49] George Marsden made a similar argument after studying Beecher. He noted that these New England preachers advocated moral reform because God decreed a special purpose for America, a manifest destiny, to change the world through their vision and holiness: "The effect of such a view of the national destiny was that evangelicals were thoroughly convinced that it was their

---

48. There is evidence that the commitment of the ministry to the movement waxed and waned. "The ministry twenty years since, were pioneers in reform. Their cooperation is again soundly invoked, and cannot longer be withheld. Again, the cause of sobriety asks, as indispensable, the aid of the moral groundwork and stimulus which first set the temperance cause in motion and without which it can never permanently live and prosper." "New Demands of Temperance," *Watchman & Reflector*, 24 January 1856, 2. Hampel noted the decrease in the devotion on the part of pastors to the temperance cause: "The infidelity of several lecturers and newspaper editors, the carnival atmosphere of the meetings, and the taunting of wine drinking church members all had cooled the once fervent ministerial commitment to the anti-drink crusade." Hampel, *Temperance and Prohibition*, 154.

49. Byron C. Lambert, "The Rise of the Anti-Mission Baptists: Sources and Leaders, 1800–1840 (A Study in American Religious Individualism)" (PhD diss., University of Chicago, 1957) 11.

most solemn duty to mind everyone else's moral business; otherwise, the entire nation would suffer for the sins of a few."[50] Beecher appealed for moral reform in grandiose terms. In *Plea for the West*, written in 1835, he called the church to action but he directed his rhetoric, characteristically, toward the country as a whole: "But if this nation is, in the providence of God, destined to lead the way in the moral and political emancipation of the world, it is time she understood her high calling, and were harnessed for the work."[51] Though the church had officially been disestablished, a new type of establishment took place in the early nineteenth century. The benevolent societies were the new religious state, enforcing the precepts and principles of the church and threatening the freedoms of the young republic.

Beecher, and other activists cut from the same cloth, had many detractors. The line between Beecher's religious nationalism and the denominational cooperation undergirding the benevolent movement was, for some Christians, too thin. "Primitive" Baptists refused to have anything to do with benevolent societies, which encroached, they believed, on their hard-won civil rights as independent churches. In the benevolent empire, both the purity of the church and the separation of church and state were being threatened. They saw, according to Byron Lambert:

> an exciseman in every shadow of extracongregational cooperation, and a state church in the minutes of every intercongregational missionary endeavor. Add to this ecclesiastical gun-shyness the patriotic fervor of the Revolutionary period, the enthusiasm whipped up in a war, the novelty of their experiment in a new government, the seemingly endless space (political as well as geographical) given to them, the seriousness with which they took their ideals of liberty and their own abilities to

50. George M. Marsden, *The Evangelical Mind and the New School Presbyterian Experience: A Case Study of Thought and Theology in Nineteenth-Century America* (New Haven, CT: Yale University Press, 1970) 23.

51. Lyman Beecher, *A Plea for the West*, 2nd ed. (Cincinnati: Truman & Smith, 1835) 11. These ideas are reflected in the perspective of Daniel Walker Howe, who argued that after Beecher lost the fight to keep together church and state through an established religion, he united them through benevolent societies. "A well-known fact about Lyman Beecher is that he fought hard to retain the establishment of religion in Connecticut but, after losing that fight in 1818, became rapidly reconciled to disestablishment. The benevolent societies served the purpose of collective religious and moral dedication more effectively than an established church, he decided." See Daniel Walker Howe, *The Political Culture of the American Whigs* (Chicago: The University of Chicago Press, 1979) 58.

use it, and one begins to see even at this distance how the Baptist churches often became antinomian and unruly.[52]

Antimission Baptists, as they came to be called, cherished autonomy above unity, specifically, the autonomy of the local church.[53]

They were not the only Baptists, however, to object to temperance reform. Dissent came from several different quarters. Some quarreled with the reformers' use of Scripture, arguing the Bible lacked a direct injunction to warrant the temperance crusade. Others contended that the temperance reform movement violated one's liberty of conscience. Both arguments deserve to be examined for they betray a Baptist conscience captive to scripture and skeptical of the temperance movement's foundation.

First, some Baptists reasoned that without a biblical text enjoining participation in a temperance society, Christians ought to keep their distance. As the editors of the *Religious Herald* reported in 1828, those who refused to join societies did so because they insisted, "there is neither precept nor example in the Bible for them; and they suppose that the formation of societies for any object where the Scriptures do not sanction them, is attempting to regulate the world better than God has done

52. Lambert, "Rise of the Anti-Mission Baptists," 53. Lambert devoted his dissertation to uncovering and evaluating some of the most notable antimission Christians. One of his arguments is that they did not all share an identity. "In some ways it would be more accurate to say there were anti-Missionisms in those years; each of the numerous leaders, armed with his own program of attack against the missionary societies then in existence, had a strong force of supporters behind him." Representatives included Elias Smith and John Leland among the Baptists. The Quaker, Elias Hicks, the Deist Anne Royall, the freethinker Robert Dale Owen also joined the anti-mission cause, along with Methodists Lorenzo Dow, Peter Cartwright and Freeborn Garrettson. Ibid., iv.

53. Besides rejecting mission societies, antimission Baptists also opposed seminaries and Sunday schools. Daniel Parker is a prominent example of the anti-missionary movement, described by Wimberly as the figure who "coalesced the prevailing sentiments of antimissionism in the West." Dan B. Wimberly, *Frontier Religion: Elder Daniel Parker, His Religious and Political Life* (Austin, TX: Eakin, 2002) 149. See also Daniel Parker, *A Public Address to the Baptist Society and Friends of Religion* (Vincennes, IN: Stout & Osborn, 1820). Parker developed a "two-seed" theology to defend his antimissionary stance. He reasoned from Genesis 3:15 that since the church consists of God's elect and its members have God's seed and societies consist of individuals without God's seed, then societies should not be embraced as agencies for the fulfillment of God's mission. See Daniel Parker, *Views on the Two Seeds* (Vandalia, IL: Robert Blackwell, 1826). February 8, 1828, the editors of the *Religious Herald* rebuked the Kehukee Association for its recent decision to exclude from their pulpits pastors committed to missions societies. *Religious Herald*, 8 February 1828, 19.

it." The editors disagreed and cited Jeremiah 35 as proof. In this chapter God commended the Recabites for heeding the command of their father, Jonadab, to abstain from wine. This biblical reference was not only an example of "filial respect worthy of imitation" but proof that God approved of temperance.[54] If God approved of temperance, they argued, then surely he condoned any necessary means of fighting temperance, societies included. Christians also appealed to the Apostle Paul to defend their support of the society movement. One correspondent with the *Religious Herald* cited Paul in Romans 14:21: "'It is good not to drink wine, nor any thing whereby thy brother stumbles, or is offended, or is made weak.'"[55] If it is "good not to drink wine" then it must be good to join a society that encouraged citizens to abstain. Nothing could be clearer, these Baptist reformers argued. In passages like Jeremiah 35 and Romans 14, they poured an exegetical foundation to buttress their acceptance of temperance societies.

Some reformers, however, saw no need for exegetical support. Indirect arguments sufficed. They asserted that the Bible commended the society movement and refused to defend their conclusion with proof texts. In fact, "S," in 1828, argued that looking for explicit statements in defense of the temperance movement required an overly rigid, literalist reading of Scripture. This line of argument, he reasoned, would ultimately lead one to conclude he could only read the Bible in the original languages, its purest and most "legitimate" form:

> Those who make the objection admit, I suppose, no rules for practice except they be literally transcribed from the word of God. It does not, however, follow by any means, that all rules, professing to be obtained from the word of God, must necessarily be literally transcribed in order to make them legitimate. If that were true, than our present version of the scriptures would be literally illegitimate; because it has been translated from the original languages.[56]

Similarly, J. H., writing from Mississippi to Philadelphia's *Christian Index*, lamented the "many professors of religion [who] do not approve more generally, and join temperance societies" out of the conviction they lack

---

54. "A Scripture Example of a Temperance Society," *Religious Herald*, 29 August 1828, 134.

55. J. H., "Temperance Societies Approved," *The Christian Index*, 19 May 1832, 306.

56. S. [pseud.], "On Intemperance," *Religious Herald*, 12 December 1828, 93.

any biblical warrant. For J. H., and no doubt numerous other reformers, it sufficed to know that Scripture did not prohibit the formation of societies.[57]

While all arguments against the temperance movements among Baptists found their way to the touchstone of Scripture, a second category of disagreements concerned liberty of conscience. Several Baptists did not see enough biblical evidence to require the signing of an abstinence pledge. According to their reading of Scripture, Christians were free to disagree on this very point.

In a series of letters published by the *Religious Herald* in 1850, correspondents debated the biblical basis of temperance and A. M. Poindexter, an influential Southern Baptist pastor in Virginia, concluded that the most one can argue is that moderate drinking was sometimes wrong. William D. Straughan offered a counterpoint. He suggested that to love his neighbor, the faithful Christian must support temperance:

> Here we differ, and here we must differ, until you convince me that you are right, and then I will frankly confess that I am wrong. I must believe there is a law, which God has given, that forbids me to drink this "liquid fire" as a beverage. This law is the foundation of all other divine laws, and the foundation from which flows all that are good and merciful. This law requires me to love God with all my soul, strength, and mind, and my neighbor as myself.—This is the law of love. Here it is expressed by Christ himself. "Jesus said unto him (the lawyer,) thou shalt love the Lord thy God with all thy heart, and with all thy soul, and with all they mind. This is the first and great commandment, and the second is like unto it, thou shalt love they neighbor as thyself. On these two commandments hang all the law and the prophets." This law forbids me to do anything that does not glorify God, or that tends to injure my fellow-man. If I, (either by precept or example,) exert a prejudicial influence upon the community, I am guilty of a transgression of this law.—And it not only makes it obligatory upon me to glorify God in my acts, but I am bound to labor, instrumentally, to ameliorate the condition of mankind. This is the work of love.[58]

Poindexter seemed unimpressed with Straughan's reasoning. When asked to comment upon the morality of theatres and gambling, Poindexter

57. J. H., "Temperance Societies Approved," 306.

58. William D. Straughan, "The Temperance Question," *Religious Herald*, 28 February 1850, 33.

instead returned to the topic of alcohol and reasserted his position that scripture does not condemn its consumption. This alone did not give the Christian license to drink—it was a matter of liberty and prudence. There were other biblical injunctions to be kept in mind that could make drinking immoral, such as the apostle Paul's directions regarding first century prohibitions on eating meat. Eating meat, in and of itself, was not wrong, but it could be. Drinking alcohol, likewise, was not wrong, but it could be: "If I or you were to indulge in drinking, &c., it would be with the conviction that we endangered others. But suppose another does not so believe. If independently of the consequences which we attach to the practice, he would be at liberty, then our belief that such consequences would result, cannot circumscribe his liberty. 'For why is my liberty judged of another man's conscience.'"[59]

Poindexter knew that antitemperance men did not want their liberty impinged by the movement. One writer to the *Religious Herald*, "Goliah," bewailed the temperance cause in a letter to the editor, Henry Keeling: "In truth I am provoked, unavoidably; for the fact is, my feelings are so frequently tortured by newspaper scraps, new temperance societies springing up here and there as suddenly and unexpectedly as the gourd of Jonah." And then, with a touch of humor, "O that they may all share the same fate."[60] Clearly the author felt no compulsion to join the ranks of the temperance crusaders.

Along similar lines, a Georgia pastor in June 1829 objected to the zeal of the temperance reformers. He had read in a letter that all Christians who had not signed the pledge must be "fatally wedded to their bottles." He bemoaned such generalizations: "I really wish that the advocates of temperance would be a little more guarded in their expressions, and not give the enemy so much advantage." Though he considered himself a friend of temperance, he took exception to the total abstinence cause:

59. A. M. Poindexter, "The Temperance Question," *Religious Herald*, 21 March 1850, 45.

60. Goliah [pseud.], "Of New Things, Called Old," *Religious Herald*, 13 February 1829, 21, Goliah outright rejected the call of the temperance societies to total abstinence: "But in the mean time are we to be harassed incessantly with the Christian obligations to self-denial and the forces of example? To be sure our blessed Saviour said something about such matters, but as to his saying that precept without example was as the body without the spirit, it is certain that he never in so many words said it, and I humbly hope, never meant to convey it by any allowed application of his principles; at any rate I can feel no irresistible reason for being stirred upon such points at this remote day."

"There are precious brethren who have not experienced any change in their sentiments, and who think it would be more in conformity with the word of God for our 'total abstinence' people, 'to take a little wine,' than to deal in such invectives against those who feel inclined to use it in moderation.'"[61] He defended the liberty to drink moderately.

When an antitemperance society formed in Norfolk, Virginia, in 1833 to advocate for liberty of conscience, the editors of the *Herald* quickly attacked: "It was scarcely to be presumed that such a work of reform as the Temperance cause, such a combined and powerful attack on one of the most powerful engines of the Prince of this world to ensure the souls of men, as intemperance, could be effected without arousing a powerful and determined opposition."[62] Those who argued for the liberty to drink, found themselves working against a movement that, already by 1833, was in full force. In Baptist life, those who publicly supported the antitemperance movement to defend their personal rights of liberty of conscience were a small but significant minority. Baptists were divided and never more vehemently than over the mission of the church.

Temperance and Church Division

The most vocal opponents of the temperance movement did not question the foundation of the movement as much as they lamented its effect. They worried that in the din of religious nationalism, the mission of the church and the power of the gospel were being ignored. These Baptist critics fought the method of the movement on three grounds. First, they debated the union of churches and temperance societies. Second, they questioned the phenomena of "test-churches," that is churches which made a commitment to the cause of temperance a condition of membership. Third, some Baptists disputed the calling of the church as an agent

61. "Temperance Societies Admonished," *Columbian Star*, 11 July 1829, 29. The *Star* disagreed with vehemence, "notwithstanding what our correspondent has said, we are of the full and decided opinion, that no christian, Baptist or otherwise, can innocently use even a little, unless as medicine."

62. "An Anti-Temperance Society of Temperance Men," *Religious Herald*, 9 August 1833, 123. The antitemperance society referred to the proper use of alcohol as one of the "gifts of Deity." This view had precedents. The Dover Association in 1801, in a circular letter, described liquor to be both a "creature of God" and "designed by Heaven as a blessing to man." Quoted by Pearson, *Liquor and Anti-Liquor*, 38.

of social reform. These discussions stirred controversy and fueled dissent for decades.

Many Baptists thought churches should unite with and in fact displace temperance societies. They were jealous to keep the temperance effort under the banner of the church. The Boston Baptist Association recommended to its congregations in 1830 that they become temperance societies and "adopt such measures as shall secure universal and entire abstinence from inebriating liquors."[63] The Georgia Baptist pastor mentioned above noted that though he had nothing against societies in principle, he knew many Baptists who thought it "rather degrading" to join them: "They are of opinion that every religious society is a temperance society, and are therefore desirous that the religion of Christ should have all the credit of making people temperate."[64] These Baptists argued that the church ought to engage in social reform directly. They expressed no fear of the church veering from its core mission. Quite the contrary, the church is about spiritual salvation and physical restoration. M. Ellison, likewise, writing to the *Religious Herald* in 1851, concluded reform could best be accomplished through the church: "Let the church do her duty, and there is no longer need for other temperance organizations."[65]

Some Baptists took the opposite view, rejecting the union of church and temperance society. They believed that separation best served the church and the cause of temperance. These Baptists reasoned that societies are essentially civic organizations that must remain open to Christians and non-Christians. Therefore, a church whose membership is restricted to believers only cannot be a temperance society. J. H., writing to Philadelphia's *Christian Index* in 1832, described the temperance society as "a mixed multitude." He commended the composite status of benevolent societies on pragmatic grounds, noting that "civilization leans upon religious morality. It becomes necessary in this respect to unite and combine our efforts for the suppression of this prevailing evil." Thus, Christians ought to be willing to unite "with our neighbors and fellow citizens for the promotion and advancement of the common good."[66] J. H. saw a distinction between the sacred realm of the congregation and the secular business and membership of the benevolent society. He emphasized the

63. *Minutes*, Boston Baptist Association, 1830, 8.

64. "Temperance Societies Admonished," *Religious Herald*, 11 July 1829, 29.

65. M. Ellison, "Should Christians Unite with Sons of Temperance," *Religious Herald*, 17 July 1851, 113.

66. J. H., "Temperance Societies Approved," *Christian Index*, 9 May 1832, 306.

societies' role in promoting a moral civilization and not promulgating the Christian gospel.

Those who believed temperance societies should be severed from the church risked being criticized for advocating a secular cause. They drew the ire of reformers who saw the temperance movement as a means of spreading the gospel. Furthermore, many congregations promoted themselves as institutions, ordained by God, for the moral reformation of America. The ministers and churches who believed promoting temperance to be a part of their mission looked down upon those who advocated the separation of church and society.

Those who argued that the church is a temperance society risked secularizing the church. Congregations that served as societies blurred the distinction between their temporal and spiritual ministry. Some churches responded by folding the temperance movement into one of the church's core missions: upholding membership standards. Christians could disagree over whether the church should be a society but all could agree that each local church had the responsibility to purify its rolls. The "test-church" controversy arose when some Baptists used this reasoning to argue that a commitment to the temperance cause ought to be a test or qualification of church membership.[67]

On February 21, 1833, the Second Baptist Church in Richmond, Virginia, decided to hold its members accountable to the principles of the temperance movement:

> Resolved, that in future any members of this Church, who shall drink ardent spirits—or shall offer it to his friend in drink— when sickness does not require it—or who shall make a business of selling it to be drunk by persons in good health, shall be considered guilty of immoral conduct, and liable to be cited before the Church.[68]

The test church was not strictly a southern phenomenon. Baptists in the North had called for modifications of church covenants years earlier. In 1833 the First Providence Baptist Church of Rhode Island reported to the Warren Baptist Association, "This, as well as other churches in

67. Variations of the test-church first arose in the eighteenth century. The Elkhorn Baptist Association entertained a query from a local church regarding whether to accept into membership a person who sold alcohol. The association concluded the individual should be welcomed into the congregation without hesitation. See *Minutes*, Elkhorn Baptist Association, 1796, 473.

68. "Temperance Church," *Religious Herald*, 1 March 1833, 31.

Providence belonging to the Association, receive no members without a pledge to abstain from the use of ardent spirits."[69] It was in Virginia, however, that the issue of excluding members for refusing to adhere to the temperance cause became a heated controversy in the 1830s. Opposition to test churches must have surfaced for the *Herald* came to the defense of a Richmond church's action. Every Baptist admitted the church's right to exclude drunkards, the question at hand concerned whether moderate drinking of ardent spirits also could be prohibited. This case seemed clear to the *Herald's* editors:

> Has the church a right to decide on the morality or immorality of any practice of which her members are guilty . . . Are not ardent spirits used for sensual gratification, or as a stimulate or excitement. Can they be innocently used for any of these purposes? Is not the use of ardent spirits, in the smallest quantity, contrary to some of the plainest precepts of the Bible? Can Christians' gravity, temperance, sober-mindedness, non-conformity to the world be maintained by the moderate drinker? Has not the use of ardent spirits, or any other intoxicating liquor, a tendency to banish these Christian graces and virtues from the life and practice of the professor of religion?[70]

"Moderator" objected. He saw the test church as an unwarranted association between gospel ministry and social reformation: "The union of Church and Temperance societies, are repugnant to the genius and spirit of our Republican institutions. The grand features which distinguish our government from all others, are its many checks and balances, designed to counterpoise and correct all irregularities." The author supported temperance societies and believed that the act of churches excluding members for not pledging abstinence caused division, "a rending of churches," as he put it.[71]

Advocates of test churches believed the evil of intemperance required local churches to restrict their membership to those committed to the cause. The responsibility of churches to support temperance overshadowed an individual's freedom to drink intoxicating beverages. As one correspondent asserted, when an individual applied for membership to a church, "he is no longer at liberty to live to himself. He is under law to Christ, becomes the servant of Christ, and [the church], with the

69. "Abstract from the Letters," *Minutes*, Warren Baptist Association, 1833, 10.

70. "A Temperance Church," *Religious Herald*, 8 March 1833, 34.

71. Moderator [pseud.], "Temperance," *Religious Herald*, 22 August 1834, 131.

word of Christ in her hands, must claim of him the relinquishment of all that tends to grieve the righteous, or accelerate the sinner's progress to the pit."[72] Submission to Christ required the forfeiture of personal rights. "Moderator" was right, sometimes the result proved divisive.

Such was the case in 1847 at Salem Baptist Church, part of the Dover Baptist Association, and led by Andrew Broaddus. A small group in the church advocated turning the congregation into a test church. They introduced "temperance as a rule of church discipline." The need for greater focus on temperance came not primarily because moderate drinking plagued the church but because several cases of intoxication had proven scandalous. As a result, a cadre suggested total abstinence. Broaddus encouraged the members of his congregation to seek counsel on the matter through the pages of the *Religious Herald*. Before that action could be completed, his church split. The proponents failed to win a majority and, unwilling to serve in a congregation that countenanced moderate drinking, they "took letters of dismission, withdrew from Salem church, and formed a new church, in which abstinence from intoxicating drinks" became the practice.[73]

The issue of test churches arose in North Carolina where Thomas Meredith, editor of the *Biblical Recorder*, argued against them: "We do not think that churches constituted on gospel principles, as ours claim to be, possess the constitutional right, either to authorise, or to prohibit the use of any particular sorts of food or drink—for the obvious reason, that the sin consists, not in the kind used, but in the excess committed."[74]

Likewise in 1851 the Dover Baptist Association announced: "We are opposed to what are called 'tests.'" The association's temperance committee, instead, urged its member churches to greater vigilance: "Ought not the laws of God to be of paramount consideration in advocating and perpetuating every kind of reformation, civil or religious? Then the church ought to adopt such rules and regulations as are consonant with the word of God, and concentrate her efforts and bring her influence to bear more directly upon the habitual and intemperate use of strong drink, and thus purge herself from the accursed thing." By arguing that the Bible did not

---

72. T. [pseud.], "Temperance," *Religious Herald*, 29 August 1834, 135.

73. The members of the new church distinguished between total abstinence as a "test of fellowship" and a "rule of discipline." In short, they sought to regulate the conduct, not the admission of their members as it related to temperance. See Eli Ball, "Temperance, a Rule of Discipline," *Religious Herald*, 9 September 1847, 141–42.

74. Thomas Meredith, "Query," *Biblical Recorder*, 28 August 1847, 2.

offer enough evidence to defend subscription to abstinence as a qualification for membership but urging churches to adopt "rules and regulations" bearing on temperance, the Dover Baptists put pastors and churches in the awkward position of figuring out for themselves what stipulations did merit adoption.[75]

Meredith and the Dover Baptist Association did not deny that society needed to be transformed. Nor did they deny that Christians should be at the vanguard of such a change. They simply challenged the notion that the church, as the church, should advocate such a goal through means other than those that are purely spiritual:

> Should it be said that the present state of society needs to be reformed—that the most effectual way to prevent intoxication is to prevent the use of intoxicating liquors, etc.—we reply, this may all be very true. But still it may not be true that our churches are the proper places to carry on the work of such reforms.—Besides, our churches generally contain strifes and controversies enough, growing out of matters properly belonging to their jurisdiction, without subjecting them to the endless contentions incident to societies organized for purposes of social reform.[76]

A correspondent to the *Christian Watchman* shared similar concerns about the church being embroiled in humanitarian causes in an 1845 an essay entitled, "Social Reform, Not Christianity." He feared that the mission of the church had been eclipsed. He penned his words when the embers from the Second Great Awakening were barely smoldering and his words betrayed a spirit unimpressed with the social conscience of his peers. The temperance movement was to him a means of theological compromise instead of evangelical cooperation. The promise of social reform was ruined by the reality of doctrinal erosion:

> According to this theory, the Christian is no longer one, who receiving the Bible as his infallible guide, repents of sin and

75. Baptists in Rhode Island did not appear to suffer the same ambivalence. For nearly thirty years, the Warren Baptist Association reported the work of individual churches devoted to the cause of fighting intemperance. So, for example, in 1833, Somerset church in Rhode Island noted that "The cause of Temperance occupies its appropriate place; a matter in which we are unanimously agreed." "Abstract from the Letters," *Minutes*, Warren Baptist Association, 1833, 10. The church at New Shoreham, in 1849, described itself as being "active in the cause of Temperance," *Minutes*, Warren Baptist Association, 1849, 7. And in 1864, the Warren Association resolved to commit itself to the cause of temperance. *Minutes*, Warren Baptist Association, 1864, 8.

76. Meredith, "Query," 2.

believes in Christ, and aspires after immortality in a life of obedience to God and love to man. All the distinctive doctrines of the
cross are discarded or misstated, and the Christian is declared to
be one who, wholly irrespective of his religious creed, possesses
much of the milk of human kindness, in whom the kindly sympathies of our nature are in lively exercise, and who labors most
zealously and madly for the deliverance of man from social mis-
eries. The ideas of God and accountability, of heaven and hell, of
the atonement and regeneration and sanctification, of faith and
pardon, of prayer and holy living, are ridiculed as abstractions,
and are struck out to foist in a system of temporal improvements
under the name of gospel . . .. It is true that Christianity legiti-
mately promotes the temporal elevation of mankind, but then
this is, so to speak, rather its incidental benefit than its main
design, which is to save sinners from eternal wrath.[77]

The popularity of the temperance movement muffled the voices of
Baptists who wanted churches to extricate themselves from social reform
and, specifically, from the strategies employed by most reformers. J. C.,
Meredith, and later, Boyce, represented a minority position. Most leaders, from their platforms as editors, pastors, and chairmen of temperance
committees in associations, pleaded with anyone who would listen to
adopt the temperance cause and encouraged individuals and churches to
engage in the movement.

The voices of dissent could not compete. In 1836 the Charleston
Baptist Association in South Carolina issued a plea to Christians and
non-Christians, "to all lovers of good order and of human kind," to suppress intemperance. Be it the drunkard in need of rebuke and reformation, the Christian in need of encouragement to act, or the humanitarian
whose sympathies aligned with the temperance cause. The association
in Charleston, like the association in Dover, served the church. Its delegates, largely pastors, who attended this meeting, understood that the
temperance reformation was consonant with the mission of the church.
A concern for individual salvation had to include a concern for society
at large. Such statements paved the way for an overt political activism.
When it came to temperance reform, most pastors and churches came
to believe they had a public responsibility to serve a constituency larger
than their own congregation. Most Baptists had become sympathetic to
the cause of social reform; many had become social reformers.

77. J. C., "Social Reform, Not Christianity," *Christian Watchman*, 25 July 1845, 118.

Temperance and Politics

Political action was not the primary means employed by Baptists to promote the temperance movement, but it was not ignored. Baptists in fact often chose a political path. From the beginning of the movement but with increasing intensity as the movement progressed, direct social action—attempts by temperance reformers to change society's laws—attracted their attention.

Baptists indicated before the temperance movement started in full force that political action might be necessary. Eventually they decided to place pressure both on the conscience of American citizens and the levers of political power. As early as 1822, in one of the *Columbian Star's* first articles on the temperance crusade, the editors noted the necessity of government involvement and the inadequacy of a strategy that sought only to persuade the individual: "All our religious institutions, all our charitable and pauperism societies, all preaching and praying will not eradicate this wretched and awful evil, unless government interpose." The price of whiskey was too low not to be drunk, the editor argued, necessitating a tax.[78] In 1829 the *Star* included a report from the Jasper County Temperance Society, which resolved not to vote for any candidate known to use ardent spirits "with a view to gain election."[79] While the society's decision fell short of actually changing the law, it exceeded mere moral suasion. The temperance crusade was moving in the direction of political activism.

Reformers continued to lay a foundation for political reform in temperance addresses such as that presented by Dr. William Goodwin and published in the *Religious Herald* in 1832. Speaking to the Laurel Spring Temperance Society on July 4, Goodwin addressed the "virtue, health, happiness, [and] well being of society." Drunkenness is a matter of public concern: "The welfare and happiness of ourselves and our posterity depend in a great degree upon the preservation of good government and good order in society."[80] Goodwin made temperance reform a matter of civic discourse. If intemperance threatened "good government" then

78. "Intemperance," *Columbian Star*, 28 September 1822, 3.

79. "Jasper County Temperance Society," *Columbian Star and Christian Index*, 26 December 1829, 405.

80. "An Address delivered to the Laurel Spring Temperance Society," *Religious Herald*, 17, 24 August 1832, 125–26, 132.

those with an interest in the well-being of society must consider the necessity of a political solution.

Baptists in the North moved haltingly but steadily in the direction of political activism. In February 1826 the *Watchman* reprinted an article by William Collier calling for a paper devoted to the cause of benevolence, the *National Philanthropist*, which ran from 1826 through 1829. Besides the periodical, Collier suggested a society organized to petition Congress "to regulate duties on distilleries and ardent spirits, domestic and foreign, as might appear best calculated to promote the temperance and prosperity of the nation."[81] In 1833 the editors of the *Watchman* expressed displeasure at the discussion held by the Young Men's Temperance Society in Boston, when John Calhoun, Lucius M. Sargeant, and William Sullivan each spoke to the importance of government intervention for the sake of the virtue of America. Without condemning political action entirely, the editors lamented the lack of "homage . . . awarded to Christianity" in the proceedings.[82] Political issues heated up when in 1834 the Massachusetts legislature rejected a bill allowing towns to prohibit the licensing of liquor stores. The *Watchman* printed a letter to the editor opposing the legislature's action: "The people now have all the power; and it is for them to say, whether in opposition to their interest and that of their children, and in spite of their remonstrances these pauper, crime, disease, and death-causing manufactories, shall continue to be forced on them or not."[83] In 1838 the *Watchman* edged closer to supporting political action itself, noting that Massachusetts was well situated to outlaw the licensing of bars, but it still warned "legislative enactments in a moral cause, are worse than anything without moral power."[84] By 1838 the editors of the *Watchman* were willing to sanction a combination of political activism combined with moral suasion.

Passage of the Fifteen Gallon Law in July of 1838 by the Massachusetts legislature left the editors of the *Christian Watchman* in a dilemma. The law prohibited the sale of ardent spirits in quantities under fifteen gallons not intended for medicinal purposes—a true victory for temperance.[85] The editors had committed themselves to largely remain detached

81. William Collier, "Prospectus of a Weekly Paper," *Christian Watchman*, 10 February 1826, 39.

82. "Another Temperance Meeting," *Christian Watchman*, 8 March 1833, 38.

83. "Pleadings for Temperance," *Christian Watchman*, 28 March 1834, 50.

84. "The New License Law," *Christian Watchman*, 20 July 1838, 114.

85. Hampel, *Temperance and Prohibition*, 57.

from political issues but now the reformers had won a decisive victory
for the temperance movement: "How, then, shall our influence be exerted
on the present occasion, in regard to this law?" asked the editors. They
concluded that their support of the law and its enforcement should be
clear, public, and unrestrained due to the severity of the damage wrought
by drunkenness. Those who objected to legislating morality had simply
failed to grapple with the horrors wrought by abusing the bottle:

> We want, then, to go to them in the spirit of love, in the name
> of humanity and religion, and take them by the hand, and lead
> them through the tenements of poverty, the miserable garrets
> and cellars of intemperance, wretchedness and crime;—to con-
> duct them to alms houses, the hospitals, the jails, the peniten-
> tiaries, and the insane retreats, in our land;—to point them to
> the broken-hearted fathers, mothers, wives and sisters, which
> intemperance has made;—and in view of these facts, to ask
> them if they can oppose a law which originated in the purest
> motives, and the most exalted views, and which if heartily sup-
> ported and faithfully executed, will shed unnumbered blessings
> on our State, and cause its benign influences to be felt through-
> out the world.[86]

A government which chose to ignore the morality of its people, the
Watchman's editors insisted, might as well declare itself a tyranny since
a democracy populated by vicious citizens will soon find itself unable to
govern. "But happily the freemen of this State know that such a course
on the part of their legislators would be as gross a neglect of their proper
duties, as an attempt to coerce men into virtue, would be an absurd and
fruitless assumption."[87] The Fifteen Gallon Law made Boston Baptists
willing supporters of both social reform and political action.

With the passage of the Fifteen Gallon Law, interest in political
activity began to spread. The Charleston Baptist Association in 1840
encouraged every Christian to oppose "employing spirituous liquors to
influence elections . . . and to withhold his suffrage from every candidate,
who is known to resort to such measures."[88] A few years later, the same
association supported "every consistent means" to suppress intemperance. Given its willingness to encourage Christians to vote against anti-
temperance candidates, it is likely that "every consistent means" included

86. "The New License Law," *Christian Watchman*, 27 July 1838, 118.

87. "New License Law," *Christian Watchman*, 17 August 1838, 130.

88. *Minutes*, Charleston Baptist Association, 1840, 3–4.

political action.[89] Virginia entertained the issue of licensing bars in the 1840s. The *Herald* suggested the matter come before the people in an 1846 editorial.[90] The temperance committee of the Dover Baptist Association, also in 1846, resolved to form a subcommittee of three with the responsibility of memorializing the legislature with the purpose of leaving it to the voters of each county whether the sale of ardent spirits be permitted in that district.[91]

Another legislative victory, this time in Maine, encouraged Baptists, North and South, to continue their legislative battles. Passed in 1851, the Maine law prohibited the traffic of liquor throughout the state and is the first, statewide prohibition law.[92] Massachusetts, in 1852, passed its own prohibitory act. At the time, it garnered the support of a number of Baptist churches. The Boston South Baptist Association gave the sweeping legislation its stamp of approval:

> Resolved, That this Association humbly acknowledges its sense of gratitude to God for giving to our State a law known as "An Act Concerning the Manufacture and Sale of Spirituous or Intoxicating Liquors," and that we cordially approve of its faithful execution.[93]

Toward the end of the year, no doubt with this landmark bill in mind, the *Watchman* wrote about the government's responsibility to, at times, impinge upon the rights of the individual. Some may have thought that the periodical had once again blurred the line between church and state. However, the editors undoubtedly saw it as their role to make the state's duties clear. They argued that government is more than an earthly institution. God gave it the responsibility to ensure the morality of its populace: "The best moral condition and safety of its citizens, it is bound to seek, and, so far as possible, is bound to secure. Every vice which preys on the purity and peace of society, it must guard; and if need be, war against." Whether the attack came from gamblers, perjurers, swindlers, the lewd, or slanderers, the government had the right and responsibility

89. *Minutes*, Charleston Baptist Association, 1848, 11.

90. "Licensing Dram Shops: Why Not Leave It to the People?" *Religious Herald*, 15 January, 1846, 10. See Pearson, *Liquor and Anti-Liquor*, 122–23.

91. "Report of the Committee on Temperance," *Minutes*, Dover Baptist Association, 1846, 10.

92. Liquor could still be manufactured for medicinal purposes and for export. See Hanley, *Temperance and Prohibition*, 146.

93. *Minutes*, Boston South Baptist Association, 1852, 9.

to intercede—statutorily if necessary. In declaring the responsibility of the state to inculcate morality, the state admitted continuity with its colonial past. The theocracy may have been overthrown, but some of its principles remained alive and well: "In this respect, we have not outgrown the Puritan fathers." To ignore the responsibility of government to stamp out intemperance and, by implication, the role of the church to urge the government to play its role, is to resign society to a life of barbarity.[94]

As the nineteenth-century progressed Baptists seemed more comfortable turning toward the state to make whatever gains possible. In 1853 the Tennessee Concord Baptist Association noted that the intemperance crisis demanded "the enactment of a stern prohibitory law, positively forbidding the sale of ardent spirits as a beverage, and enforced by severe penalties."[95] William A. Whitsitt chaired the temperance committee which led the association to resolve that "as patriots, philanthropists, and christians, we believe it incumbent upon us to use all laudable efforts to secure the passage of this law." They expected pastors to carry these demands into the pulpit. These Tennessee Baptists embraced political activism. Likewise, in 1855 the New York Oneida Baptist Association regretted "the fearful ravages which intemperance has made in our enlightened land" and therefore resolved it to be incumbent upon "every Christian to exert his entire influence to aid the constituted authorities in enforcing the recently enacted Prohibitory Liquor Law."[96] Even in Virginia, a letter to the editor of the *Religious Herald* in 1856 suggests the popularity of legislative action among some Baptists.[97]

Most Baptists in the North and the South remained convinced that the church and the state had a role to play in ridding society of intemperance. Persuading sinners to give up intoxicating drink would always be central to the overall strategy because evangelism and the temperance cause went hand-in-hand. Evangelism was social reform, which made Baptists willing social reformers. But it did not stop there. Long before the prohibition movement of the 1870s that culminated in the eighteenth

---

94. "The Morals of Legislation," *Christian Watchman* 23 December 1852, 206.

95. *Minutes*, Concord Baptist Association, 1853, 11.

96. *Minutes*, Oneida Baptist Convention, 1855, 9.

97. "W" writing to the editor argued that the movement for prohibition became so popular that it all but killed the Sons of Temperance, a temperance society that depended upon its members agitating for temperance at the grass roots level. See W. [pseud.], "A Word to Sons of Temperance," *Religious Herald*, 15 May 1856, 74.

amendment to the federal constitution, many Baptists pressed for political support of their moral convictions.

Nonetheless, while select issues like temperance drove Baptists into the political realm, their first and most cherished method of social reform remained the transformation of the individual. They promoted the gospel as a vehicle of personal and public virtue. They engaged in political activism when necessary. Politics and piety went hand-in-hand.

8

Conclusion

THE MISTAKEN NOTION THAT Baptist piety had very little to do with earthly matters transcends historical discussions. The idea permeates popular culture. Truman Capote offered a compelling image of heaven in his classic short story "A Christmas Memory": "I've always thought a body would have to be sick and dying before they saw the Lord. And I imagined that when He came it would be like looking at the Baptist window: pretty as colored glass with the sun pouring through, such a shine you don't know it's getting dark." For the speaker, "Baptist" and "heaven" went hand-in-hand. Capote's point, much like that of Walt Whitman a hundred years earlier, is that God was to be experienced in the here and now. A spirituality that depends upon the future for its vindication, or even its culmination—characterized by the Baptist window in Capote's narrative—is unworthy of human dignity. Capote and Whitman wanted a religion they perceived to be of some earthly good.

Historians of social reform have had their own criticisms of Baptist spirituality. They do not contest that spirituality or a preeminent concern with salvation rested at the heart of Baptist life. Samuel S. Hill Jr. argued in his epilogue to John Lee Eighmy's now classic *Churches in Cultural Captivity*: "All studies on the religion practiced by Southern people concluded, the primary presupposition and concerns of popular religion are individualistic, centering on the salvation of each soul."[1] The claim, if sweeping, is difficult to contest. Yet Eighmy, Hill, and others have argued more than merely that southern religion promoted individual piety. They

---

1. John Lee Eighmy, *Churches in Cultural Captivity: A History of the Social Attitudes of Southern Baptists*, with an introduction and epilogue by Samuel S. Hill Jr. (Knoxville: University of Tennessee Press, 1972) 201.

insisted that by privileging individual piety Christians shortchanged the evangelical social conscience. This is the dominant premise of Eighmy's project: "Whether the theme is social responsibility, the nature of the church, basic theology, or the meaning of salvation, Southern Protestants think dominantly in individualistic terms. Images of theology and mission are thus not social in character."[2] The spiritual impulse, Eighmy and others argued, kept southern Baptists from committing themselves to social causes.

I have challenged such understandings of Baptist spirituality and social engagement. I have done this in two basic ways. First, I have tried to show that for Baptists spirituality or personal piety was never far removed from social action. I have disputed the notion that for Baptists, North and South, a dominant concern about the salvation of souls relegated social reform to secondary importance. They prized both. Throughout these chapters, I have drawn attention to themes of caution and withdrawal in Baptist life, themes that certainly fit the reigning thesis that spirituality actually impeded social reform. Nonetheless, Baptists regularly intended that evangelism and discipleship do more than bless the church—they serve the nation.

C. C. Goen dismissed such reasoning as naïve.[3] The antislavery reformers, he argued, should have known that conversions would not change society. At another time in history, Goen might have been right, but in the context of the Second Great Awakening the belief that real reform could come through personal transformation seemed a reasonable expectation. Baptists maintained that personal piety produced social change. Kathryn Teresa Long argued that the revival of 1857–1858 represented a turning point in the history of revivalism and social reform. From this point forward, reformers would spiritualize their expectations when it came to revivals and recalibrate their goals: "Any needed social transformation would result from the cumulative personal reforms of regenerate individuals and from the direct, supernatural intervention of

---

2. Ibid. For similar characterizations of the "spirituality inhibits social reform" thesis see Kenneth K. Bailey, *Southern White Protestantism in the Twentieth Century* (New York: Harper & Row, 1964) 43; Samuel S. Hill Jr., *The South and the North in American Religion* (Athens: The University of Georgia Press, 1980) 8; and C. C. Goen, *Broken Churches, Broken Nation: Denominational Schisms and the Coming of the American Civil War* (Macon, GA: Mercer University Press, 1985) 163–64.

3. Goen, *Broken Churches*, 163.

God."[4] Long presented a compelling argument that reformers of this era failed to capitalize on the momentum inaugurated by a national revival to generate a significant political victory. What she did not notice was that American Baptists had always counted on the cumulative effects of regeneration in individual lives. No sudden change gripped them in the mid-nineteenth century. Baptists and other evangelicals were simply trading on methods adopted for almost a century of American life.

No historian deserves more credit for uncovering the importance of religion in inspiring social reform than Timothy L. Smith.[5] Scholars continue to follow his lead when describing the importance of evangelicalism in the nineteenth century. I have benefited from Smith's analysis but have also been led to view the social effects of the Second Great Awakening in a different way. Whereas Smith saw the revivalism and social reform through the lens of the Oberlin Theology of Charles Finney, I have seen it through the Calvinism of nineteenth-century Baptists like Boston's Samuel Stillman and Barton Stow, and Virginia's Abner Clopton and John Broadus. Each lived during the rise of revivalism and the benevolent empire. Each advocated for the social welfare of their community. Their role in the social reform movement should not be overstated, but neither should it be obscured by the towering shadow of Finney.

Second, I have suggested that Baptists also engaged in direct social reform. They did not merely wait for society to change as evangelism had its intended effect. They raised their political voices, signed their memorials, and challenged their church members to support the state for the sake of society's welfare. Eighmy conceded that southern Baptists had a social conscience: "Southern Baptists, from their colonial beginnings, have responded to social issues more significantly than is generally recognized."[6] He pinpointed the split over slavery as the moment the denomination came "to terms with its environment." Like Long, he marked the mid-nineteenth century as an important turning point in evangelical thought. Prior to this turning point, he seemed to suggest, Baptists were "not captive" to the culture. Their activities showed lives and ministries responsive to the social needs of their environment. However, with the exception of a brief and secondary treatment of antislavery advocates Da-

4. Kathryn Teresa Long, *The Revival of 1857–58: Interpreting an American Religious Awakening* (New York: Oxford, 1998) 125.

5. Timothy L. Smith, *Revivalism and Social Reform in Mid-Nineteenth Century America* (New York: Abingdon, 1957).

6. Eighmy, *Churches in Cultural Captivity*, x.

vid Barrow and Carter Tarrant, Eighmy dropped any further exploration of the social conscience of Baptists prior to the mid-nineteenth century.

This book resolves that omission. I have presented Baptists, both northern and southern, not simply as ministers, newspaper editors, and churchmen interested in evangelism, but often as social reformers, anxious to deliberate over, engage in, and influence the social and political issues of the day. Sometimes this resulted in social welfare, like the Baptist church in Savannah, Georgia, forming a poverty relief committee when the city failed to take action. Sometimes it resulted in directives, as when the Charleston Baptist Association of South Carolina recommended its delegates withdraw their support from any candidates who used "spirituous liquors" to win an election. Occasionally it meant criticizing the federal government. So Thomas Meredith, editor of North Carolina's *Biblical Recorder*, angered some of his readers when he publicly opposed the Mexican War.

None of these examples are meant to deny the strong, otherworldly spiritual impulse in Baptist life. They show, instead, a diversity of opinion. As Christine Heyrman argued, "evangelicalism has never been a static, monolithic structure of belief and that its adherents have never been an undifferentiated mass."[7] Baptists wrestled with two competing interests— the spiritual and social goals of the church. Civil crises often drove this competition into the background. Baptists acted directly, socially, and politically. Baptists considered their personal piety to be consistent with and in fact necessary for the public welfare. They did not, however, always depend solely upon their piety. At times, when the occasion demanded it, they spoke up or acted out immediately.

Hugh Heclo has argued that the results of nineteenth-century Christian social engagement persist into the present: "Despite misgivings about marrying Christianity to various worldly projects to do good, there have been few doubts about a larger bond that has grown over the centuries. It is the bond uniting Christianity and the democratic faith in the political society that is America."[8] To be a Christian today is to remain committed to a "sanctified vision of the Nation's mission."[9] Heclo rightly assessed the ambivalence that existed among evangelicals during the Sec-

7. Christine Leigh Heyrman, *Southern Cross: The Beginnings of the Bible Belt* (New York: Knopf, 1997) 254.

8. Hugh Heclo, ed., *Christianity and American Democracy* (Cambridge, MA: Harvard University Press, 2007) 76.

9. Ibid.

ond Great Awakening, a tension between social reform that derived from the spiritual as opposed to the political experience. Baptists, from the Revolution to the Civil War, from the North and the South, contributed to the creation of this vision. They advocated a practical spirituality. They insisted their personal piety have public effects. They believed that virtue was both God-given and gospel-induced, and they preached that the success and well-being of the nation depended on its broad diffusion. In so doing, they contributed to a religious national identity, an identity that persists today.

Bibliography

Abbot, Abiel. *An Address Delivered before the Massachusetts Society for Suppressing Intemperance*. Cambridge, MA: Hilliard and Metcalf, 1815.

———. *A Discourse Delivered Before the Members of the Portsmouth Female Asylum, On the Lord's Day, August 9, 1807*. Portsmouth, NH: Stephan Sewall, 1807.

———. *Traits of Resemblance in the People of the United States of America*. Haverhill, MA: Moore & Stebbins, 1799.

Adams, Ezra Eastman. *The Pulpit a Civilizer*. New Hampshire: n.p.,1860.

Ahlstrom, Sydney E. *A Religious History of the American People*. New Haven, CT: Yale University Press, 1972.

Albaugh, Gaylord P. *History and Annotated Bibliography of American Religious Periodicals and Newspapers*. 2 vols. Worcester, MA: American Antiquarian Society, 1994.

Andrew, John A., III. *From Revivals to Removal: Jeremiah Evarts, the Cherokee Nation, and the Search for the Soul of America*. Athens: University of Georgia Press, 1992.

Angus, Joseph. *Christian Churches, the Noblest Form of Social Life: The Representatives of Christ on Earth, the Dwelling Place of the Holy Spirit*. London: Jackson, Walford & Hodder, 1864.

Anonymous. "To the People of the United States." Virginia Society for Promoting the Observance of the Christian Sabbath. N.p., n.d.

Armitage, Thomas. *The Funeral Sermon on the Death of Rev. Spencer Houghton Cone . . . Sept. 16, 1855*. New York: Holman & Gray, 1855.

Asplund, John. *The Annual Register of the Baptist Denomination*. Goodlettsville, TN: Church History and Research Archives, 1791. Reprint, 1979.

Atherton, John. *Christian Social Ethics: A Reader*. Cleveland: Pilgrim, 1994.

Ayers, Edward L., and John C. Willis, eds., *The Edge of the South: Life in Nineteenth-Century Virginia*. Charlottesville: University Press of Virginia, 1991.

———. *Vengeance and Justice: Crime and Punishment in the Nineteenth-Century American South*. New York: Oxford University Press, 1984.

Backus, Charles. *The Folly of Man's Choosing This World For His Portion*. Boston: Samuel Hall, 1796.

Backus, Isaac. *An Abridgement of the Church History of New England from 1602 to 1804*. Boston: E. Lincoln, 1804.

———. *An Appeal to the Public for Religious Liberty*. In *Isaac Backus on Church, State, and Calvinism Pamphlets, 1754–1789*, edited by William G. McLoughlin. Cambridge, MA: Belknap, 1968.

————. *The Diary of Isaac Backus*. Edited by William G. McLoughlin. Providence, RI: Brown University Press, 1979.

————. *A History of New England: With Particular Reference to the Baptists*. New York: Arno, 1969.

————. *A History of the Baptist Warren Association in New England from the Year 1767, to the Year 1792*. N.p., 1792.

————. *The Infinite Importance of the Obedience of Faith, and of a Separation from the World, Opened and Demonstrated*. Boston: Samuel Hall, 1791.

————. *Isaac Backus on Church, State, and Calvinism; Pamphlets, 1754–1789*. Edited by William G. McGlouglin. Cambridge, MA: Belknap, 1968.

————. *The Kingdom of God, Described by His Word, with its Infinite Benefits to Human Society*. Boston: Samuel Hall, 1972.

Bacon, Joel Smith. *An Inaugural Address, Delivered in Georgetown*. Georgetown, KY: N. L. Finnell, 1830.

Bacote, Vincent E. *The Spirit in Public Theology: Appropriating the Legacy of Abraham Kuyper*. Grand Rapids: Baker Academic, 2005.

Bailey, David T. *Shadow on the Church: Southwestern Evangelical Religion and the Issue of Slavery, 1783–1860*. Ithaca, NY: Cornell University Press, 1985.

Bailey, Kenneth. *Southern White Protestantism in the Twentieth Century*. New York: Harper & Row, 1964.

Baker, Joseph. *The Question of the Age*. Nashville: South-Western, 1857.

Baker, Robert A. *Relations Between Northern and Southern Baptists*. Fort Worth, TX: n.p., 1948.

————. *The Southern Baptist Convention and Its People, 1607–1972*. Nashville: Broadman, 1974.

Baldwin, Thomas. *Brief Sketch of the Revival of Religion in Boston in 1803–1805*. Boston: Lincoln & Edmands, 1826.

————. *Christian Baptism, as Delivered to the Churches*. Boston: Lincoln & Edmands, 1812.

————. *A Discourse Delivered Before the Members of the Boston Female Asylum, September 26, 1806, Being Their Sixth Anniversary*. Boston: Russell & Cutler, 1806.

————. *The Eternal Purpose of God, the Foundation of Effectual Calling*. Boston: Manning & Loring, 1804.

————. *The Happiness of a People Illustrated and Explained*. Boston: Adams and Rhoades, 1805.

————. *Series of Letters: In Which the Distinguishing Sentiments of Baptists are Explained and Vindicated*. Boston: Manning and Loring, 1810.

————. *A Sermon, Delivered at Boston . . . at a Quarterly Meeting of Several Churches for Special Prayer*. Boston: Manning & Loring, 1799.

————. *A Sermon, Delivered Before His Excellency Caleb Strong, esq . . . May 26, 1802: Being the Day of General Election*. Boston: Young and Minns, 1802.

————. *A Sermon Delivered the Day of Public Thanksgiving*. Boston: Manning & Loring, 1795.

————. *A Sermon Preached February 15, 1802, Before the Honourable Senate and House of Representatives of the Commonwealth of Massachusetts*. Boston: Young and Minns, 1802.

Banner, Lois W. "Religious Benevolence as Social Control: A Critique of an Interpretation." *The Journal of American History* 60 (1973) 23–41.

Banner, Stuart. *The Death Penalty: An American History.* Cambridge, MA: Harvard University Press, 2002.

Baptist, Edward. *The Diary of Edward Baptist: Letters to the Pamphleteer.* N. p., 1830.

Bardaglio, Peter W. *Reconstructing the Household: Families, Sex, and Law in the Nineteenth-Century South.* Chapel Hill: University of North Carolina Press, 1995.

Barnes, Gilbert Hobbs. *The Antislavery Impulse, 1830–1844.* New York: D. Appleton-Century, 1933.

Barnes, William W. *The Southern Baptist Convention, 1845–1953.* Nashville: Broadman & Holman, 1945.

Barrow, David. "Diary of David Barrow, Pioneer Baptist Minister, Virginia–Kentucky." Archives and Special Collections, James P. Boyce Centennial Library. Southern Baptist Theological Seminary Special Collections, Louisville, Kentucky.

———. *Involuntary, Unmerited, Perpetual, Absolute, Hereditary Slavery, Examined; On the Principles of Nature, Reason, Justice, Policy, and Scripture.* Lexington, KY: D & C Bradford, 1808.

Bassett, John Spencer. *Slavery in the State of North Carolina.* Baltimore: The Johns Hopkins Press, 1899.

Bassett, Paul Merritt. "Exploring the Social Vision of the Wesleyan Movement." *Wesleyan Theological Journal* 25 (1990) 7–129.

Bates, Barnabas. *An Address Delivered at a General Meeting of the Citizens of the City of New-York to Express Their Sentiments on the Memorials to Congress.* New York: Office of the Gospel Herald, 1830.

Bauman, Michael, and David Hall, eds. *God and Caesar: Selected Essays from the 1993 Evangelical Theological Society's Convention in Washington, DC.* Camp Hill, PA: Christian Publications, 1994.

Beecher, Lyman. *Autobiography.* Vol. 1. New York: Harper & Brothers, 1866.

———. *A Plea for the West.* 2nd ed. Cincinnati: Truman & Smith, 1835.

———. *Six Sermons on the Nature, Occasions, Signs, Evils, and Remedy of Intemperance.* 10th ed. Boston: Perkins & Marvin, 1829.

Beeman, Richard, ed. *Beyond Confederation: Origins of the Constitution and American National Identity.* Chapel Hill: University of North Carolina Press, 1987.

Bender, Thomas. *Toward an Urban Vision: Ideas and Institutions in Nineteenth-Century America.* Baltimore: Johns Hopkins University Press, 1975.

Benedict, David. *An Abridgement of the General History of the Baptist Denomination in America.* Boston: Lincoln & Edwards, 1820.

Bergman, Jill, and Debra Bernardi, eds. *Our Sisters' Keepers: Nineteenth-Century Benevolence Literature by American Women.* Tuscaloosa: University of Alabama Press, 2005.

Berk, Steven. *Calvinism versus Democracy; Timothy Dwight and the Origins of American Evangelical Orthodoxy.* Hamden, CT: Archon,1974.

Bernhard, Virginia. *Slaves and Slaveholders in Bermuda, 1616–1782.* Columbia: University of Missouri Press, 1999.

Biggs, Joseph. *A Concise History of the Kehukee Baptist Association.* Tarborough, NC: George Howard, 1834.

Birdsall, Richard D. "The Second Great Awakening and the New England Social Order." *Church History* 39 (September 1970) 345–64.

Birdwhistell, Ira. *The Baptists of the Bluegrass: A History of the Elkhorn Association, 1785–1985.* Berea, KY: Berea College Press, 1985.

Birney, James Gillespie. *The American Churches, the Bulwarks of American Slavery.* Newburyport, MA: Charles Whipple, 1842. Reprint, New York: Arno, 1969.

Birney, William. *James G. Birney and His Times.* New York: D. Appleton, 1890.

Blakely, William Addison, ed. *American State Papers Bearing on Sunday Legislation.* Washington, DC: The Religious Liberty Association, 1911.

Bliss, George Ripley. *The Place of Baptists in Protestant Christendom.* Philadelphia: The Society, 1862.

Blocker, Jack S. *American Temperance Movements: Cycles of Reform.* Boston: Twayne, 1989.

Bloesch, Donald G. *The Invaded Church.* Waco, TX: Word, 1975.

Blumhoefer, Edith L., ed. *Religion, Politics, and the American Experience: Reflections on Religion and American Public Life.* Tuscaloosa: University of Alabama Press, 2002.

Bode, Frederick A. *Protestantism and the New South: North Carolina Baptists and Methodists in Political Crisis.* Charlottesville: University Press of Virginia, 1975.

Bodo, John R. *The Protestant Clergy and Public Issues, 1812–1848.* Princeton, NJ: Princeton University Press, 1954.

Bogger, Tommy L. *Free Blacks in Norfolk, Virginia, 1790–1860: The Darker Side of Freedom.* Charlottesville: University Press of Virginia, 1997.

Boles, John B. *The Great Revival, 1787–1805: The Origins of the Southern Evangelical Mind.* Lexington: University of Kentucky Press, 1972.

———. *The Irony of Southern Religion.* New York: Peter Lang, 1994.

Boyd, Jesse L. *A History of Baptists in America, Prior to 1845.* New York: American Press, 1957.

Boyer, Paul. *Mission on Taylor Street: The Founding and Early Years of the Dayton Brethren in Christ Mission.* Grantham, PA: Brethren in Christ Historical Society, 1987.

Boylan, Anne M. *Sunday School: The Formation of an American Institution, 1790–1880.* New Haven, CT: Yale University Press, 1988.

Braaten, Carl E., and Robert W. Jenson, eds. *The Two Cities of God: The Church's Responsibility for the Earthly City.* Grand Rapids: Eerdmans, 1997.

Brack, Gene M. *Mexico Views Manifest Destiny, 1821–1846: An Essay on the Origins of the Mexican War.* Albuquerque: University of New Mexico Press, 1975.

Brackney, William H. *Baptists in North America.* Malden, MA: Blackwell, 2006.

———. *A Genetic History of Baptist Thought.* Macon, GA: Mercer University Press, 2004.

Brantly, William T. "The Pure Church, Characterized by Spirituality." *Baptist Pamphlets,* vol 2. Philadelphia: American Baptist Publication Society, 1854.

Bremner, Robert H. *The Public Good: Philanthropy and Welfare in the Civil War Era.* New York: Alfred A. Knopf, 1980.

Broadus, John A. "Address to Berryville Total Abstinence Society." May 1846. Broadus-Mitchell Family Papers. Archives and Special Collections, James P. Boyce Centennial Library, Southern Baptist Theological Seminary Special Collections, Louisville, Kentucky.

———. "On Sensation Preaching." Manuscript Notebook. The John A. Broadus Collection. Archives and Special Collections, James P. Boyce Centennial Library, Southern Baptist Theological Seminary Special Collections, Louisville, Kentucky.

Brockway, Duncan. "More American Temperance Song-Books." *Hymn* 22 (1971) 54–56.

———. "More American Temperance Song-Books." *Hymn* 25 (1974) 82–84.

Brown, Christopher Leslie. *Moral Capital: Foundations of British Abolitionism*. Chapel Hill: University of North Carolina Press, 2006.

Brown, Stewart J. "Reform, Reconstruction, Reaction: The Social Vision of Scottish Presbyterianism." *Scottish Journal of Theology* 44 (1991) 489–517.

Brownson, Orestes. *New Views of Christianity, Society, and the Church*. N.p., 1836.

Burch, Walter Jarrett. "A Historical and Theological Inquiry into the Impact of Adeil Sherwood in the Establishment of Georgia Baptist Institutions." PhD diss., Southern Baptist Theological Seminary, 2001.

Burgess, Roger. "Whatever Happened to the Temperance Movement?" *Christian Century* 82 (1965) 984–87.

Burin, Eric. *Slavery and the Peculiar Institution: A History of the American Colonization Society*. Gainesville: University Press of Florida, 2005.

Burkitt, Lemuel. *A Concise History of the Kehukee Baptist Association*. Halifax, NC: A. Hodge, 1803. Revised by Henry L. Burkitt, Philadelphia: Lippincott, 1850.

Burns, Eric. *The Spirits of America: A Social History of Alcohol*. Philadelphia: Temple University Press, 2004.

Bush, Russ L., and Thomas J. Nettles, eds. *Baptists and the Bible*. Rev. ed. Nashville: Broadman & Holman, 1999.

Bushman, Richard. *The Refinement of America: Persons, Houses, Cities*. New York: Vintage, 1993.

Buss, Dietrich. "The Millennial Vision as Motive for Religious Benevolence and Reform: Timothy Dwight and the New England Evangelicals Reconsidered." *Fides et Historia* 16 (1983) 18–34.

Callender, John. *An Historical Discourse, on the Civil and Religious Affairs of the Colony of Rhode Island*. 1843. Reprint, Freeport, NY: Books for Libraries, 1971.

Carpenter, Joel A. *Revive Us Again: The Reawakening of American Fundamentalism*. New York: Oxford University Press, 1997.

Carson, Donald A. *Christ and Culture Revisited*. Grand Rapids: Eerdmans, 2008.

Carter, Stephen L. *The Culture of Disbelief: How American Law and Politics Trivialize Religious Devotion*. New York: Anchor, 1993.

Carwardine, Richard. *Evangelicals and Politics in Antebellum America*. New Haven, CT: Yale University Press, 1993.

Case, Shirley Jackson. *The Social Triumph of the Ancient Church*. London: George Allen & Unwin, 1934.

Cashdollar, Charles D. "The Social Implications of the Doctrine of Divine Providence, RI: A Nineteenth-Century Debate in American Theology." *Harvard Theological Review* 71 (1978) 265–84.

Catherwood, Christopher. *Whose Side is God On? Nationalism and Christianity*. London: SPCK, 2003.

Chase, Irah. *The Value of a Soul: A Sermon Preached December 28, 1825 at the Ordination of Mr. James D. Knowles*. Boston: Lincoln & Edmands, 1826.

Cherry, Conrad, ed. *God's New Israel: Religious Interpretations of American Destiny*. Chapel Hill: University of North Carolina Press, 1998.

Christian Watchman and *Watchman-Examiner*. Boston, Massachusetts. 1819–1860.

Church, Pharcellus. *Antioch: or, The Increase of Moral Power in the Church of Christ*. Boston: Gould, Kendall, & Lincoln, 1843.

————. *Seed-Truths, or, Bible-Views of Mind, Morals, and Religion*. New York: Sheldon, 1871.

Chute, Anthony L. *A Piety Above the Common Standard: Jesse Mercer and the Defense of Evangelistic Calvinism*. Macon, GA: Mercer University Press, 2004.

Clarke, Thomas Erskine. "Thomas Smyth: Moderate of the Old South." ThD thesis, Union Theological Seminary, 1970.

Clements, Keith W. *A Patriotism for Today: Dialogue with Dietrich Bonhoeffer*. Bristol, UK: Bristol Baptist College, 1984.

Clopton, Abner W., and Eli Ball, eds. *Wisdom's Voice to the Rising Generation: Being a Selection of the Best Addresses and Sermons on Intemperance*. Philadelphia: n.p., 1828.

Coffey, John J. "A Political History of the Temperance Movement in New York State, 1808–1920." PhD diss., Pennsylvania State University, 1976.

Coker, Joe L. "A Bibliography of American Temperance Hymnals, 1835–1934." *Hymn* 51 (2000) 28–36.

————. *Liquor in the Land of the Lost Cause: Southern White Evangelicals and the Prohibition Movement*. Lexington: The University of Kentucky Press, 2007.

Cole, Charles C., Jr. *The Social Ideas of Northern Evangelicals*. New York: Columbia University Press, 1964.

Coleman, Peter J. *The Transformation of Rhode Island, 1790–1860*. Providence, RI: Brown University Press, 1963.

Columbian Star and *Christian Index* . Washington, DC (1822–1827); Philadelphia, PA, (1827–1833); and Washington, Penfield, Macon, and Atlanta, GA (1833–1865).

Cone, Edward W. *Some Account of the Life of Spencer Houghton Cone: A Baptist Preacher in America*. New York: Livermore & Rudd, 1856.

Cone, Spencer Houghton. *The Bible, its Excellence, and the Duty of Distributing it in its Purity: With a History of Bible Societies*. New York: E. H. Tripp, 1852.

————. *A Summary of the Faith and Practice with the Articles of the Covenant, of the First Baptist Church, in the City of New York*. New York: John Gray, 1841.

Conforti, Joseph. "Edwardsians, Unitarians, and the Memory of the Great Awakening, 1800–1840." In *American Unitarianism: 1805–1865*, edited by Conrad Edick Wright, 31–50. Boston: Northeastern University Press, 1989.

Congressional Temperance Society. *First Annual Report of the Congressional Temperance Society . . . Held at the Capitol in Washington City, February 25, 1834*. Washington, DC: Jacob Gideon, Jr, 1834.

Cook, Joseph B. *The Good and Faithful Servant . . . A Funeral Sermon Occasioned by the Much Lamented Death of the Rev. Richard Furman*. Charleston, SC: South Carolina Baptist Convention, 1826.

Cornelius, Janet Duitsman. *When I Can Read My Title Clear: Literacy, Slavery, and Religion in the Antebellum South*. Columbia: University of South Carolina Press, 1991.

Cousins, Norman. *"In God We Trust": The Religious Beliefs and Ideas of the American Founding Fathers*. New York: Harper & Row, 1958.

Crane, C. B. "The Spiritual Constitution of the Christian Church." In *The Madison Avenue Lectures*. Philadelphia: American Baptist Publication Society, 1867.

Creed, Brad. "John Leland and Sunday Mail Delivery: Religious Liberty, Evangelical Piety, and the Problem of a 'Christian Nation.'" *Fides et Historia* 33 (2001) 1–11.

Crofts, Daniel. *Old Southampton: Politics and Society in a Virginia County, 1834–1869.* Charlottesville: University Press of Virginia, 1992.

Cromartie, Michael, ed. *Caesar's Coin Revisited: Christians and the Limits of Government.* Washington, DC: Ethics and Public Policy Center, 1996.

Cully, Kendig Brubaker, and F. Nile Harper, eds. *Will the Church Lose the City?* New York: World Publishing, 1969.

Curry, Thomas J. *Farewell to Christendom: The Future of Church and State in America.* Oxford: Oxford University Press, 2001.

Cyclopedia of Temperance, Prohibition and Public Morals. Cincinnati: The Methodist Book Concern, 1917.

D'Costa, Gavin. *Theology in the Public Square: Church, Academy and Nation.* Malden, MA: Blackwell, 2005.

Dagg, J. L. *Manual of Theology and Church Order.* 2 vols. Charleston, SC: Southern Baptist Publication Society, 1858. Reprint, Harrisonburg, VA: Gano, 1990.

Dahlberg, Bruce T. "Before Emancipation: Massachusetts Baptists and the Nineteenth-Century Antislavery Struggle." *American Baptist Quarterly* 21 (2002) 51–64.

Daly, John Patrick. *When Slavery Was Called Freedom: Evangelicalism, Proslavery, and the Causes of the Civil War.* Lexington: University Press of Kentucky, 2002.

Danforth, John. *Faith and Politics: How the "Moral Values" Debate Divides America and How to Move Forward Together.* New York: Viking, 2006.

Dargan, Edwin Charles. *Ecclesiology: A Study of the Church.* 2nd ed. Louisville, KY: Charles T. Dearing, 1905.

———. *Society, Kingdom and Church.* Philadelphia: American Baptists Publication Society, 1907.

Davis, David Brion. *Inhuman Bondage: The Rise and Fall of Slavery in the New World.* New York: Oxford University Press, 2006.

———. *The Problem of Slavery in the Age of Revolution, 1770–1823.* Ithaca, NY: Cornell University Press, 1975.

Davis, Derek H. *Religion and the Continental Congress, 1774–1789.* Oxford: Oxford University Press, 2000.

Davis, George Harron. *Between Caesar and Jesus.* New York: T. Y. Crowell, 1899.

Davis, Lawrence. *Immigrants, Baptists, and the Protestant Mind in America.* Urbana: University of Illinois Press, 1973.

Dawson, Joseph M. *Baptists and the American Republic.* Nashville: Broadman, 1956.

Dayton, Donald W. *Discovering an Evangelical Heritage.* New York: Harper & Row, 1976.

Demy, Timothy J., and Gary P. Stewart. *Politics and Public Policy: A Christian Response.* Grand Rapids: Kregel, 2000.

Djupe, Paul A., and Christopher P. Gilbert. *The Prophetic Pulpit: Clergy, Churches, and Communities in American Politics.* Oxford: Rowman & Littlefield, 2003.

Dorrien, Gary J. *The Making of American Liberal Theology: Idealism, Realism, and Modernity, 1900–1950.* Louisville, KY: John Knox, 2003.

Dreisbach, Daniel L. "Bills Reported by the Committee of Revisors Appointed by the General Assembly of Virginia in 1776, 18 June 1779." In *Thomas Jefferson and the Wall of Separation between Church and State,* appendix 3. New York: New York University Press, 2002.

Dubois, Laurent. *Avengers of the New World: The Story of the Haitian Revolution.* Cambridge, MA: Belknap, 2005.

Dumbauld, Edward, ed. *The Political Writings of Thomas Jefferson*. New York: Harper & Row, 1955.

Durkheim, Emile. *The Elementary Forms of Religious Life: A Study in Religious Sociology*. Translated by Joseph Ward Swain. London: George Allen & Unwin, 1915. Reprint, New York: Free Press, 1995.

Dusing, Michael Lee. "The Relation of the Second Great Awakening to Social Reform Movements in America." ThM thesis, Columbia University, 1991.

Dwight, Timothy. *The Charitable Blessed: A Sermon Preached in the First Church in New-Haven, August 8, 1810*. New Haven, CT: Sidney's, 1810.

———. *The Duty of Americans, at the Present Crisis: Illustrated in a Discourse, Preached on the Fourth of July, 1798*. New Haven, CT: Thomas and Samuel Green, 1798.

Earle, Jonathan Halperin. *Jacksonian Antislavery and the Politics of Freesoil, 1824–1854*. Chapel Hill: University of North Carolina Press, 2004.

Eaton, George Washington. *Claims of Civil and Ecclesiastical History as Indispensable Branches of Ministerial Education*. Utica, NY: Bennett, Backus, & Hawley, 1841.

———. *An Inaugural Address: Delivered in the Chapel of the Hamilton Literary & Theological Seminary, June 4, 1834*. Utica, NY: Bennett & Bright, 1835.

Eberly, Don E., "Preface." In *The Content of America's Character: Recovering Civic Virtue*. Lanham, MD: Madison, 1995.

Edwards, Wendy J. Deichmann. *Forging an Ideology for American Missions: Josiah Strong and Manifest Destiny*. Cambridge, MA: Currents in World Christianity Project, 1998.

———. "Manifest Destiny, the Social Gospel and the Coming Kingdom: Josiah Strong's Program of Global Reform, 1885–1916." In *Perspectives on the Social Gospel*, edited by Christopher H. Evans, 81–116. Lewiston, NY: Edwin Mellen, 1999.

Egerton, Douglas R. *He Shall Go Out Free: The Lives of Denmark Vesey*. Lanham, MD: Rowman & Littlefield, 2004.

Eighmy, John Lee. *Churches in Cultural Captivity: A History of Social Attitudes of Southern Baptists*. With an introduction and epilogue by Samuel S. Hill Jr. Knoxville: University of Tennessee Press, 1972.

Elmore, F. H. *Correspondence Between the Hon. F. H. Elmore, One of the South Carolina Delegation in Congress, and James G. Birney, One of the Secretaries of the American Anti-Slavery Society*. New York: American Anti-Slavery Society, 1838.

Emmons, William, Ashel Langworthy, and Ely Moore. *Authentic Biography of Col. Richard M. Johnson, of Kentucky*. New York: H. Mason, 1833.

Engeman, Thomas S., and Michael P. Zuckert, eds. *Protestantism and the American Founding*. Notre Dame: University of Notre Dame Press, 2004.

Ericson, David F. *The Debate over Slavery: Antislavery and Proslavery Liberalism in Antebellum America*. New York: New York University Press, 2000.

Ernst, William J. "Urban Leaders and Social Change: The Urbanization Process in Richmond, Virginia, 1840–1880." PhD diss., University of Virginia, 1978.

Eslinger, Ellen. "The Brief Career of Rufus W. Bailey, American Colonization Society Agent in Virginia." *The Journal of Southern History* 1 (February 2005) 39–74.

Essig, James D. *The Bonds of Wickedness: American Evangelicals Against Slavery, 1770–1808*. Philadelphia: Temple University Press, 1982.

———. "The Lord's Free Man: Charles G. Finney and His Abolitionism." In *Abolitionism and American Religion*, edited by John R. McKivigan, 319–39. New York: Garland, 1999.

Estes, Todd. *The Jay Treaty Debate, Public Opinion, and the Evolution of Early American Political Culture.* Amherst: University of Massachusetts Press, 2006.

Evarts, Jeremiah, ed. *An Account of Memorials Presented to Congress During its Last Session, By Numerous Friends of Their Country and its Institutions.* New York: Published at the Request of Many Petitioners, 1829.

Farmer, James Oscar. *The Metaphysical Confederacy: James Henley Thornwell and the Synthesis of Southern Values.* Macon, GA: Mercer University Press, 1986.

Faust, Drew Gilpin. "Evangelicalism and the Meaning of the Proslavery Argument: The Reverend Thornton Stringfellow of Virginia." *Virginia Magazine of History and Biography* 85 (January 1977) 3–17.

Ferguson, John. "In Honor of Robert Raikes." *Baptist Quarterly* 28 (1980) 342–54.

Finkelman, Paul, ed. *Religion and Slavery.* New York: Garland, 1989.

Finley, John Miller. "Edwin Charles Dargan: Baptist Denominationalist in a Changing South." PhD diss., Southern Baptist Theological Seminary, 1984.

First Annual Report of the General Union for Promoting the Observance of the Christian Sabbath. New York: J. Collord, 1829.

Flowers, Betsy. "Southern Baptist Evangelicals or Social Gospel Liberals? The Woman's Missionary Union and Social Reform. 1888–1928." *American Baptist Quarterly* 19 (2000) 106–28.

Flynt, Wayne J. *Alabama Baptists: Southern Baptists in the Heart of Dixie.* Tuscaloosa: University of Alabama Press, 1998.

———. "Southern Baptists and Reform: 1890–1920." *Baptist History and Heritage* 7 (1972) 211–23.

———. "Southern Baptists: Rural to Urban Transition." *Baptist History and Heritage* 16 (1981) 24–34.

Forbes, Robert P. "Slavery and the Evangelical Enlightenment." In *Religion and the Antebellum Debate over Slavery,* edited by John R. McKivigan and Mitchell Snay, 68–108. Athens: University of Georgia Press, 1998.

Forrester, Duncan B. *Christian Justice and Public Policy.* Cambridge: Cambridge University Press, 1997.

Foster, Charles I. *An Errand of Mercy: The Evangelical United Front, 1790–1837.* Chapel Hill: University of North Carolina Press, 1960.

Freehling, William W. *Prelude to Civil War: The Nullification Controversy in South Carolina, 1816–1836.* New York: Harper & Row, 1966.

Frelinghuysen, Theodore. *Speech of Mr. Frelinghuysen on His Resolution Concerning Sabbath Mails in the Senate of the United States, May 8, 1830.* Washington, DC: Rothwell & Ustick, 1830.

Frick, John W. *Theatre, Culture, and Temperance Reform in Nineteenth-Century America.* New York: Cambridge University Press, 2003.

Friedman, Jean E. *The Enclosed Garden: Women and Community in the Evangelical South, 1830–1900.* Chapel Hill: University of North Carolina Press, 1985.

Friedman, Lawrence J. *Gregarious Saints: Self and Community in American Abolitionism, 1830–1870.* Cambridge: Cambridge University Press, 1982.

Fristoe, William. *A Concise History of the Ketocton Baptist Association.* Staunton, VA: William Gilman Lyford, 1808. Reprint, Stephens, VA: Commercial Press, 1978.

Fuller, Richard. *The Benevolence of the Gospel Toward the Poor.* Baltimore: G. F. Adams, 1848.

Fuller, Wayne Edison. *Morality and the Mail in Nineteenth-Century America.* Urbana: University of Illinois Press, 2003.

Furman, Richard. *Address Delivered before the Rhode Island Historical Society.* Providence, RI: B. Cranston, 1844.

———. *America's Deliverance and Duty: a Sermon, Preached at the Baptist Church, in Charleston, South-Carolina, on the Fourth of July, 1802.* Charleston, SC: W. P. Young, 1802.

———. *Exposition of the Views of the Baptists Relative to the Coloured Population in the United States.* 2nd ed. Charleston, SC: A. E. Milner, 1833.

———. *The Glory of Zion: A Discourse, Delivered Before the Welsh Neck Baptist Association.* Charleston, SC: Walker & James, 1854.

———. *Rewards of Grace Conferred on Christ's Faithful People; a Sermon, Occasioned by the Decease of the Rev. Oliver Hart.* Charleston, SC: J. M'Iver, 1796.

———. *A Sermon on the Constitution and Order of the Christian Church.* Charleston, SC: Markland & M'Iver, 1791.

Gammell, William. *A History of American Baptist Missions in Asia, Africa, Europe and North America.* Boston: Gould & Lincoln, 1854.

———. *William Gammell, LL.D.; A Biographical Sketch.* Cambridge, MA: Riverside, 1890.

Gano, John. *Biographical Memoirs of the Late Rev. John Gano.* New York: Southwick & Hardcastle, 1806.

Garrett, James Leo, Jr. *Systematic Theology: Biblical, Historical, and Evangelical.* Vol 2. Richland Hills, TX: Bibal, 1991.

Gaustad, Edwin Scott. *Faith of Our Fathers: Religion and the New Nation.* Waco, TX: Baylor University Press, 1987.

———. "Our Country: One Century Later." In *Liberal Protestantism: Realities and Possibilities,* edited by Robert S. Michaelsen and Wade Clark Roof, 85–101. New York: Pilgrim, 1986.

———, ed. *Religious Issues in American History.* New York: Harper & Row, 1968.

Genovese, Eugene D. *A Consuming Fire: The Fall of the Confederacy in the Mind of the White Christian South.* Athens: University of Georgia Press, 1998.

———. *From Rebellion to Revolution: Afro-American Slave Revolts in the Making of the Modern World.* Baton Rouge: Louisiana State University, 1979.

———. *The Slaveholder's Dilemma: Freedom and Progress in Southern Conservative Thought, 1820–1860.* Columbia: University of South Carolina Press, 1992.

George, Timothy, and David S. Dockery, eds. *Baptist Theologians.* Nashville: Broadman, 1990.

Georgia Analytical Repository. Savannah, Georgia. 1802–1803.

Gettleman, Marvin E. *The Dorr Rebellion: A Study in American Radicalism: 1833–1849.* New York: Random House, 1973.

Gewehr, Wesley M. *The Great Awakening in Virginia, 1740–1790.* Durham, NC: Duke University Press, 1930.

Gillette, A. D. *Sermon on the Death of Rev. S. H. Cone, D.D.* New York: Pruden & Roberts, 1855.

Gilpin, W. Clark. *Public Faith: Reflections on the Political Role of American Churches.* St. Louis: CBP, 1990.

Ginzberg, Lori D. "'Moral Suasion is Moral Balderdash': Women, Politics, and Social Activism in the 1850s." *Journal of American History* 73 (1986) 601–22.

————. *Women and the Work of Benevolence: Morality, Politics, and Class in the Nineteenth-Century United States.* New Haven, CT: Yale University Press, 1990.

Glock, Charles Y., and Rodney Stark. *Religion and Society in Tension.* Chicago: Rand McNally, 1965.

Goen, G. C. *Broken Churches, Broken Nation: Denominational Schisms and the Coming of the Civil War.* Macon, GA: Mercer University Press, 1985.

Goodwin, Everett C., ed. *Baptists in the Balance: The Tension Between Freedom and Responsibility.* Valley Forge, PA: Judson, 1997.

Gordon-McCutchan, R. C. "Great Awakenings." *Sociological Analysis* 44 (1984) 83–95.

Gould, Philip. *Barbaric Traffic: Commerce and Antislavery in the Eighteenth-Century Atlantic World.* Cambridge, MA: Harvard University Press, 2003.

Graham, Elaine, and Esther D. Reed. *The Future of Social Ethics: Essays on the Work of Ronald H. Preston, 1913–2001.* New York: Continuum, 2004.

Graham, Preston D., Jr. *A Kingdom Not of This World: Stuart Robinson's Struggle to Distinguish the Sacred from the Secular during the Civil War.* Macon, GA: Mercer University Press, 2002.

Gray, Edgar Harkness. *Assaults Upon Freedom! Or, Kidnapping an Outrage Upon Humanity and Abhorrent to God.* Shelburne Falls, MA: D. B. Gunn, 1854.

————. *A Cloud on the Church: A Sermon Delivered Before the Franklin County Baptist Association in Coleraine, Mass.* Greenfield, MA: Merriam & Mirick, 1846.

————. *A Discourse on the Imperative Duties of the Hour, Delivered in the E Street Baptist Church, Washington, DC* Washington, DC: H. Polkinhorn, 1863.

Greene, L. F., ed. *The Writings of John Leland.* New York: Arno, 1969.

Gribbin, William. *The Churches Militant: The War of 1812 and American Religion.* New Haven, CT: Yale University Press, 1973.

Griffin, Clifford S. *Their Brothers' Keeper: Moral Stewardship in the United States, 1800–1865.* New Brunswick, NJ: Rutgers University Press, 1960.

Grimke, Thomas Smith. *Address On the Patriot Character of the Temperance Reformation.* Charleston, SC: Observer Office, 1833.

————. *The Temperance Reformation the Cause of Christian Morals: An Address Given Before the Charleston Temperance Society.* Charleston, SC: Observer Officer, 1834.

Groody, Daniel G., ed. *The Option for the Poor in Christian Theology.* Notre Dame, IN: University of Notre Dame Press, 2007.

Guelzo, Allen. "An Heir or a Rebel? Charles Grandison Finney and the New England Theology." *Journal of the Early Republic* 17 (1997) 61–94.

————. "Oberlin Perfectionism and Its Edwardsian Origins, 1835–1870." In *Jonathan Edward's Writings: Text, Context, Interpretation,* edited by Stephen J. Stein, 159–74. Bloomington: Indiana University Press, 1996.

Gusfield, Joseph. *Symbolic Crusade: Status Politics and the American Temperance Movement.* Urbana: University of Illinois Press 1963.

Gushee, David, ed. *Toward a Just and Caring Society: Christian Responses to Poverty in America.* Grand Rapids: Baker, 1999.

Habig, Brian, and Les Newsom. *The Enduring Community: Embracing the Priority of the Church.* Jackson, MS: Reformed University Press, 2001.

Hall, David W. *The Genevan Reformation and the American Founding.* Lanham, MD: Lexington, 2003.

Hall, Robert. *Modern Infidelity Considered with Respect to its Influence on Society.* Charlestown, MA: Samuel Ethridge, 1801.

Hallock, William A. *"Light and Love": A Sketch of the Life and Labors of Rev. Justin Edwards.* New York: American Tract Society, 1855.

Hambrick-Stowe, Charles E. *Charles G. Finney and the Spirit of American Evangelicalism.* Grand Rapids: Eerdmans, 1996.

Hamburger, Philip. *Separation of Church and State.* Cambridge, MA: Harvard University Press, 2002.

Hamilton, James E. "The Church as Universal Reform Society: The Social Vision of Asa Mahan." *Wesleyan Theological Journal* 25 (1990) 42–56.

Hammett, John S. *Biblical Foundations for Baptist Churches: A Contemporary Ecclesiology.* Grand Rapids: Kregel, 2005.

Hammond, John L. *The Politics of Benevolence: Revival Religion and American Voting Behavior.* Norwood, NJ: Ablex, 1979.

———. "Revival Religion and Antislavery Politics." *American Sociological Review* 39 (1974) 175–86.

Hampel, Robert L. *Temperance and Prohibition in Massachusetts, 1813–1852.* Ann Arbor, MI: UMI Research Press, 1982.

Handy, Robert T. *A Christian America: Protestant Hope and Historical Reality.* 2nd ed. New York: Oxford University Press, 1984.

———, ed. *The Social Gospel in America, 1870–1920.* New York: Oxford University Press, 1966.

Hankins, Barry. *The Second Great Awakening and the Transcendentalists.* Westport, CT: Greenwood, 2004.

———. "Southern Baptists and Northern Evangelicals: Cultural Factors and the Nature of Religious Alliances." *Religion of American Culture* 7 (1997) 271–98.

———. *Uneasy in Babylon: Southern Baptists and American Culture.* Tuscaloosa: University of Alabama Press, 2002.

Hanley, Mark Y. *Beyond a Christian Commonwealth: The Protestant Quarrel with the American Republic, 1830–1860.* Chapel Hill: University of North Carolina Press, 1994.

Harper, Keith. *The Quality of Mercy: Southern Baptists and Social Christianity, 1890–1920.* Tuscaloosa: University of Alabama Press, 1996.

Harrold, Stanley. *The Rise of Aggressive Abolitionism: Addresses to the Slaves.* Lexington: University Press of Kentucky, 2004.

Hart, D. G. "Christianity and Liberalism in a Postliberal Age." *Westminster Theological Journal* 56 (1994) 329–44.

———. *Defending the Faith: J. Gresham Machen and the Crisis of Conservative Protestantism in Modern America.* Grand Rapids: Baker, 1995.

———, ed. *Reckoning with the Past: Historical Essays on American Evangelicalism from the Institute for the Study of American Evangelicals.* Grand Rapids: Baker, 1995.

———. *Recovering Mother Kirk.* Grand Rapids: Baker, 2003.

———. *A Secular Faith: Why Christianity Favors the Separation of Church and State.* Chicago: Ivan R. Dee, 2006.

Hart, Oliver. *America's Remembrancer, with Respect to Her Blessedness and Duty.* Philadelphia: T. Dobson, 1791.

———. *A Gospel Church Portrayed, and Her Orderly Service Pointed Out.* Trenton, NJ: Isaac Collins, 1791.

———. *A Humble Attempt to Repair the Christian Temple: A Sermon, Shewing the Business of Officers and Private Members in the Church of Christ.* Philadelphia: Robert Aitken, 1785.

Harvey, Hezekiah. *Memoir of Alfred Bennett, First Pastor of the Baptist Church, Homer, N.Y.* New York: Edward H. Fletcher, 1852.

Harvey, Paul. *Politics and Religion in the White South.* Lexington: University of Kentucky Press, 2005.

———. *Redeeming the South: Religious Cultures and Racial Identities among Southern Baptists, 1865–1925.* Chapel Hill: University of North Carolina Press, 1997.

Hatch, Nathan O. *The Democratization of American Christianity.* New Haven, CT: Yale University Press, 1989.

Hayden, Lucien. "The Pure Church, Characterized by Spirituality." In *Baptist Pamphlets* 2, edited by George W. Anderson. Philadelphia: American Baptist Publication Society, 1854.

Haynes, Dudley C. *The Baptist Denomination.* New York: Sheldon, Blakeman, 1856.

Heidler David S., and Jeanne T. Heidler. *The Mexican War.* Westport, CT: Greenwood, 2006.

Helco, Hugh, ed. *Christianity and American Democracy.* Cambridge, MA: Harvard University Press, 2007.

Helco, Hugh, and Wilfred M. McClay, eds. *Religion Returns to the Public Square: Faith and Policy in America.* Baltimore: Johns Hopkins University Press, 2003.

Henry, Carl F. H. "Christianity and Social Reform." *Moravian Theological Seminary Bulletin* (1960) 17–33.

———. *The Uneasy Conscience of Modern Fundamentalism.* Grand Rapids: Eerdmans, 2003.

Herbert, David. *Religion and Civil Society: Rethinking Public Religion in the Contemporary World.* Burlington, VT: Ashgate, 2003.

Heyrman, Christine Leigh. *Southern Cross: The Beginnings of the Bible Belt.* New York: Alfred A. Knopf, 1997.

Hickey, Donald R. *The War of 1812: A Forgotten Conflict.* Urbana: University of Illinois Press, 1989.

Hill, Samuel S., Jr. *The South and the North in American Religion.* Athens: University of Georgia Press, 1980.

Hirrel, Leo P. *Children of Wrath: New School Calvinism and Antebellum Reform.* Lexington: University Press of Kentucky, 1998.

Hiscox, Edward Thurston. *The Baptist Directory: A Guide to the Doctrines and Practices of Baptist Churches.* New York: Sheldon, 1876.

Hobbie, Peter Hairston. "Ernest Trice Thompson: Prophet for a Changing South." PhD diss., Union Theological Seminary in Virginia, 1987.

Holifield, E. Brooks. *Gentleman Theologians: American Theology in Southern Culture, 1795–1860.* Durham, NC: Duke University Press, 1978.

———. "The Penurious Preacher? Nineteenth-Century Clerical Wealth: North and South." *Journal of the American Academy of Religion* 58 (Spring 1990) 17–36.

———. *Theology in America: Christian Thought from the Age of the Puritans to the Civil War.* New Haven, CT: Yale University Press, 2003.

Holland, Matthew S. *Bonds of Affection: Civic Charity and the Making of America, Winthrop, Jefferson, and Lincoln.* Washington, DC: Georgetown University Press, 2007.

Holmes, Oliver W. "Sunday Travel and Sunday Mails: A Question Which Troubled Our Forefathers." *New York History* 20 (October 1939) 413–15.

Hoppe, Leslie J. *There Shall Be No Poverty among You: Poverty in the Bible*. Nashville: Abingdon, 2004.

Horton, James Oliver. *Slavery and the Making of America*. Oxford: Oxford University Press, 2005.

Hovey, Alvah. "The Bible the Only Standard of Christian Doctrine and Duty." In *The Madison Avenue Lectures*. Philadelphia: American Baptist Publication Society, 1867.

———. *A Memoir of the Life and Times of the Rev. Isaac Backus, A. M.* Boston: Gould & Lincoln, 1859.

Howe, Daniel Walker. "The Evangelical Movement and Political Culture in the North during the Second Party System." *Journal of American History* 77 (March 1991) 1216–39.

———. *The Political Culture of the American Whigs*. Chicago: The University of Chicago Press, 1979.

———. "Religion and Politics in the Antebellum North." In *Religion and American Culture: From the Colonial Period to the Present*, edited by Mark A. Noll and Luke E. Harlow, 121–45. 2nd ed. Oxford: Oxford University Press, 2007.

Hudson, Winthrop S., ed. *Baptist Concepts of the Church*. Philadelphia: Judson, 1959.

———. *Baptists in Transitions: Individualism and Christian Responsibility*. Valley Forge, PA: Judson, 1979.

Hughey, Michael W. *Civil Religion and Moral Order: Theoretical and Historical Dimensions*. Westport, CT: Greenwood, 1983.

Hunter, James Davidson. *Evangelicalism: The Coming Generation*. Chicago: University of Chicago Press, 1987.

Huston, James L. "The Experiential Basis of the Northern Antislavery Impulse." *Journal of Southern History* 56 (1990) 609–40.

Hutchinson, William R. "Americanness of the Social Gospel: An Inquiry in Comparative History." *Church History* 44 (1975) 367–81.

———. *The Modernist Impulse in American Protestantism*. Durham, NC: Duke University Press, 1992.

Hutson, James H. *Church and State in America: The First Two Centuries*. Cambridge: Cambridge University Press, 2008.

———, ed. *Religion and the New Republic: Faith in the Founding of America*. Lanham, MD: Rowman & Littlefield, 2000.

Hyma, Albert. *Christianity and Politics: A History of the Principles and Struggles of Church and State*. Philadelphia: J. B. Lippincott, 1938.

Israel, Charles A. *Before Scopes: Evangelicalism, Education, and Evolution in Tennessee, 1870–1925*. Athens: University of Georgia Press, 2004.

Jackson, Henry. *An Account of the Churches in Rhode Island*. Providence, RI: G. H. Whitney, 1854.

Jackson, Luther P. "Religious Instruction of Negroes, 1830–1860, with Special Reference to South Carolina." In *Religion and Slavery*, edited by Paul Finkelman, 190–232. New York: Garland, 1989.

Jay, William. *An Historical Discourse, Delivered in the Central Baptist Meeting House, Newport, R. I., January 8, 1854*. Newport, RI: Cranston & Norman, 1854.

———. *Miscellaneous Writings on Slavery*. Boston: John P. Jewett, 1853.

Jeter, Jeremiah Bell. *A Memoir of Abner W. Clopton, A. M.: Pastor of Baptist Churches in Charlotte County, Virginia*. Richmond, VA: Yale & Watt, 1837.

———. "Mission on Baptists." In *The Madison Avenue Lectures*. Philadelphia: American Baptist Publication Society, 1867.

———. *The Recollections of a Long Life*. Richmond, VA: Religious Herald, 1891.

John, Richard R. *Spreading the News: The American Postal System from Franklin to Morse*. Cambridge, MA: Harvard University Press, 1995.

Johnson, Byron L. *Need is Our Neighbor*. New York: Friendship, 1966.

Johnson, Kelly S. *The Fear of Beggars: Stewardship and Poverty in Christian Ethics*. Grand Rapids: Eerdmans, 2007.

Johnson, Paul. *The Early American Republic, 1789–1829*. New York: Oxford University Press, 2007.

———. *The Shopkeeper's Millennium: Society and Revivals in Rochester, New York, 1815–1837*. New York: Hill & Wang, 1978.

Johnson, Richard M. "In Senate of the United States." 20th Congress. Washington, DC: United States Senate, 1829.

———. *Sunday Mail*. 21st Congress. Washington, DC: Duff Green, 1830.

Jones, Charles Colcock. *The Religious Instruction of the Negroes in the United States*. Savannah: Thomas Purse, 1842.

Jones, Jonathan Milner. "The Making of a Vice President: The National Political Career of Richard M. Johnson." PhD diss., University of Memphis, 1998.

Jones, Joseph H. *History of the Baltimore Association*. Baltimore: T. A. Rhoades, 1872.

Jones, Lawrence Neale. *African Americans and Christian Churches, 1619–1860*. Cleveland: Pilgrim, 2007.

Jones, Samuel. *A Century Sermon: Delivered in Philadelphia at the Opening of the Philadelphia Baptist Association, October 6, 1807*. Philadelphia: Bartram & Reynolds, 1807.

Julius, Kevin C. *The Abolitionist Decade, 1829–1838: A Year by Year History of Early Events in the Anti-Slavery Movement*. Jefferson, NC: McFarland, 2004.

Kaufman, Peter Iver. *Redeeming Politics*. Princeton, NJ: Princeton University Press, 1990.

Kennedy Lionel H., and Thomas Parker. *An Official Report of the Trials of Sundry Negroes Charged with an Attempt to Raise an Insurrection in the State of South Carolina*. Charleston, SC: James R. Schenck, 1822.

Kimball, Gregg David. "Place and Perception: Richmond in Late Antebellum America." Ph.D. diss., University of Virginia, 1997.

Kling, David W. *A Field of Wonders: The New Divinity and Village Revivals in Northwestern Connecticut, 1792–1822*. University Park: Pennsylvania State University Press, 1993.

Knowles, James Davis. *Perils and Safeguards of American Liberty*. Boston: Lincoln & Edmands, 1828.

Kramnick, Issack, and R. Laurence Moore. *The Godless Constitution: The Case against Religious Correctness*. New York: Norton, 1996.

Kraynak, Robert. *Christian Faith and Modern Democracy: God and Politics in the Fallen World*. Notre Dame: University of Notre Dame Press, 2001.

Krout, John Allen. *The Origins of Prohibition*. New York: Russell & Russell, 1953.

Kuklick, Bruce. *American Religious Thought of the Eighteenth and Nineteenth Century*. New York: Oxford University Press, 1987.

————. *A History of Philosophy in America, 1720–2000*. Oxford: Oxford University Press, 2001.

Kuykendall, John W. *"Southern Enterprize": The Work of National Evangelical Societies in the Antebellum South*. Westport, CT: Greenwood, 1982.

Lambert, Byron C. "The Rise of the Anti-Mission Baptists: Sources and Leaders, 1800–1840 (A Study in American Religious Individualism)." PhD diss., University of Chicago, 1957.

Lambert, Frank. *The Founding Fathers and the Place of Religion in America*. Princeton, NJ: Princeton University Press, 2003.

Laurie, Bruce. *Beyond Garrison: Antislavery and Social Reform*. Cambridge: Cambridge University Press, 2005.

Lazerow, Jama. "Religion and Labor Reform in Antebellum America: The World of William Field Young." *American Quarterly* 38 (1986) 265–86.

Leland, John. *Discourses on Various Subjects*. London: Johnson & Dodsley, 1769.

————. *Free Thoughts on War*. Pittsfield, MA: Phinehas Allen, 1816.

————. *An Oration Delivered at Cheshire, Massachusetts, July 5th, 1802, On the Celebration of American Independence*. Hudson, NY: Charles Holt, 1802.

————. *Part of a Speech Delivered on the First Jubilee*. Pittsfield, MA: Phinehas Allen, 1826.

————. *Politics Sermonized, Exhibited in Ashfield, on July 4th, 1806*. Springfield, MA: Andrew Wright, 1806.

————. *Short Sayings on Times, Men, Measures and Religion*. Pittsfield, MA: Phinehas Allen, 1830.

Leonard, Bill J. *Baptist Ways: A History*. Valley Forge, PA: Judson, 2003.

————. "Southern Baptists and the Separation of Church and State." *Review and Expositor* 2 (1986) 195–207.

Lindsay, Alexander Dunlop. *The Churches and Democracy*. London: Epworth, 1934.

Link, William A. *A Hard Country and a Lonely Place: Schooling, Society, and Reform in Rural Virginia, 1870–1920*. Chapel Hill: University of North Carolina Press, 1986.

Lipset, Seymour Martin. "Religion and Politics in the American Past and Present." In *Religion and Social Conflict*, edited by Robert Lee and Martin E. Marty, 69–126. New York: Oxford University Press, 1964.

Long, Kathryn Teresa. *The Revival of 1857–58: Interpreting an American Religious Awakening*. New York: Oxford University Press, 1998.

Longfield, Bradley J. *The Presbyterian Controversy: Fundamentalists, Moderates, and Modernists*. New York: Oxford University Press, 1993.

Loveland, Anne C. "Evangelicalism and 'Immediate Emancipation' in American Antislavery Thought." In *Abolitionism and American Religion*, edited by John R. Mckivigan, 2–18. New York: Garland, 1999.

————. *Southern Evangelicals and Social Order, 1800–1860*. Baton Rouge: Louisiana State University, 1980.

Luker, Ralph E. "Social Gospel and the Failure of Racial Reform, 1877–1898." *Church History* 46 (1977) 80–99.

MacCormac, Earl R. "The Transition from Voluntary Missionary Society to the Church as a Missionary Organization among American Congregationalists, Presbyterians, and Methodists." PhD diss., Yale University, 1961.

MacIntyre, Alisdair. *After Virtue: A Study in Moral Theory*. 3rd ed. Notre Dame: University of Notre Dame Press, 2007.

Maddex, Jack P. "From Theocracy to Spirituality: The Southern Presbyterian Reversal on Church and State." *Journal of Presbyterian History* 54 (1976) 438–57.

———. "Proslavery Millennialism: Social Eschatology in Antebellum Southern Calvinism." *American Quarterly* 31 (1979) 46–62.

Magnuson, Norris. *Salvation in the Slums: Evangelical Social Work, 1965–1920.* Metuchen, NJ: Scarecrow, 1977.

Manly, Basil, Sr. Papers. Archives and Special Collections. James P. Boyce Centennial Library. Southern Baptist Theological Seminary Special Collections. Louisville, Kentucky.

Mann, Horace. *Two Lectures on Intemperance: I. The Effects of Intemperance on the Poor and Ignorant. II. The Effects of Intemperance on the Rich and Educated.* Syracuse, NY: Hall, Mills, 1852.

Marion, Forrest L. "The Gentleman Sabbatarians: The Sabbath Movement in the Upper South, 1826–1836." PhD diss., University of Tennessee, Knoxville, 1998.

Marsden, George M. *The Evangelical Mind and the New School Presbyterian Experience: A Case Study of Thought and Theology in Nineteenth-Century America.* New Haven, CT: Yale University Press, 1970.

———. *Fundamentalism and American Culture: The Shaping of Twentieth Century Evangelicalism, 1870–1925.* Oxford: Oxford University Press, 1980.

———. "The Gospel of Wealth, the Social Gospel, and the Salvation of Souls in Nineteenth Century America." In *Protestantism and Social Christianity*, edited by Martin E. Marty, 10–21. New York: K. G. Saur, 1992.

Marsden, George M., and Nathan O. Hatch. *The Search for Christian America.* Colorado Springs: Helmeis & Howard, 1989.

Marty, Martin E., ed. *Protestantism and Social Christianity.* New York: K. G. Saur, 1992.

Mason, Lowance. *A House Divided: The Antebellum Slavery Debates in America, 1776–1865.* Princeton, NJ: Princeton University Press, 2003.

Massachusetts Constitutional Convention. *Constitution.* Boston: Benjamin Edes & Son, 1780.

Mathews, Donald G., ed. *Abolitionism and American Religion.* New York: Garland, 1999.

———. "Charles Colcock Jones and the Southern Evangelical Crusade to Form a Biracial Community." *The Journal of Southern History* 3 (August 1975) 299–320.

———. *Religion in the Old South.* Chicago: University of Chicago Press, 1977.

———. "The Second Great Awakening as an Organizing Process, 1780–1830: An Hypothesis." *American Quarterly* 21 (Spring 1969) 23–43.

———. *Slavery and Methodism: A Chapter in American Morality, 1780–1845.* Princeton, NJ: Princeton University Press, 1965.

———. *The War Against Proslavery Religion: Abolitionism and the Northern Churches, 1830–1865.* Ithaca, NY: Cornell University Press, 1984.

Mathews, Donald G., and Mitchell Snay, eds. *Religion and the Antebellum Debate over Slavery.* Athens: University of Georgia Press, 1998.

Mathisen, Robert R. "Evangelicals and the Age of Reform, 1870–1930: An Assessment." *Fides et Historia* 16 (1984) 74–85.

———, ed. *The Role of Religion in American Life: An Interpretive Historical Anthology.* Dubuque, IA: Kendall/Hunt, 1994.

Maxcy, Jonathan. *American Eloquence: Consisting of Orations, Addresses, and Sermons: Being the Literary Remains of the Rev. Jonathan Maxcy, With a Memoir of His Life by Romeo Elton.* New York: A. V. Blake, 1845.

———. *An Oration, Delivered before the Providence Association of Mechanics and Manufacturers.* Providence, RI: Bennett Wheeler, 1795.

———. *A Sermon, Preached in Boston, at the Annual Convention of the Warren Association.* Boston: Manning & Loring, 1797.

Mays, Blanche. *The Proper Relationship of Church and State as Viewed and Held by Baptists.* Nashville: Baptist Sunday School Board, 1929.

McBeth, H. Leon, ed. *A Sourcebook for Baptist Heritage.* Nashville: Broadman, 1990.

McCafferey, James M. *Army of Manifest Destiny: The American Soldier in the Mexican War, 1846–1848.* New York: New York University Press, 1992.

McCann, Dennis P., and Patrick D. Miller, eds. *In Search of the Common Good.* New York: T. & T. Clark, 2005.

McCormick, Richard L. *The Party Period and Public Policy: American Politics from the Age of Jackson to the Progressive Era.* New York: Oxford University Press, 1986.

McDannell, Colleen. *Religions of the United States in Practice.* 2 vols. Princeton, NJ: Princeton University Press, 2001.

McElroy, Robert W. *The Search for an American Public Theology: The Contribution of John Courtney Murray.* New York: Paulist, 1989.

McKanan, Dan. *Identifying the Image of God: Radical Christians and Nonviolent Power in the Antebellum United States.* Oxford: Oxford University Press, 2002.

McKenna, George. *The Puritan Origins of American Patriotism.* New Haven, CT: Yale University Press, 2007.

McKivigan, John R. "The Sectional Division of the Methodist and Baptist Denominations as Measures of Northern Antislavery Sentiment." In *Religion and the Antebellum Debate over Slavery*, edited by John R. McKivigan and Mitchell Snay, 343–63. Athens: University of Georgia Press, 1998.

McLellan, David. *Political Christianity: A Reader.* London: SPCK, 1997.

McLoughlin, William G., ed. *The American Evangelicals, 1800–1900.* New York: Harper & Row, 1968.

———. "Introduction." In *Isaac Backus on Church, State, and Calvinism Pamphlets, 1754–1789*, edited by William G. McLoughlin. Cambridge, MA: Belknap, 1968.

———. *Isaac Backus and the American Pietistic Tradition.* Boston: Little, Brown, 1967.

———. *Modern Revivalism: Charles Grandison Finney to Billy Graham.* New York: Ronald, 1959.

———. *Revivals, Awakenings, and Reform: An Essay on Religion and Social Change in America, 1607–1977.* Chicago: The University of Chicago Press, 1978.

McTyeire, Holland Nimmons, ed. *Duties of Masters to Servants: Three Premium Essays.* Charleston, SC: Southern Baptist Publication Society, 1851.

Mead, Sydney. *Nation with the Soul of a Church.* New York: Harper & Row, 1975.

Mecklenburg, George. *Bowing the Preacher Out of Politics.* New York: Fleming H. Revell, 1928.

Mell, Patrick Hues. *Baptism in Its Mode and Subjects.* Charleston, SC: Southern Baptist Publication Society, 1854.

———. *Calvinism: An Essay Read Before the Georgia Baptist Ministers' Institute at Marietta, Ga., August 13, 1868.* Atlanta: Geo. C. Conner, 1868.

———. *Church Polity.* Atlanta: Jas. P. Harrison, 1878.

———. *Life of Patrick Hues Mell, By His Son, P. H. Mell, Jr.* Louisville, KY: Baptist Book Concern, 1895.

Mercer, Jesse. *History of the Georgia Baptist Association.* Washington, GA: Georgia Baptist Association, 1848. Reprint, 1980.

———. *Jesse Mercer's Pulpit: Preaching in a Community of Faith and Learning.* Edited by Wilfred C. Platt Jr. and Douglas E. Thompson. Macon, GA: Mercer University Press, 2006.

Merrill, John L. "The Bible and the American Temperance Movement: Text, Context, and Pretext." *Harvard Theological Review* 81 (1988) 145–70.

Meyer, Leland Winfield. *The Life and Times of Colonel Richard M. Johnson of Kentucky.* New York: Columbia University Press, 1932.

Meyer, Paul R. "Fear of Cultural Decline: Josiah Strong's Thoughts about Reform and Expansion." *Church History* 42 (1973) 396–405.

Michaelsen, Robert S. *The American Search for Soul.* Baton Rouge: Louisiana State University Press, 1975.

Minutes. Boston Baptist Association, Massachusetts. 1812–1847.

Minutes. Boston North Baptist Association, Massachusetts. 1849–1870.

Minutes. Boston South Baptist Association, Massachusetts. 1849–1870.

Minutes. Charleston Baptist Association, South Carolina. 1775, 1777, 1788–1860, 1865, 1867–1869.

Minutes. Concord Baptist Association. Tennessee. 1812–1847, 1849, 1851–1854, 1856, 1859, 1866.

Minutes. Dover [Separate] Baptist Association, Virginia. 1809–1841, 1843–1846, 1849–1859, 1862–1866, 1867–1870.

Minutes. Elkhorn Baptist Association, Kentucky. 1785–1870.

Minutes. Great Crossing Baptist Church. Lexington, Kentucky. 1813–1861.

Minutes. Kehukee Baptist Association, North Carolina. 1769–1772, 1828, 1853–1854, 1856.

Minutes. Ketocton [Regular] Baptist Association, Virginia. 1798, 1808, 1814, 1820, 1826, 1829, 1835, 1840, 1873.

Minutes. North-District Association, Kentucky. 1802, 1805.

Minutes. Oneida Baptist Association, New York. 1824–1826, 1828–1831, 1833–1834, 1838, 1840–1846, 1848–1853, 1855–1858, 1860–1862, 1865–1868.

Minutes. Sandy Creek Baptist Association, North Carolina. 1835, 1861.

Minutes. Warren Baptist Association Minutes, Rhode Island. 1769–1870.

Moore, Moses Nathaniel. "Righteousness Exalts a Nation: Black Clergymen, Reform, and New School Presbyterianism." *American Presbyterians* 70 (1992) 222–38.

Moore, R. Laurence. "Religion, Secularization, and the Shaping of the Culture Industry in Antebellum America." *American Quarterly* 41 (June 1989) 216–42.

———. *Religious Outsiders and the Making of Americans.* New York: Oxford University Press, 1986.

Moore, Russell D. *The Kingdom of Christ: The New Evangelical Perspective.* Wheaton, IL: Crossway, 2004.

Moorhead, James H. *American Apocalypse: Yankee Protestants and the Civil War.* New Haven, CT: Yale University Press, 1978.

———. "Social Reform and the Divided Conscience of Antebellum Protestantism." *Church History* 48 (1979) 416–30.

Morris, Jeremy. *F. D. Maurice and the Crisis of Christian Authority*. Oxford: Oxford University Press, 2005.

Mueller, William A. *Church and State in Luther and Calvin*. Garden City, NY: Anchor, 1965.

Muller, Dorothea R. "Josiah Strong and the Social Gospel: A Christian's Response to the Challenge of the City." *Journal of the Presbyterian Historical Society* 39 (1961) 150–75.

———. "The Social Philosophy of Josiah Strong." *Church History* 28 (1959) 183–201.

Müller-Fahrenholz, Geiko. *America's Battle for God: A European Christian Looks at Civil Religion*. Grand Rapids: Eerdmans, 2007.

Mullin, Robert Bruce. *The Puritan as Yankee: The Life of Horace Bushnell*. Grand Rapids: Eerdmans, 2002.

Myers, Robert Manson, ed. *The Children of Pride: Selected Letters of the Family of the Rev. Dr. Charles Colcock Jones*. New Haven, CT: Yale University Press, 1972.

Najar, Monica. "'Meddling with Emancipation': Baptists, Authority, and the Rift over Slavery in the Upper South." *Journal of the Early Republic* 25 (Summer 2005) 157–86.

Nash, Ronald H. *Social Justice and the Christian Church*. Lima, OH: Academic Renewal, 2002.

Nettles, Thomas J. *The Baptists: Key People Involved In Forming a Baptist Identity*. 3 vols. Scotland: Christian Focus, 2005–2006.

———. *By His Grace and For His Glory: A Historical, Theological, and Practical Study of the Doctrines of Grace in Baptist Life*. Grand Rapids: Baker, 1986.

Neuhaus, Richard John. *The Naked Public Square: Religion and Democracy in America*. Grand Rapids, Eerdmans, 1984.

Neuhaus, Richard John, and Michael Cromartie, eds. *Piety and Politics: Evangelicals and Fundamentalists Confront the World*. Washington, DC: Ethics and Public Policy Center, 1987.

Newman, Richard S. *The Transformation of American Abolitionism: Fighting Slavery in the Early Republic*. Chapel Hill: University of North Carolina Press, 2002.

Nichols, James Hastings. *Democracy and the Churches*. Philadelphia: Westminster, 1951.

Niebuhr, H. Richard. *Christ and Culture*. New York: Harper Colophon, 1975.

Noll, Mark A. *America's God: From Jonathan Edwards to Abraham Lincoln*. New York, 2002.

———. *The Civil War as a Theological Crisis*. Chapel Hill: University of North Carolina Press, 2006.

———. "The Earliest Protestants and the Reformation of Education." *Westminster Theological Journal* 43 (1980) 97–131.

———. "From the Great Awakening to the War for Independence: Christian Values in the American Revolution." *Christian Scholar's Review* 12 (1983) 99–110.

———, ed. *God and Mammon: Protestants, Money, and the Market, 1790–1860*. Oxford: Oxford University Press, 2002.

———. *One Nation under God? Christian Faith and Political Action in America*. San Francisco: Harper & Row, 1988.

———. *The Rise of Evangelicalism: The Age of Edwards, Whitefield and the Wesleys*. Downers Grove, IL: InterVarsity, 2003.

———. *The Scandal of the Evangelical Mind*. Grand Rapids: Eerdmans, 1994.

Noll, Mark A., and Luke E. Harlow, eds. *Religion and American Politics: From the Colonial Period to the Present.* 2nd ed. New York: Oxford University Press, 2007.

Norman, R. Stanton. *The Mission of Today's Church: Baptist Leaders Look at Modern Faith Issues.* Nashville: Broadman & Holman Academic, 2007.

Norton, Anne. *Alternative Americas: A Reading of Antebellum Political Culture.* Chicago: University of Chicago Press, 1986.

Novak, Michael. "The Cultural Roots of Virtue and Character." In *The The Content of America's Character: Recovering Civic Virtue.* Lanham, MD: Madison, 1995.

O'Brien, John T. "Factory, Church, and Community: Blacks in Antebellum Richmond." *Journal of Southern History* 44 (November 1978) 509–36.

O'Donovan, Oliver. *The Desire of the Nations: Rediscovering the Roots of Political Theology.* New York: Cambridge University Press, 1999.

O'Donovan, Oliver, and Joan Lockwood O'Donovan. *Bonds of Imperfection: Christian Politics, Past and Present.* Grand Rapids: Eerdmans, 2004.

Oliver, E. H. *The Social Achievements of the Christian Church.* Toronto: Board of Evangelism and Social Service of the United Church of Canada, 1930.

Ott, Thomas O. *The Haitian Revolution, 1789–1804.* Knoxville: University of Tennessee Press, 1973.

Parker, Daniel. *A Public Address to the Baptist Society and Friends of Religion.* Vincennes, IN: Stout & Osborn, 1820.

———. *Views on the Two Seeds.* Vandalia, IL: Robert Blackwell, 1826.

Parkinson, William. *Jubilee: A Sermon, Containing a History of the Origin of the First Baptist Church in the City of New York.* New York: n.p., 1813.

Pearson, C. C., and J. Edwin Hendricks. *Liquor and Antiliquor in Virginia, 1616–1919.* Durham, NC: Duke University Press, 1967.

Pease, William H., and Jane H. Pease. *The Web of Progress: Private Values and Public Styles in Boston and Charleston, 1828–1843.* New York: Oxford University Press, 1985.

Peat, J. B., *The Baptists Examined.* Chicago: Church & Goodman, 1868.

Pegram, Thomas R. *Battling Demon Rum: The Struggle for a Dry America, 1800–1933.* Chicago: Ivan R. Dee, 1998.

Pendleton, Othniel Alsop. *The Influence of the Evangelical Churches Upon Humanitarian Reform: A Case-Study Giving Particular Attention to Philadelphia, 1790–1840.* Philadelphia: n.p., 1947.

Perry, Lewis, and Michael Fellman, eds. *Antislavery Reconsidered: New Perspectives on the Abolitionists.* Baton Rouge: Louisiana State University Press, 1989.

Pivar, David. *Purity Crusade: Sexual Morality and Social Control, 1868–1900.* Westport, CT: Greenwood, 1973.

Plant, Raymond. *Politics, Theology, and History.* Cambridge: Cambridge University Press: 2001.

Porterfield, Amanda, ed. *American Religious History.* Malden, MA: Blackwell, 2002.

Priest, Gerald L. "The Abel Morgans's Contribution to Baptist Ecclesiology in Colonial America." *Detroit Baptist Seminary Journal* 8 (2003) 49–68.

Proceedings of the Southern Baptist Convention, May 11–15, 1888. Atlanta: Jas. P. Harrison, 1888.

Queen, Edward L., II. *In the South the Baptists are the Center of Gravity: Southern Baptists and Social Change, 1930–1980.* New York: Carlson, 1991.

Raboteau, Albert J. *Slave Religion: The "Invisible Institution" in the Antebellum South.* New York: Oxford University Press, 1978.

Rasmussen, Larry, ed. *Reinhold Niebuhr: Theologian of Public Life.* Minneapolis: Fortress, 1988.

Raucher, Alan. "Sunday Business and the Decline of Sunday Closing Laws: A Historical Overview." *Journal of Church and State* 36 (1994) 13–33.

Rauschenbusch, Walter. *Christianity and the Social Crisis.* New York: Macmillan, 1907.

———. *Christianity and the Social Crisis in the 21st Century: The Classic that Woke Up the Church.* New York: HarperCollins, 2007.

———. *A Theology for the Social Gospel.* New York: Macmillan, 1917. Reprint, Nashville: Abingdon, 1945.

Rawls, John. *The Law of Peoples.* Cambridge, MA: Harvard University Press, 1999.

Religious Herald. Richmond, Virginia. 1828–1860.

Richards, Peter Judson. "'A Clear and Steady Channel': Isaac Backus and the Limits of Liberty." *Journal of Church and State* 43 (2001) 447–82.

Ripley, Henry Jones. *Church Polity: A Treatise on Christian Churches and the Christian Ministry.* Boston: Graves & Young, 1867.

Robertson, Archibald Thomas. *Life and Letters of John Albert Broadus.* Harrisonburg, VA: Gano, 1987.

Robinson, E. B. "The Relation of the Church and the Bible." In *The Madison Avenue Lectures.* Philadelphia: American Baptist Publication Society, 1867.

Rogers, James A. *Richard Furman: Life and Legacy.* Macon, GA: Mercer University Press, 2001.

Rogers, William. *A Sermon Occasioned by the Death of the Rev. Oliver Hart.* Philadelpha: Lang & Ustick, 1796.

Rosenburg, R. B. "John Davis Williams: A Forgotten Virginia Baptist Minister." *Virginia Baptist Register* 22 (1983) 1092–1106.

Rossing, John P. "A Cultural History of Nineteenth Century American Sabbath Reform Movements." PhD diss., Emory University, 1994.

Roth, John K. *Private Needs, Public Selves: Talk about Religion in America.* Urbana: University of Illinois Press, 1997.

Rumbarger, John J. *Profits, Power, and Prohibition: Alcohol Reform and the Industrializing of America, 1800–1930.* New York: State University of New York Press, 1989

Russell, C. Allyn. *Rhode Island Baptists, 1825–1931.* N.p., 1969.

Ryan, Susan M. *The Grammar of Good Intentions: Race and Antebellum Culture of Benevolence.* Ithaca, NY: Cornell University Press, 2003.

Ryland, Garnett. *The Baptists of Virginia, 1699–1926.* Richmond, VA: Whittet & Shepperson, 1955.

Samson, G. W. "Church Polity." In *The Madison Avenue Lectures.* Philadelphia: American Baptist Publication Society, 1867.

———. *Memorial Discourse on the Life and Character of Rev. Joel Smith Bacon.* Washington, DC: Judd & Detweiler, 1870.

Sandlund, Vivien. "'A Devilish and Unnatural Usurpation': Baptist Evangelical Ministers and Antislavery in the Early Nineteenth Century, A Study of the Ideas and Activism of David Barrow." *American Baptist Quarterly* 13 (1994) 262–77.

———. "Robert Breckinridge, Presbyterian Antislavery Conservative." *Journal of Presbyterian History* 78 (2000) 145–54.

Sandoz, Ellis, ed. *Political Sermons of the American Founding Era, 1730–1805*. 2 vols. Indianapolis: Liberty Fund, 1991.

Schultz, Stanley K. "Temperance Reform in the Antebellum South: Social Control and Urban Order." *The South Atlantic Quarterly* 83 (1984) 323–39.

Schweiger, Beth Barton. *The Gospel Working Up: Progress and Pulpit in Nineteenth-Century Virginia*. New York: Oxford, 2000.

Semple, Robert B. *A History of the Rise and Progress of the Baptists in Virginia*. Richmond, VA: Pitt & Dickinson, 1894.

Shain, Barry Alan. *The Myth of American Individualism: The Protestant Origins of American Political Thought*. Princeton, NJ: Princeton University Press, 1994.

Silbey, Joel H., et al. *The History of American Electoral Behavior*. Princeton, NJ: Princeton University Press, 1978.

Smidt, Corwin E. *Pulpit and Politics: Clergy in American Politics at the Advent of the Millennium*. Waco, TX: Baylor University Press, 2004.

Smith, Billy G., ed. *Down and Out In Early America*. University Park: Pennsylvania State University Press, 2004.

Smith, Christian. *American Evangelicalism: Embattled and Thriving*. Chicago: University of Chicago Press, 1998.

Smith, Gary Scott. "Conservative Presbyterians: The Gospel, Social Reform, and the Church in the Progressive Era." *American Presbyterians* 70 (1992) 93–110.

———. "The Cross and the Social Order: Calvinist Strategies for Social Improvement, 1870–1920." *Fides et Historia* 17 (1984) 39–55.

———. "Reassessing the Relationship Between Religion and Social Reform." *Christian Scholar's Review* 14 (1985) 319–34.

Smith, J. A. *Memoir of Rev. Nathaniel Colver*. Boston: Durkee & Foxcroft, 1873.

Smith, Timothy L. *Revivalism and Social Reform: American Protestantism on the Eve of the Civil War*. Expanded edition. Baltimore: Johns Hopkins University Press, 1980.

Smucker, Donovan E. *The Origins of Walter Rauschenbusch's Social Ethics*. Montreal: McGill-Queen's University Press, 1994.

Snay, Mitchell. *Gospel of Disunion: Religion and Separatism in the Antebellum South*. New York: Cambridge University Press, 1993.

Snyder, Robert Arthur. "William T. Brantly (1787–1845) A Southern Unionist and the Breakup of the Triennial Convention." PhD diss., Southern Baptist Theological Seminary, 2005.

Solberg, Winton U. *Redeem the Time: The Puritan Sabbath in Early America*. Cambridge, MA: Harvard University Press, 1977.

Spain, Rufus B. *At Ease in Zion: Social History of Southern Baptists, 1865–1900*. Tuscaloosa: University of Alabama Press, 2003.

Spann, J. Richard., ed. *The Church and Social Responsibility*. New York: Abingdon-Cokesbury, 1953.

Spears, John Randolph. *The American Slave Trade: An Account of its Origin, Growth, and Suppression*. Port Washington, NY: Kennikat, 1900.

Speicher, Anna M. *The Religious World of Antislavery Women: Spirituality in the Lives of Five Abolitionist Lecturers*. Syracuse, NY: Syracuse University Press, 2000.

Spencer, Carole D. "Evangelism, Feminism, and Social Reform: The Quaker Woman Minister and the Holiness Revival." *Quaker History* 80 (1991) 24–48.

Spencer, J. H. *A History of Kentucky Baptists, from 1769–1885.* Vol. 1. Cincinnati: J. R. Baumes, 1885. Reprint, Lafayette, TN: Church History Research & Archives, 1976.

Spencer, Jon Michael. "Moral Abolitionism in an Antislavery Hymnal." *Reformed Liturgy and Music* 21 (1987) 148–51.

Staples, William G. *Castles of Our Conscience: Social Control and the American State, 1800–1985.* New Brunswick, NJ: Rutgers University Press, 1985.

Staudenraus, P. J. *The African Colonization Movement, 1816–1865.* New York: Columbia University Press, 1961.

Stauffer, John. *The Black Hearts of Men: Radical Abolitionists and the Transformation of Race.* Cambridge, MA: Harvard University Press, 2002.

Staughton, William. *Compassion to the Poor Recommended.* Philadelphia: Bartholomew Graves, 1810.

Stillman, Samuel. *Charity Considered in a Sermon Preached at Charlestown, June 24, 1785.* Boston: T. & J. Fleet, 1785.

———. *A Discourse Delivered Before the Members of the Boston Female Asylum, Friday, Sept. 25, 1801.* Boston: Russell & Cutler, 1801.

———. *A Good Minister of Jesus Christ: A Sermon, Preached in Boston, September 15, 1797, at the Ordination of the Rev. Mr. Stephen Smith Nelson.* Boston: Manning & Loring, 1797.

———. *A Sermon Delivered the Day of Annual Thanksgiving.* Boston: Manning & Loring, 1795.

———. *A Sermon Preached Before the Honorable Council, and the Honorable House of Representatives of the State of Massachusetts-Bay, in New England, at Boston, May 26, 1779.* Boston: T. & J. Fleet, 1779.

———. *A Sermon Preached for a National Fast.* Boston: Manning & Loring, 1799.

———. *Thoughts on the French Revolution: A Sermon, Delivered November 20, 1794: Being the Annual Day of Thanksgiving.* Boston: Manning & Loring, 1795.

Stockbridge, John C. *A Memoir of Rev. Baron Stow.* Boston: Lee & Shepard, 1894.

Stout, Jeffrey. *Democracy and Tradition.* Princeton, NJ: Princeton University Press, 2003.

Stowe, Lyman Beecher. *Saints, Sinners, and Beechers.* New York: Blue Ribbon, 1934.

Strange, Sammie Pedlow. "Baptists and Religious Liberty: 1700–1900." PhD diss., Southern Baptist Theological Seminary, 2006.

Stringfellow, Thornton. *Slavery: Its Origin, Nature and History.* Alexandria, VA: n.p. 1860.

Strong, Douglas M. *They Walked in Spirit: Personal Faith and Social Action in America.* Louisville, KY: Westminster John Knox, 1997.

Strong, Josiah. *My Religion in Everyday Life.* New York: Baker & Taylor, 1910.

———. *The New Era or the Coming Kingdom.* New York: Baker & Taylor, 1893.

———. *Our Country: Its Possible Future and its Present Crisis.* Rev. ed. New York: Baker & Taylor, 1891.

Sutton, William R. "The Influence of Nathaniel W. Taylor on Revivalism in the Second Great Awakening." *Religion and American Culture* (Winter 1992) 23–48.

Swatos, William H. "The Faith of the Fathers: On the Christianity of Early American Sociology." *Sociological Analysis* 44 (1983) 33–52.

Sweeney, Douglas A. "Edwards and His Mantle: The Historiography of the New England Theology." *New England Quarterly* 71 (1998) 97–110.

Sweeney, Douglas A., and Allen C. Guelzo, eds. *The New England Theology: From Jonathan Edwards to Edwards Amasa Park*. Grand Rapids: Baker Academic, 2006.

Sweet, William Warren, *Religion on the American Frontier: The Baptists, 1783–1830*. New York: Cooper Square, 1931.

Swierenga, Robert P. "Ethnoreligious Political Behavior in the Mid-Nineteenth Century: Voting, Values, Cultures." In *Religion and American Politics: From the Colonial Period to the Present*, edited by Mark Noll, 145–68. 2nd ed. Oxford: Oxford University Press, 2007.

Tait, L. Gordon. *The Piety of John Witherspoon: Pew, Pulpit, and Public Forum*. Louisville, KY: Geneva, 2001.

Tarrant, Carter *The Substance of a Discourse Delivered in the Town of Versailles*. Lexington, KY: D. Bradford, 1806.

Taylor, Adam. *Memoirs of the Rev. Dan Taylor*. Boston: Wilkins, Derby, Noble, 1820.

Taylor, Dan. *A Circular Letter on the Necessity and Importance of Right Order and Good Government in the Churches of Christ*. Wisbech, UK: W. Nicholson, 1781.

———. *A Compendious View of the Nature and Importance of Christian Baptism for the Use of Plain Christians*. London: W. C. Drake, 1824.

———. *Entertainment and Profit United: Easy Verses on Some of the Chief Subjects of Christianity for the Use of Poor Children and Youth*. London: R. Hawes, c. 1770.

———. *Fundamentals of Religion in Faith and Practice*. Leeds: n.p., 1775.

———. *An Humble Essay on Christian Baptism*. London: J. W. Pasham, 1777.

———. *A Letter on the Duties of Church Members to Each Other*. London: R. Hawes, c. 1790.

———. *Rules and Observations for the Enjoyment of Health and Long Life*. Leeds: G. Wright, c. 1700.

———. *Strictures on the Rev. Stephen Addington's Late Summary of the Christian Minister's Reasons for Baptizing Infants, and for Administering the Ordinance by Sprinkling or Pouring Water in Two Letters to the Author*. London: J. W. Pasham, 1777.

Taylor, James Barnett. *Virginia Baptist Ministers*. 2 vols. 3rd ed. Philadelphia: J. B. Lippincott, 1859.

Thiemann, Ronald F. *Constructing a Public Theology: The Church in a Pluralistic Culture*. Louisville, KY: Westminster John Knox, 1991.

Thomas, Ray. *Daniel and Abraham Marshall: Pioneer Baptist Evangelists to the South*. Springfield, MO: Particular Baptist, 2006.

Thompson, E. T. *Changing Emphases in American Preaching: The Stone Lectures for 1943*. Philadelphia: Westminster, 1943.

———. *The Changing South and the Presbyterian Church in the United States*. Richmond, VA: John Knox, 1950.

———. *Plenty and Want: The Responsibility of the Church*. 2 vols. Nashville: Joint Season of Witness Presbyterian Church, U.S., 1966.

———. *Presbyterians in the South: 1607–1861*. Vol 1. Richmond, VA: John Knox, 1963.

———. *The Sermon on the Mount and Its Meaning for Today*. Richmond, VA: John Knox, 1961.

———. *The Spirituality of the Church: A Distinctive Doctrine of the Presbyterian Church in the United States*. Richmond, VA: John Knox, 1961.

———. *Through the Ages: A History of the Christian Church*. Richmond, VA: CLC, 1965.

Thompson, James J., Jr. *Tried as by Fire: Southern Baptists and the Religious Controversies of the 1920s*. Macon, GA: Mercer University Press, 1982.

Tillinghast, George. *An Oration, Commemorative of the Nineteenth Anniversary of American Independence*. Providence, RI: Carter & Wilkinson, 1794.

Tinder, Glenn E. *The Political Meaning of Christianity: An Interpretation*. Baton Rouge: Louisiana State University Press, 1989.

Tocqueville, Alexis. *Democracy in America*. Translated and edited by Harvey C. Mansfield and Delba Winthrop. Chicago: University of Chicago Press, 2000.

Torbet, Robert G. *A History of the Baptists*. 3rd ed. Valley Forge, PA: Judson, 1963.

Troeltsch, Ernst. *The Social Teaching of the Christian Churches*. 2 vols. Translated by Oliver Wyon. London: Allen & Unwin, 1931. Reprint, Louisville, KY: Westminster, 1992.

Tyler, Alice Felt. *Freedom's Ferment: Phases of American Social History to 1860*. Minneapolis: University of Minnesota Press, 1944.

Tyrell, Ian R. "Drink and Temperance in the Antebellum South: An Overview and Interpretation." *Journal of Southern History* 48 (Fall 1982) 485–510.

———. "Drink and the Process of Social Reform: From Temperance to Prohibition in Antebellum America, 1813–1860." PhD diss., Duke University, 1974.

———. *Sobering Up: From Temperance to Prohibition in Antebellum America, 1800–1860*. Westport, CT: Greenwood, 1979.

Valentine, Foy. *The Cross in the Marketplace*. Waco, TX: Word, 1966.

———. *Southern Baptists and the Contemporary Racial Crisis*. Nashville: Christian Life Commission of the Southern Baptist Convention, 1966.

Van Broekhoven, Deborah Bingham. "Suffereing with Slaveholders: The Limits of Francis Wayland's Antislavery Witness." In *Religion and the Antebellum Debate over Slavery*, edited by John R. McKivigan and Mitchell Snay, 196–220. Athens: University of Georgia Press, 1998.

Van Ruler, Arnold A. *Calvinist Trinitarianism and Theocentric Politics: Essays Toward a Public Theology*. Lewiston, NY: Edwin Mellen, 1989.

Van Till, Kent A. *Less Than Two Dollars a Day: A Christian View of Poverty and the Free Market*. Grand Rapids: Eerdmans, 2007.

Vedder, Henry C. *A Short History of Baptists*. London: Baptist Tract and Book Society, 1897.

Walters, Ronald G. *American Reformers, 1815–1860*. Rev. ed. New York: Hill & Wang, 1997.

Washington, George. "Farewell Address." In *The Writings of George Washington*, edited by Jared Sparks, 12:214–35. Boston: Little, Brown, 1855.

———. "To the General Committee, Representing the United Baptist Churches in Virginia. May, 1789." In *The Writings of George Washington*, edited by Jared Sparks, 12:154–55. Boston: Little, Brown, 1855.

———. "To the Synod of the Reformed Dutch Church in North America, October, 1789." In *The Writings of George Washington*, edited by Jared Sparks, 12:166–67. Boston: Little, Brown, 1855.

Wayland, Francis. *An Address, Delivered Before the Providence Association for the Promotion of Temperance, October 20, 1831*. Boston: Lincoln & Edmands, 1832.

———. *The Death of Ex-Presidents* in *Occasional Discourses*. Boston: J. Loring, 1833.

———. *A Discourse Delivered in the First Baptist Church, Providence, R. I.: On the Day of Public Thanksgiving, July 21, 1842*. Providence, RI: H. H. Brown, 1842.

——. *A Discourse in Commemoration of the Character and Services of Rev. James Nathaniel Granger, D. D.* Providence, RI: George H. Whitney, 1857.

——. *A Discourse in Commemoration of the Life and Character of Moses Brown Ives.* Providence, RI: Knowles, Anthony, 1857.

——. *The Duties of an American Citizen.* Boston: J. Loring, 1825.

——. *The Duty of Obedience to the Civil Magistrate: Three Sermons Preached in the Chapel of Brown University.* Boston: Little & Brown, 1847.

——. *The Elements of Moral Science.* Boston: Gould & Lincoln, 1867.

——. *Encouragements to Religious Effort.* Philadelphia: American Sunday School Union, 1830.

——. *Letters on the Ministry of the Gospel.* Boston: Gould & Lincoln, 1863.

——. *Notes on the Principles and Practices of Baptist Churches.* New York: Sheldon, Blakeman, 1857.

——. *Occasional Discourses.* Boston: J. Loring, 1833.

——. *Sermons to the Churches.* New York: Sheldon, Blakeman, 1858.

Wayland, Francis, and Richard Fuller. *Domestic Slavery Considered as a Scriptural Institution: In a Correspondence Between the Rev. Richard Fuller, the Rev. Francis Wayland.* New York: Lewis Colby, 1845.

Wayland, Francis, and H. L. Wayland. *A Memoir of the Life and Labors of Francis Wayland.* 2 vols. New York: Sheldon, 1867.

Welch, Claude. *Protestant Thought in the Nineteenth Century.* Vol. 1. New Haven, CT: Yale University Press, 1972.

Wellman, Judith. *The Road to Seneca Falls: Elizabeth Cady Stanton and the First Woman's Rights Convention.* Urbana: University of Illinois Press, 2004.

Wells, David F. *Losing Our Virtue: Why the Church Must Recover Its Moral Vision.* Grand Rapids: Eerdmans, 1998.

White Ronald C., Jr., and Howard C. Hopkins. *The Social Gospel: Religion and Reform in Changing America.* Philadelphia: Temple University Press, 1976.

Whitehead, John Walter. "The Church, Its Relation to God and to Culture: An Essay in Constructive Ecclesiology Through an Exposition and Evaluation of H. Richard Niebuhr's Thought." PhD diss., Vanderbilt University, 1971.

Whitener, Daniel Jay. *Prohibition in North Carolina, 1715–1945.* Chapel Hill: University of North Carolina Press, 1945.

Wigglesworth, Michael. "God's Controversy with New England." In *God's New Israel: Religious Interpretations of American Destiny,* edited by Conrad Cherry, 42–53. Chapel Hill: University of North Carolina Press, 1998.

Wilburn, James R., ed. *Faith and Public Policy.* Lanham, MD: Lexington, 2002.

Wilkinson, Henry C. *Bermuda from Sail to Steam: The History of the Island from 1784 to 1801.* Vol. 2. London: Oxford University Press, 1973.

Willey, Larry G. "John Rankin, Antislavery Prophet, and the Free Presbyterian Church." *American Presbyterians* 72 (1994) 157–71.

Williams, William R. "The Church in Its Relation to the State." *The Madison Avenue Lectures.* Philadelphia: American Baptist Publication Society, 1867.

Williamson, Douglas J. "The Rise of the New England Methodist Temperance Movement." *Methodist History* 21 (October 1982) 3–28.

Wills, Gregory A. *Democratic Religion: Freedom, Authority, and Church Discipline in the Baptist South, 1785–1900.* New York: Oxford University Press, 1997.

————. "The First Hundred Years of Baptist Home Missions in America: Civilization, Denominationalism, and Americanization." In *Baptists and Mission: Papers from the Fourth International Conference on Baptist Studies*, edited by Ian M. Randall and Anthony Cross, 130–48. Milton Keynes, UK: Paternoster, 2008.

Wilson, Charles Reagan. *Baptized in Blood: The Religion of the Lost Cause, 1865–1920.* Athens: University of Georgia Press, 1980.

Wimberly, Dan B. *Frontier Religion: Elder Daniel Parker, His Religious and Political Life.* Austin, TX: Eakin, 2002.

Winchcole, Dorothy Clarke. *The First Baptists in Washington, DC, 1802–1952.* Washington, DC: First Baptist Church, 1952.

Witte, John, Jr. "'A Most Mild and Equitable Establishment of Religion': John Adams and the Massachusetts Experiment." In *Religion and the New Republic: Faith in the Founding of America*, edited by John Witte Jr., 213–52. Lanham, MD: Rowman & Littlefield, 2000.

Wolever, Terry. *The Life and Ministry of John Gano, 1727–1804.* Springfield, MO: Particular Baptist, 1998.

Woodward, E. L. *The Age of Reform, 1815–1870.* Oxford: Clarendon, 1962.

Wyatt-Brown, Bertram. "The Antimission Movement in the Jacksonian South: A Study in Regional Folk Culture." *The Journal of Southern History* 36 (November 1970) 501–29.

————. *Lewis Tappan and the Evangelical War against Slavery.* Baton Rouge: Louisiana State University Press, 1997.

Yager, Arthur. *Sketch of the Life of William Calmes Buck.* Louisville, KY: C. T. Dearing, 1906.

Yarbrough, Jean M. *American Virtues: Thomas Jefferson on the Character of a Free People.* Lawrence: University Press of Kansas, 1998.

Yoder, John Howard. *The Politics of Jesus.* Grand Rapids: Eerdmans, 1994.

Young, Robert Jeffrey. *Proslavery and Sectional Thought in the Early South, 1740–1829.* Columbia: University of South Carolina Press, 2006.

Zink-Sawyer, Beverly Ann. "The Preachers and the Suffragists: The Role of Preachers and Suffragists in the Ideological Transformation of the Woman Suffrage Movement in the United States." PhD diss., Vanderbilt University, 1997.

Index